D0761024

ATLAS OF NAZI GERMANY

ATLAS OF NAZI GERMANY

Michael Freeman

Consulting Editor: Tim Mason

Macmillan Publishing Company
NEW YORK

Macmillan Publishing Company.
866 Third Avenue, New York, NY 10022

Library of Congress Catalog Card Number: 87-12261

Printed and bound in Great Britain

printing number
1 2 3 4 5 6 7 8 9 10

Library of Congress Cataloging-in-Publication Data

Freeman, Michael, 1950–
    An atlas of Nazi Germany.

    Bibliography: p.
    1. Germany — Historical geography. 2. Germany — Historical geography — maps. 3. Germany — History — 1933–1945. I. Mason, Tim. II. Title.
DD256.5.F73354 1987 911′.43 87-12261
ISBN 0-02-910681-8

Contents

Foreword

Mainstream historians do not usually attach much importance to visual images. Their source materials are for the most part written documents, and they produce books which are above all to be read. To try to understand social and political history is to engage in an activity which is above all literary. It is the words which count. The illustrations contained in works of history are perhaps a little more numerous now than they were fifteen years ago, but they are still normally very few and very conventional and are in every sense separate from the text. Modern historians may use old photographs to give an impression of what people, streets, workplaces or warfare looked like, but they seldom use them as evidence or discuss their messages.

Meanwhile new historical specialisms are arising, which, modelled it seems upon the history of art, do indeed give appropriate importance to the history of design, of photography, the cinema and television etc., but tend to carry their subject matter away from the concerns of the general historian. Such specialists have a lot to say about how to analyse images from the past, much less about the use of images in enhancing historical understanding. The visual component in the process of learning about the past thus tends to be underestimated and neglected all round.

In this respect Michael Freeman's book about Nazi Germany is innovative. It is much more than a historical atlas: he has succeeded in representing most of the important themes in the political, economic and military history of the Third Reich in the form of diagrams, charts, graphs and tables, as well as of maps and photographs. These images are an integral part of what he has written on each theme. His historical summaries comment on the visual

material, and the images document part of his exposition or argument. He has composed the book in a highly self-conscious and deliberate manner which has involved much research and a great deal of painstaking revision in order to reach the best possible relationship between text and image on each spread of pages.

The book is intended for sixth-formers, university students and serious general readers. (Those looking for another picture book on Nazi Germany should stop reading here.) And they will be among the best judges of the value of his approach. Professional experts on recent European history will find some useful summaries of recent research and debates, and they may also extend their knowledge of the geography of Germany; above all, however, they may come to appreciate, as I have done, how complicated historical issues can be illuminated and clarified when they are presented as a combination of image and prose, diagram and description.

Perhaps it is helpful to give an example of this from my own work. In the past fifteen years some historians of Nazi Germany have come to attach great significance to the fluidity of the institutions of the dictatorship. The processes of decision-making and the channels of command were anything but uniform and clear, and the various ministries, party agencies, military and police authorities devoted great energy and ingenuity to competing with each other for a greater share of the expanding dictatorial powers of the regime. These conflicts probably (not every historian agrees) had a considerable influence over the policies finally sanctioned or chosen by Hitler. The relevant facts and the interpretations to which they give rise are complicated and often technical; many detailed monographs have been written around the theme, but it remains very difficult to give a summary account of this aspect of the Third Reich which is intelligible to non-experts. Such accounts, my own included, are all too often congested and allusive, strenuous efforts to make language adequate to the tortuous growth processes of the regime and its policies *in general.* How much clearer all this becomes when we are presented with a series of maps and diagrams which turn 'overlapping jurisdictions' and 'confused patterns of power and

responsibility' into visual realities. The abstract nouns gain enormously from being illustrated.

This is the main reason why I believe that Michael Freeman's book will be useful and instructive. He makes difficult and important topics accessible to readers who may not yet know a great deal about Nazi Germany, without in any way condescending to them in the manner typical of popularisers.

Tim Mason
Rome, September 1986

Preface and Acknowledgements

This book started life over an impromptu lunchtime discussion with David Croom in the spring of 1984. It was originally intended as a short, popular exposition on the Third Reich, but under Tim Mason's editorial eye and as a result of a certain internal momentum, it turned out to be rather more serious in intent and coverage. However, restrictions of time and money rendered it impossible to make a comprehensive search for *original cartographic* materials. None of the relevant American archives was searched, for example. In Germany, the only repository examined was the Bundesarchiv, which proved to have a disappointingly restricted set of material relating specifically to the National Socialist regime, although it is clear that some items lie in special archival groups like the Speer Collection. The greater body of original cartographic sources has been found, in fact, in Oxford, in the map collections of the Bodleian Library and the School of Geography. Some of these materials were collected in the normal run of accessions, notably up to 1939. Other material was acquired relatively recently from the Directorate of Military Survey. Some also derives from the period during the war when the School of Geography was a centre of naval intelligence work, particularly for the compilation of some of the *Admiralty Handbooks*, although those covering Germany were completed in Cambridge where, unhappily, few records survive. For the rest of the book's illustrative material, it will become immediately apparent that, apart from official printed sources such as the *Statistisches Jahrbuch*, there is a heavy reliance on existing published work. The range of this is enormous and was a primary cause of the extension from one to two years in the time taken to complete the book. It is the individuals whose names are credited on the illustrations who warrant the first acknowledgement. Without their research and writing effort, the book would have been a far more difficult task. If the results of their research have been misdirected or misused in any way, I can but offer apologies and beg the chance to rectify it in later editions. Special thanks must go also to the librarians and library staffs who have assisted me in searches for literature, particularly Rosamund Campbell at St Antony's College, Oxford, which houses a remarkable special collection on the Third Reich, and Elspeth Buxton at the School of Geography. Gordon Smith, of Keble College, Oxford, suggested various improvements to the text, particularly in those parts dealing with the war. David Croom, of Croom Helm, has been a marvellous stimulant to the project, in material as well as mental ways. However, my deepest gratitude must be reserved for Tim Mason, who has been ever patient, always exacting in comment and criticism, and adept at giving encouragement when interest or confidence flagged. I absolve him of all responsibility for any weaknesses in the book. It is first and foremost my own creation. But it would have been measurably inferior without his enormous fund of knowledge, his scholarship and his acuteness of perception.

The illustrations have all been drawn by Jayne Lewin, who has handled the task with characteristic patience and good sense. The transformations from author's 'roughs' into finished products have sometimes been remarkable to see.

I am also grateful to Andrew Goudie, Professor of Geography at Oxford, for the general support that he has enabled me to have in the

School of Geography there. The University of Oxford has also helped by making travel funds available for my research in Germany.

Photographs are reproduced by courtesy of the following institutions:

pp. 10, 36, 45, 46, 61, 87, 88, 100, 126, 144, 186:— The Imperial War Museum
p. 185:— The Robert Harding Picture Library

p. 82:— Weidenfeld and Nicholson
The Bodleian Library, Oxford:—
p. 60 (Per 17007 c. 35, 1938, p. 145)
p. 74 (Per 17007 c. 35, 1938, p. 38)
p. 81 (Per 17007 c. 35, 1938, p. 242)
p. 90 (Per 17007 c. 35, 1938, p. 48)
p. 91 (Per 17007 c. 35, 1938, p. 45)
    (Per 17007 c. 35, 1938, p. 347)
p. 97 (1170 c. 5, 1934, p. 30)

Abbreviations

BVP	Bayerische Volkspartei — Bavarian People's Party
DAF	Deutsche Arbeitsfront — German Labour Front
DAW	Deutsche Ausrüstungswerke GmbH — German Armaments Works: a division of the SS organisation
DEST	Deutsche Erd und Steinwerke GmbH — German Earth and Stone Works: a division of the SS organisation
DNVP	Deutschnationale Volkspartei — German National People's Party
DVP	Deutsche Volkspartei — German People's Party
EHER-Verlag	NSDAP's central publishing house in Munich
GBA	Generalbevollmächtigen für den Arbeitseinsatz — General Plenipotentiary for Labour Allocation
Gestapo	Geheime Staatspolizei — Secret State Police
HJ	Hitler Jugend — Hitler Youth organisation
KdF	Kraft durch Freude — Strength through Joy: the leisure organisation of the German Labour Front (DAF)
KPD	Kommunistische Partei Deutschlands — German Communist Party
KRIPO	Kriminalpolizei — Criminal Police
NSBO	Nationalsozialistische Betriebszellenorganization — Nazi factory cell organisation
NSDAP	Nationalsozialistische Deutsche Arbeiter Partei — National Socialist German Workers' Party (Nazi Party)
NSKK	Nationalsozialistische Kraftfahrer Korps — National Socialist Motor Transport Corps
OKW	Oberkommando der Wehrmacht — Armed Forces High Command
RFSS	Reichsfuehrer–SS — Himmler's title as SS Chief
RKFDV (or RKF)	Reichskommissar für die Festigung deutschen Volkstums — Reich Commissar for the Strengthening of German Nationhood
RSHA	Reichssicherheitshauptamt — Main Reich Security Office, the apex of the SS organisation
RUSHA	Rasse- and Siedlungs-Hauptamt — SS main office for race and settlement
SA	Sturmabteilungen — Storm Troopers: the strong-arm squads of the Nazi Party
SD	Sicherheitsdienst — Security Service of the SS
SPD	Sozialdemokratische Partei Deutschlands — German Social Democratic Party
SS	Schutzstaffeln — guard detachments: more widely, the Nazis' elite formations
USCHLA	Untersuchungs- und Schlichtungs-Ausschuss — NSDAP investigation and arbitration committee
WVHA	Wirtschafts und Verwaltungshauptamt — the chief SS economic and administrative office

Introduction

Anyone writing about the Third Reich for the first time does so with trepidation. For not only is the literature, in German as well as in English, vast in range and in depth, but it is characterised by intense and sometimes bitter controversy. The Third Reich has now been located within an almost bewildering variety of interpretative frames, many of which seem to be poles apart. In some eyes it might appear churlish for a newcomer to say that the entire field begins to read like a never-ending Agatha Christie novel, yet it remains true that the succession of events and processes continues to be re-examined, re-sorted and relocated to make for new readings of the plot such that any intelligible denouement becomes steadily more remote.[1] This is not to cast doubt on the quality of scholarship in much work on the Third Reich, nor is it intended to belittle the persuasiveness and intellectual sophistication of the analytical frames within which some of that work is set. However, no new observer can fail to be struck by the apparent willingness of some writers to apply logical reasoning to a regime which in both its leading persona and its structures was frequently illogical, to engage in *ex post facto* interpretations, to ride slipshod over questions of equifinality, and to confine their perspectives within statistical prisons. Nor has the literature on the Third Reich been insulated from the pitfalls of social scientific method as developed and applied in many arts disciplines from about 1960. The predisposition to look for facts to fit particular theories, often treating those facts as having independent existence, is clearly evident in some of the literature of that time.

None of this is to say that the present volume does not suffer weaknesses. However, its purpose is of a rather different kind. It seeks to provide a graphic presentation of the outward face and inward structures of the Third Reich and, where applicable, the manner of their evolution. In some respects it bears comparison with the recent upsurge of literature seeking to summarise and review the state of thinking on the regime, although in nothing like so comprehensive or acute a fashion. But in other respects it strikes relatively new ground in attempting to portray features of the Third Reich in ways which provide an immediacy of communication that is achieved only with much more difficulty in the consecutive form of prose. It is a remarkable and, in this writer's view, disconcerting feature of a vast body of the literature on the Third Reich that it is so lacking in graphic, even tabular, presentation. Broszat's penetratingly seductive analysis, *The Hitler state*, for example, confines its graphic presentation to Nazi election performance, a single linkage diagram of party–state relations, and tables on the sociological structure of party membership and on political and other crimes.[2] Hidden in both text and footnotes, though, is much statistical and other material which, if it could have been suitably presented, would have lent a greater immediacy and clarity to many of the facets being analysed. The argument has been put that the complexity and constant state of flux of so many structures and organisations of the Third Reich make invalid any even semi-formal articulation of them. But the obverse of this argument is that such features lend even greater force to some form of graphic presentation. It may be the case that, metaphorically speaking, the movement of the chess pieces on the board steadily reconstitutes the rules of the game, but this does not render any less valid the identification of the pieces, or of their pattern on the board at any one time and the circum-scribing effects that result.

It is not just with 'graphicacy', though, that this book is concerned. More fundamentally, it attempts to expose some of the geographical dimensions of the Third Reich. This does not primarily mean the compilation of a sort of 'place' inventory, although there are elements on this — for example where organisations such as the SS established new enterprises. Nor does it mean a primary focus on sets of geographical distributions, although once again there are examples of this, as in Part Four. It refers most of all to conceptions of *relative* as distinct from *absolute* space, to *relations* in geographical space; in plainer terms to the tensions and dis-sonances that incongruent administrative areas generate, for example; to the so-called 'friction of distance' as an ingredient of locational deci-sions and as an inhibitor on actions and on efficiency, economic or otherwise.

The most startling geographical feature of the Third Reich was undeniably the scale of its territorial extension and areal conquest. By 1942 it constituted one of the most rapidly made land empires in history. It was over 3,200 km from the German naval bases on the west coast of France to the Russian front in the Don Basin. The furthest longitudinal extent of 'Versailles' Germany was only about 950 km, and that distance was interrupted by the Polish corridor. For an advanced capitalist state like Germany, there were very evident merits in resource terms of such an extended land base. And the drive for 'Lebensraum' has been seen by various commentators as a seeking for just such resources, whether arising from internal resource crises or from ideological visions about a new German national realm.[3] Some of these additional resource bases were quickly assimil-ated by cartels like the chemical giant, IG-Farben, and the Hermann Goering industrial combine. In the war, the SS became a com-petitor for such bases — as part of Himmler's attempt to build up an independent industrial capacity for the SS following the 'state within a state' syndrome. And, from 1942, Speer's legen-dary War Ministry made determined efforts to

systematise the utilisation of annexed and con-quered resource groupings. But advanced industrial states are not made from the simple accumulation of coal, mineral and manufactur-ing bases, however numerous. They are created, too, through the emergence of complex linea-ments of communication, from the working out of myriad systems of comparative advantage, involving production linkages and trading reciprocities of multitudinous form. This pro-vided one of the major difficulties under which the expanded Third Reich laboured. Already in 1938/9 the communications system of Germany proper was strained from the expan-sions and reorientations that Hitler's rearma-ment and autarkic policies imposed upon the economy.[4] With the territorial annexations of that period and, later, territorial conquests, the problems intensified. Of course, the regime could utilise the communications systems of annexed or occupied countries (though much less easily in Russia, where the wider railway gauge was a severe impediment), but these, and more critically the systems of trade relations, had evolved in the context of largely indepen-dent national development. They did not read-ily interlock into a new style of European indus-trial economy which was targeted towards German needs and the German core area, following a neocolonial system of resource assemblage. The Reichsbahn was soon to regis-ter these strains as locomotives, rolling stock and manpower were eked out over an increas-ingly diffuse network, and as trans-European line-hauls accumulated in number and scale as the war progressed.[5] The extensive autobahn system that Nazi planners envisaged for Central Europe offered a potential solution, but the German autobahn system itself remained very incomplete at the outbreak of war and the completed sections, anyway, were equivocally economic in their objective.[6] Given the Third Reich's transport problems, one would have expected autobahn construction to have been given some priority after 1939; in practice, new construction was almost entirely abandoned.[7]

The exigencies of war, of course, wove their own pattern into these difficulties of resource transfer and assembly. The war fronts required a continuous stream of supplics of materials, food and men. Where attrition formed the primary mould of combat, the front became a bottomless sink into which materials and men were poured. So as trainloads of requisitioned resources and conscripted foreigners rumbled into Germany from former countries of Europe, there was a counter-stream of troops and weaponry.

As the Third Reich evolved, therefore, especially after 1936, it was attempting to forge entirely new sets of spatial relations, yet it was never fully able to service or realise these, and in this respect it can be argued that distance produced its own tyranny. Time proved too short to remould the diverse economic–industrial bases of the annexed and conquered territories into a unitary, pan–German system and to evolve a complementary profile of communication and trade infrastructures. The way the traditional dominance of the Ruhr was maintained to the very end of the war demonstrates the regime's relative bankruptcy in remodelling the European economic–industrial realm to meet its purposes more clearly. The Ruhr's position was a very evident strategic weakness, as 1944 and 1945 were to prove.[8] But it also became progressively sub-optimal in location terms as the frontiers of the Reich expanded. The development of a more easterly industrial complex, on the scale of the Ruhr, would have made real sense in terms of the economics and logistics of location. The pitfalls of such argument, though, is that it ascribes to the Third Reich a dominance of economic purpose which was manifestly absent. Economic optima and economic consistency were frequently and increasingly compromised by ideological designs. In this way thousands of skilled Jews were deported from vital German and Polish war factories midway through the war for extermination in camps like Auschwitz.[9] But even in its progressive drive to liquidate Europe's Jews, the regime was caught in the same distance web as that experienced in the economic–industrial system. SS demands for deportation trains to service points as far afield as south-west France and southern Greece merely exacerbated the Reichsbahn's many problems.

As the Third Reich grew in areal extent, posing all kinds of problems of spatial reintegration on a Europe-wide scale, it was upholding concepts of territory and maintaining maladjusted systems of territorial administration which could only frustrate the difficulties. The singular power of the Gauleiters, in the style of territorial chieftains, was quite alien to the operation of an advanced industrial state. Speer and his Armaments Ministry soon found this out to their cost when efforts were begun to harness industrial production more clearly towards the needs of war.[10] In the Gauleiters' view, their territories were not intended to be subservient to any central or Reich authority. The interests of the local party and the well-being of the local population were their primary and sovereign concerns, not the wider workings of the German state, either in peace or in war. Similar centrifugal or divergent tendencies were characteristic of occupied territories where party strongmen sometimes wielded even greater powers than their counterparts in the Reich proper. The Reichskommissariat of the Ukraine under Erich Koch (contemporaneously Gauleiter of East Prussia) was a particular case in point. And the occupied territories presented an entirely separate problem in the way they each displayed variant patterns of government. In this sense, Hitler's great land empire was more a loose federation under the overarching eye of his leadership than a clearly regulated, purposive colonial realm.

The administration of Germany proper and, later, of the Greater German Reich presented another series of limitations. It was not only the 'Gau-kingdoms' which distracted from orderly *national* government, but the way so few departments of Reich administration operated congruent administrative field systems, a feature that the rapid breakdown of cabinet government tended to cement. Even more critically, none of these systems bore any relationship to the Gaue, which were modelled on the Reichstag electoral districts of the 1920s and left largely unchanged to the end of the war. To add to this complexity, moreover, the military operated its own distinctive regional system which was later replicated in the SS.

Then there were still the remnants of the Länder which, although emasculated of separated political power in the *Gleichschaltung* of spring 1933, remained as bases for the administration of education and other social services. The outcome was thus a veritable maze of overlapping and often conflicting jurisdictions. And the Nazi practice of appointing regional party leaders to approximately parallel state offices added to the confusion rather than reducing it. Some Gauleiters, for example, quickly seized this as a pretext for pursuing their own designs by claiming direct Fuehrer-authority over and above the traditional administrative apparatus of the state.

If the Third Reich as a geographical or spatial entity was so riddled with discordant and disintegrative tendencies, either deriving from the character of its administration or from the forced exigencies of massive territorial accretion and the productive and operational demands of war, one is led inexorably towards the 'functionalist' interpretation of the Nazi regime as identified with Broszat in particular,[11] who, along with others,[12] has already pointed to certain elements of the geographical chaos here described. The Third Reich was no *tabula rasa* on which the intentions of its leadership could be fulfilled without restriction. It was contoured and embarriered in such a way that action was circumscribed and intention frustrated. At the same time, the paths of economic autarky, areal conquest and war invoked certain fundamental alterations in the relationships of the German productive machine to the geographical environment, the means for which were never fully or properly assembled. The 'friction of distance' became an increasingly stark restricting force in this process, making the Third Reich into an unwieldy empire for which grandiose Nazi plans for continental autobahns and super broad-gauge railways held ironic prophesy.

Notes

1. This has been reflected in the early 1980s by a miniature flood of books seeking to summarise, review and evaluate the mass of different viewpoints and approaches. See, for example, J. Hiden and J. Farquharson, *Explaining Hitler's Germany* (1983); K. Hildebrand, *The Third Reich* (1984) — first published in German in 1979; I. Kershaw, *The Nazi dictatorship: problems and perspectives of interpretation* (1985).

2. M. Broszat, *The Hitler state: the foundation and development of the internal structure of the Third Reich* (1981) — first published in German in 1969.

3. See the discussion in Kershaw, *Nazi dictatorship*, pp. 78-80.

4. See H. P. S. Matthews and P. O'Mahony, 'Germany in April 1939', unpublished report in the library of Oxford University Institute of Economics and Statistics, part II, pp. 25-7; see also M. Robbins, 'The Third Reich and its railways' — review article on Eugen Kreidler's 'Die Eisenbahnen im Machtbereich der Achsenmächte während des Zweiten Weltkrieges', *Journal of Transport History*, new series, 5 (1979), pp. 83-90.

5. On 15 December 1942, 54 out of 260 trains crossing German frontiers outwards were locomotive coal trains — Robbins, 'The Third Reich and its railways'.

6. See R.J. Overy, 'Transportation and re-armament in the Third Reich', *Historical Journal*, 16 (1973).

7. Ibid.

8. See A.S. Milward, *The German economy at war* (1965), ch. 7; in 1944, of the 166 million tons of German coal production, nearly 111 million were mined in the Ruhr — J.R. Gillingham, *Industry and politics in the Third Reich: Ruhr coal, Hitler and Europe* (1985), p. 58.

9. See T. Mason, 'The primacy of politics — politics and economics in National Socialist Germany' in H.A. Turner (ed.), *Nazism and the Third Reich* (1972), p. 195.

10. See Milward, *German economy*, pp. 153-5.

11. Broszat, *The Hitler state*; for an excellent discussion of this interpretation see Kershaw, *Nazi dictatorship*, pp. 65ff.

12. See, for example, J. Caplan, 'The politics of administration: the Reich Interior Ministry and the German civil service, 1933-43', *Historical Journal*, 20 (1977), pp. 707-36.

Prelude

The Weimar Republic
Versailles and the Weimar Republic

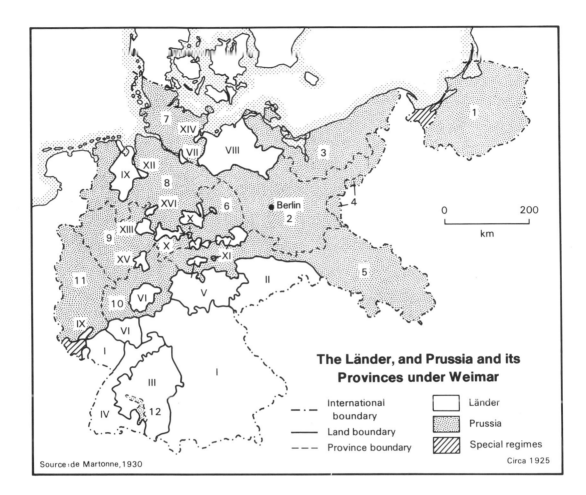

The Länder, and Prussia and its Provinces under Weimar

— · — International boundary	☐ Länder
——— Land boundary	▨ Prussia
- - - Province boundary	▨ Special regimes

Source: de Martonne, 1930

Circa 1925

Länder

I	Bavaria
II	Saxony
III	Württemberg
IV	Baden
V	Thuringia
VI	Hesse
VII	Hamburg
VIII	Mecklenburg-Schwerin
IX	Oldenburg
X	Brunswick
XI	Anhalt
XII	Bremen
XIII	Lippe
XIV	Lübeck
XV	Waldeck
XVI	Schaumburg-Lippe
XVII	(Prussia)

Prussian Provinces

1	East Prussia
2	Brandenburg
3	Pomerania
4	Grenzmark Posen Westpreussen
5	Silesia
6	Saxony
7	Schleswig-Holstein
8	Hanover
9	Westphalia
10	Hessen-Nassau
11	Rhine Province
12	Hohenzollern

The Weimar Republic

The Weimar Republic came into being in the midst of the German war defeat in the autumn of 1918. Rising popular disaffection with the military and the monarchy precipitated a revolutionary movement beginning with naval mutinies at Kiel in late October and followed by the rapid establishment of soldiers' and workers' councils throughout Germany in much the same mould as had occurred in Russia that year. By the second week of November, a reformist socialist government was in place, a republic had been declared, the Kaiser had abdicated and was in exile in Holland, and the army's war leaders had been forced from the centre stage.

The new government, however, proved hardly revolutionary in mould. It was dominated by moderate socialists (SPD) who still clung to elements of the prewar political scene. One result was that more revolutionary but minor socialist groups were quickly alienated and, later, were subject to violent suppression, with the help of newly formed army units. The threads of political continuity were reinforced when, in the first parliamentary election in early 1919, the socialists were able to form a government only with the support of the Catholic Centre Party and the Democrats.

The 'Weimar constitution' was adopted by the Reichstag, or Parliament, in August 1919. It was exceptionally democratic in that it gave the vote to all men and women at the age of 20 and, more widely, sought to uphold every possible democratic right. Governments were responsible to Parliament and there was to be a strong, popularly elected President. Provisions were also made for popular referenda. The relationship between the central government and the sovereign states of Bismarck's Reich was redefined to give much greater control at the centre. The states henceforward became *Länder*, their powers of self-administration confined to the police, the judiciary and education. In the second parliamentary chamber set up under the Weimar constitution, the *Reichsrat*, the Länder supposedly gained a broader measure of influence on government. But, in practice, the Reichsrat was subservient to the Reichstag, which was in turn somewhat overshadowed by the Reich government.

The internal political geography of Germany under the Weimar regime was among the most complicated of all contemporary European countries. Before the birth of Hitler's state, Germany was divided into no less than 17 Länder, the largest of which was Prussia, covering some 60 per cent of the country's land area and embracing some 60 per cent of its population. Prussia was itself divided into separate provinces. The remaining Länder varied wildly in size and population. Bavaria, for instance, had an area of 78,000 sq. km and a population of some 8 million, while Schaumburg-Lippe had corresponding figures of 340 and 50,000. The resulting geographical mosaic was predictably very confused. While Prussia was the dominant force across the northern half of the country and Bavaria, by virtue of its large size, likewise in the south, the small German Länder were distributed across the face of western Germany, many of them also having detached territorial outliers to add further to the confusion.

Versailles and the Weimar Republic

The Treaty of Versailles of 1919 redrew the political map of Europe on an unprecedented scale. For Germany, however, the territorial adjustments required by the Treaty were limited. Alsace-Lorraine was restored to France (having been taken from France in 1871). Minor frontier adjustments were made at Germany's expense in favour of Belgium, Czechoslovakia and Denmark. Territory was lost in the east to the recreated state of Poland, much of it land which had been seized by Prussia in the eighteenth century. But, in total, Germany had to relinquish only 13 per cent of its territory, containing approximately 10 per cent of its population. Alongside the Treaty's consequences for the Austro-Hungarian Empire, or compared with the humiliating territorial losses imposed by Germany on Russia at the earlier Treaty of Brest-Litovsk, the German state survived relatively intact, geographically, economically and politically. It deposed its dynasty, replaced monarchy by republic and in most facets retained its potential as a strong, independent nation.

The German people saw the provisions of Versailles very differently. Upon receipt of the draft terms in May 1919, the first parliamentary government of the new Republic resigned, refusing to accede to the terms. German officialdom was well aware of the likely demands of any peace treaty, but the German population at large had accumulated entirely different expectations and had not been discouraged from doing so by the government. The terms of the Treaty thus came as a profound shock. Many Germans were incensed by the detachment of East Prussia in order to create the Polish sea corridor. Equivalent bitterness arose from the requirement that Germany accept responsibility for starting the war and deliver vast reparations; many Germans believed that they had fought for defensive purposes. The related requirement of disarmament, which reduced Germany's great army to just 100,000 men and garrisoned the Rhine for 15 years was just as badly received.

Ultimately the German government had no choice but to accept the broad terms of Versailles. However, many Germans saw this as capitulation, and conservatives, who wielded the country's economic power, dissociated themselves from government and from Republic. Disruptive as the terms of Versailles were, it was not they alone which sowed the seeds of the Hitler state, or set in motion the collapse of the new Republic. It was the way the Versailles Treaty polarised German political opinion between the mild socialists, democrats and Catholic centrists who shouldered the burden it imposed and the right-wing nationalists, the conservatives and the army who were revolted by it. And because the Weimar constitution was extremely democratic in form (for example, by an elaborate system of proportional representation it allowed the fullest possible value to every vote), there was little check to the consolidation of these antipathies. Even with hindsight, though, it is not fair to say that they led inexorably to the foundation of the Nazi state. That pathway required many more ingredients and dialectical forces before its course was clearly located.

1914

1919

Russia

Lithuania

Russia

Poland

Neth.

Belg.

Czechoslovakia

France

Switz.

Austria

Hungary

Italy

Rumania

Austria-Hungary

Yugoslavia

Rumania

Serbia

Bulgaria

Bulgaria

MEMEL LAND

NORTH SCHLESWIG

EAST PRUSSIA

WEST PRUSSIA

Elbe

Berlin

Oder

Vistula

NETHERLANDS

Weser

POSEN

POLAND

BELGIUM

Rhine

EUPEN MALMEDY

UPPER SILESIA

L.

M.O

SAAR BASIN

CZECHOSLOVAKIA

LORRAINE

FRANCE

ALSACE

Danube

0   100

km

The Versailles settlement

/// Lost by Germany in 1919

···· Demilitarised territory

···· Special regimes

—·— Frontiers of 1919

SWITZ.

AUSTRIA

Source: *Adm Hbk* II

9

SA men marching through the Brandenburg Gate in Berlin on 3 March 1933.

Part One
The Rise of the Nazi Party

Adolf Hitler
The Nazi Party: Origins and Early Growth
Mein Kampf
Political Ferment: 1923
The Parliamentary Route to Power
The Road to Dictatorship
The Fuehrerprinzip
The Third Reich is Born
The Stormtroopers

Adolf Hitler

The story of how an obscure Austrian-born corporal came to be dictator of Germany is one that will never cease to intrigue students of twentieth-century European history. Hitler's dictatorship was no ordinary one, either. It was founded upon the *leader* principle, whereby allegiance was sworn to the person of the leader rather than to any party or institution of state. The pattern was forcibly expressed in the salute: 'Heil Hitler!' It found deeper manifestations in the semi-religious aura which increasingly surrounded Hitler as the Third Reich grew in strength. The cult of supreme leader was undoubtedly one to which Hitler himself aspired: his tactical manoeuvrings to take over leadership of the Nazi Party as early as 1921 are testament to this. But Hitler's authority had also to be rooted in a degree of mass acceptance by the German people. In effect the two fed upon each other, which in itself helps to explain some of the energy and dynamism the Third Reich displayed in its albeit short existence.

It has been commonplace to search Hitler's early life for clues to the man as dictator. Hitler indulged in this himself when giving accounts of the formative influences upon his character and outlook, although there is as much fiction as fact in his autobiographical writing. Until his active involvement in politics in 1919, at the age of almost 30, two influences stand out as worthy of mention. Firstly there were the years he spent in Vienna before the First World War — as a wanderer without permanent employment or trade. It was here that Hitler largely acquired the basic elements of what was to become his political ideology: nationalist, pan-German, anti-semitic, anti-Marxist. They were derived from a combination of personal contacts and reading, typically devoid of any critical appraisal, and subsequently pursued with maniacal fervour. Secondly, there were the years Hitler spent in the German Army during the First World War. For many commentators, the discipline of war and the general order of military existence helped Hitler to translate his political ideas and dreamings into realistic, practical goals. The military model was to become the operational model for National Socialism.

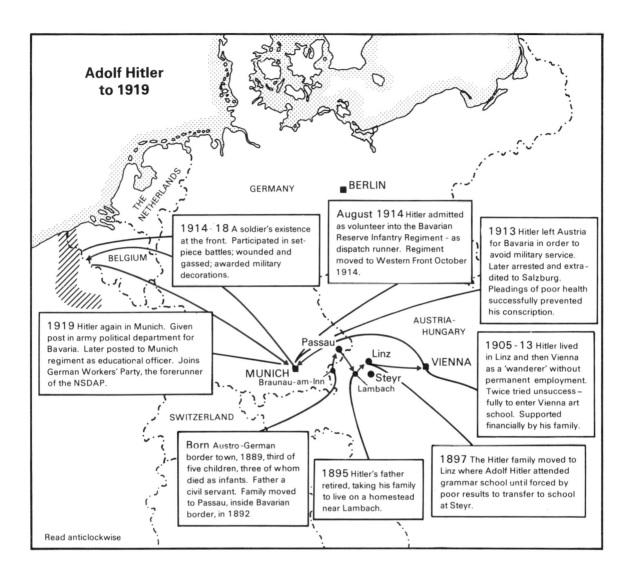

Adolf Hitler to 1919

THE NETHERLANDS

GERMANY

■ BERLIN

BELGIUM

1914-18 A soldier's existence at the front. Participated in set-piece battles; wounded and gassed; awarded military decorations.

August 1914 Hitler admitted as volunteer into the Bavarian Reserve Infantry Regiment - as dispatch runner. Regiment moved to Western Front October 1914.

1913 Hitler left Austria for Bavaria in order to avoid military service. Later arrested and extra-dited to Salzburg. Pleadings of poor health successfully prevented his conscription.

1919 Hitler again in Munich. Given post in army political department for Bavaria. Later posted to Munich regiment as educational officer. Joins German Workers' Party, the forerunner of the NSDAP.

AUSTRIA-HUNGARY

Passau

Linz

MUNICH ■
Braunau-am-Inn

Steyr
Lambach

VIENNA

1905-13 Hitler lived in Linz and then Vienna as a 'wanderer' without permanent employment. Twice tried unsuccess-fully to enter Vienna art school. Supported financially by his family.

SWITZERLAND

Born Austro-German border town, 1889, third of five children, three of whom died as infants. Father a civil servant. Family moved to Passau, inside Bavarian border, in 1892

1895 Hitler's father retired, taking his family to live on a homestead near Lambach.

1897 The Hitler family moved to Linz where Adolf Hitler attended grammar school until forced by poor results to transfer to school at Steyr.

Read anticlockwise

The Nazi Party

Origins and early growth

The Nazi Party originated from among the many nationalist, right-wing splinter groups which characterised the German-speaking political scene before and immediately following the First World War. It began life as the German Workers' Party (DAP), but membership of the DAP was small and it was to be transformed after Hitler joined and became its propaganda officer. It was largely Hitler's tutelage that placed the party on the political map — and under a new title: the National Socialist German Workers' Party (NSDAP).

The DAP and the NSDAP also represented popular mass-appeal offshoots of the Thule Society, a militant, nationalist, anti-semitic, anti-communist sect based in Munich. The sect had its own newspaper, the *Munich Observer*, and served as an important social and political arena for aspiring right-wing groups.

The early history of the Nazi Party is dominated by two themes: Hitler's drive to place the party under his own dictatorial control and the building up of a mass membership through radical reorganisation. Hitler was successful in both. He was party leader by July 1921, with dictatorial powers. By 1923 membership had mushroomed with the entry of numerous ex-soldiers and free corps members into the party and with the absorption of other rightist groups. In the meantime the party had acquired the *Munich Observer* as its official newspaper, while Hitler's accomplice, Ernst Röhm, had established the formidable paramilitary wing of the NSDAP — the SA, or Storm Troopers.

In geographical terms, the singular feature of the early Nazi Party was its highly circumscribed focus. It began life in Munich and Munich remained the seat of its activity for almost a decade. The reasons for this were mainly twofold. Bavaria was a hotbed of political dissent with highly tolerant, 'reactional' city and state governments. Hitler insisted on the primacy of the Munich party organisation as a means of ensuring his dictatorial control. Both features tended to be reinforced by the tradition of German separatism. It would be wrong, though, to give the impression that the Nazi movement penetrated no further than southern Germany. The absorption in December 1922 of the German Socialist Party (DSP), which had local centres throughout much of Germany, widened Nazi influence almost overnight. Moreover, the symbolism of the party permeated an extensive area, emphasising what was to become a vital 'engine' in the acquisition of power: mass persuasion without real political understanding or conviction.

THE GENESIS OF THE NAZI PARTY

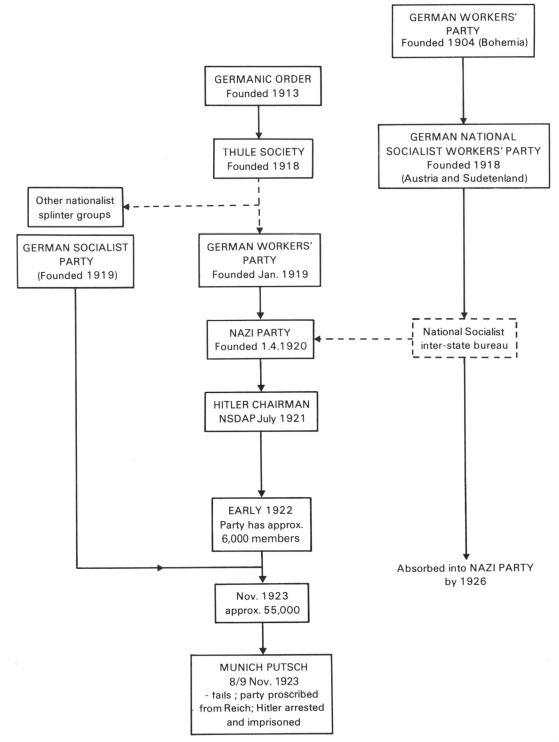

Mein Kampf

Most dictators have committed their ideas to paper to produce a universal testament in the biblical tradition. Hitler's testament was *Mein Kampf*. Part of it was written during his months in prison following the abortive *putsch*. It was published first in two volumes in 1925 and 1926. Later a popular one-volume edition appeared which became the fundamental Nazi gospel. By the time of Hitler's death over 8 million copies had been distributed or sold in Germany. Its writing is turgid and disorganised, its terminology confused and inconsistent. As an exegesis of political ideology it is both inept and unoriginal. For the enthusiast none of these things mattered. That *Mein Kampf* existed was enough. It lent a pseudo-intellectual respectability to Hitler in the popular imagination; it did not matter that thousands of copies lay unread and even unopened. For the more perceptive observer *Mein Kampf* was undoubtedly an essential vehicle to the understanding of the Hitler mind. Some commentators saw it as a blueprint of what Germany was to become. Since 1945 it has been commonplace to deride the 'appeasement lobby' for failing to give adequate attention to the message *Mein Kampf* contained. But in both instances this is to ascribe to Hitler a rationality of thought and consistency of action which he patently lacked, and his foreign policy goals appeared totally incredible in the 1920s. *Mein Kampf* is important in revealing the range of ideas upon which Hitler drew and the overall frame in which those ideas were cast. It is especially instructive on Nazi propaganda techniques and on anti-semitism. Beyond this, though, it is the barest and loosest of guides to the Nazi regime as its course unfolded.

SOME OF THE INTELLECTUAL ROOTS OF MEIN KAMPF	
Count Gobineau	nineteenth-century French racial theorist: the Aryan represented the pinnacle of racial purity.
H. S. Chamberlain	British-born writer on racism: saw race as key to history.
Hans Günther	German anthropologist, author of *Race history of the German nation*, 1922.
Heinrich Treitschke	German professor of history who glorified the state and the necessity of war.
Richard Wagner	German romantic composer whose operas recalled the heroic myths of German culture.
Karl Haushofer	German professor of geopolitics: writer on the geographical bases of political power, including *Lebensraum* concept.

(Note: Hitler was probably conversant with few of the works of these figures first-hand. Ideas were invariably acquired second-hand from self-appointed Nazi ideologists and from the lowest of the popular press.)

THE IDEOLOGY OF NATIONAL SOCIALISM

HITLER'S VIEW OF HISTORY

He took a biological interpretation which saw history as a Darwinian struggle between races. Aryans formed the highest order and were the founders of culture. Jews were the lowest order and acted as destroyers of culture. Intermarriage was viewed as devilry and likely to debase the order of races. For the Aryan race to survive, its purity had to be preserved at all costs and its social dominance intensified.

GERMANY IN HITLER'S INTERPRETATION OF HISTORY

The German homeland and its people were seen as a receptive environment for the fulfilment of such a biological view of history, notably with its long-standing pockets of anti-semitism and its latent pan-German sentiments. As the German nation stood in the 1920s, it was beholden to liberalist and economic principles. The Nazi Party, with its substitution of leadership for liberal democracy and its realisation of the fundamental racial course of history, would arrest this pattern and set Germany on a path towards European and later world domination.

THE COURSE OF GERMAN REVIVAL AND SUPREMACY

The racist vision and its conjoining with the German nation-state as defined at Versailles signalled an immediate quest for additional *Lebensraum* or 'living space'. The quest was given added urgency by the need to strike a stronger political bargaining position among the major European states. For Hitler, additional *Lebensraum* was to be found not in the nineteenth-century concept of empire but in extending the German state in Europe, in particular through a massive eastward colonisation of lands occupied by 'racially inferior' Slav and Latin peoples. Within such an expanded German homeland would emerge an elite international racial order to which all political, social and economic structures bowed and under which a progression of increasingly inferior racial groups laboured.

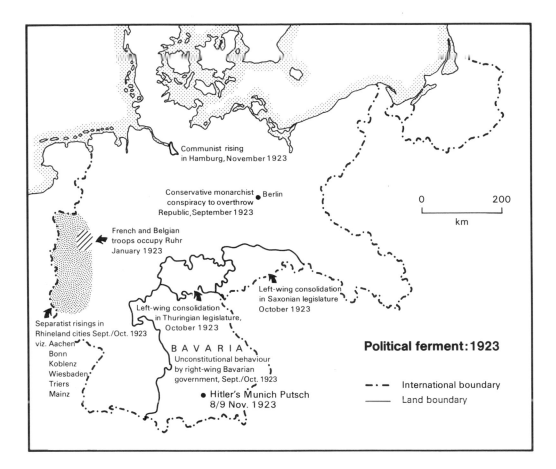

Communist rising
in Hamburg, November 1923

Conservative monarchist • Berlin
conspiracy to overthrow
Republic, September 1923

French and Belgian
troops occupy Ruhr
January 1923

Left-wing consolidation
in Saxonian legislature
October 1923

Left-wing consolidation
in Thuringian legislature,
October 1923

Separatist risings in
Rhineland cities Sept./Oct. 1923
viz. Aachen
Bonn
Koblenz
Wiesbaden
Triers
Mainz

B A V A R I A
Unconstitutional behaviour
by right-wing Bavarian
government, Sept./Oct. 1923

• Hitler's Munich Putsch
8/9 Nov. 1923

0   200
km

Political ferment: 1923

— · —   International boundary
———   Land boundary

THE INFLATION

Average monthly dollar quotations

January	1919	8.9 marks
July	1919	14.0 ··
January	1920	64.8 ··
July	1920	39.5 ··
January	1921	64.9 ··
July	1921	76.7 ··
January	1922	191.8 ··
July	1922	493.2 ··
January	1923	17,972.0 ··
July	1923	353,412.0 ··
August	1923	4,620,455.0 ··
September	1923	98,860,000.0 ··
October	1923	25,260,208,000.0 ···
November 15	1923	4,200,000,000,000.0 marks

Source: Stolper, 1940

Political Ferment: 1923

The year 1923 saw the fledgling Nazi Party at its zenith and at its nadir. The party held its first national congress in Munich in January and membership rose rapidly to reach over 50,000 by November. That same month, however, witnessed the disastrous Munich *putsch* — an attempted *coup d'état* by the Nazis which failed abysmally and led to Hitler's arrest and the banning of the party from the entire Reich.

The dramatic turnabout in NSDAP fortunes was precipitated largely by outside events, for in 1923 the Weimar Republic was plagued by external and internal crises, presenting a tantalising seedbed for dissenting political groups. In Bavaria, the seat of NSDAP political activity, the dissenting ground was rendered yet more fertile as a result of the highly equivocal attitude of its state government to that of the Reich and of the similarly disposed Bavarian Reichswehr.

From its inception the Weimar government faced formidable problems, but the most outstanding was the issue of German reparations. In 1922 the government of Chancellor Cuno requested a temporary suspension of reparations on account of the country's desperate economic plight. France refused the request and promptly occupied the Ruhr with troops. Cuno's government protested, refusing further co-operation over reparations, and stalemate prevailed. The Ruhr occupation and the passive resistance it generated spelt disaster for what little economic well-being remained in the Reich. Bankruptcy loomed, the value of the currency fell and resulted in rampant inflation, while unrest erupted all over Germany.

In the Ruhr itself, separatist movements present since the collapse of the Wilhelmine state came rapidly to the surface. By late October, open clashes were occurring in Rhineland cities. Dissent in Bavaria gathered momentum in late September with the declaration of a state of emergency and in late October with the nullification of an earlier Bavarian decree putting the Law for the Protection of the Republic into effect. In Saxony and Thuringia, meanwhile, leftist movements had advanced sufficiently to be offered representation in their respective Land governments by mid-October. The Reich government's attempts to restore its authority by peaceful means met with little success. Moreover, at a time when the loyalty of the Reichswehr to the government was under strain from a conservative monarchist conspiracy, the option of military force was less than automatic. But the communists in Saxony and Thuringia soon rescued the Reich government. By calling for resistance and violence against troops, they provided a clear excuse for the intervention of the Reichswehr, whereupon social democratic governments were quickly reinstated in both Länder. In Bavaria, though, where Hitler had already gained himself political leadership of the *Kampfbund* association of militant rightist groups, events soon developed their own momentum. At a nationalist meeting in a Munich beer hall on the evening of 8 November, attended by a host of senior state officials and military men, Hitler and his armed entourage burst in and declared the formation of a provisional Reich government. At first it seemed that the civil and military leaders had capitulated, but within 24 hours police and militia had defeated the putschists. The organisation of the *coup* had been inept: for instance, vital communication offices were left untouched; but more significant was the tenuous unity of the Bavarian right, Hitler intent upon personal dictatorship while others sought restoration of the Bavarian monarchy.

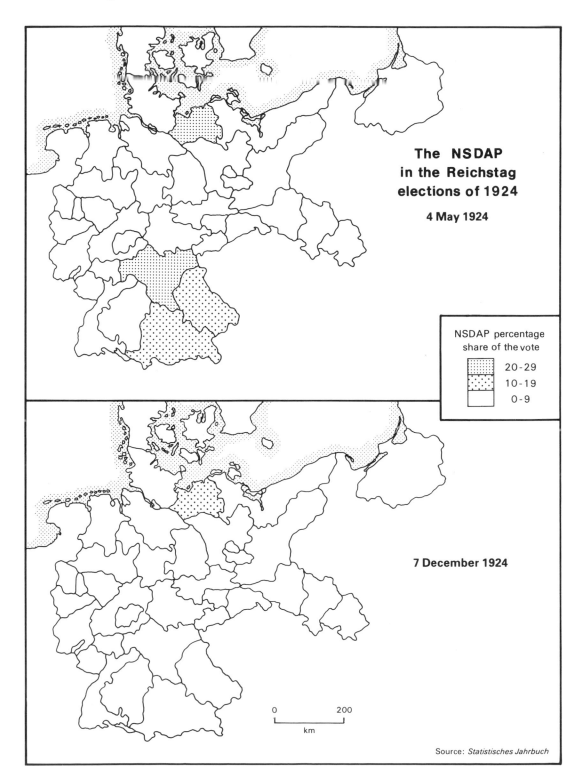

**The NSDAP
in the Reichstag
elections of 1924**

4 May 1924

NSDAP percentage
share of the vote

20 - 29
10 - 19
0 - 9

7 December 1924

0   200
km

Source: *Statistisches Jahrbuch*

The Parliamentary Route to Power

Just 13 months after the Munich *putsch*, Hitler obtained his release from Landsberg gaol only to find the remnants of his political party in chronic disarray. The tenuous bonds between the local party groups across Germany were quickly split by the failed *putsch* and separatist tendencies soon appeared. In Bavaria, the

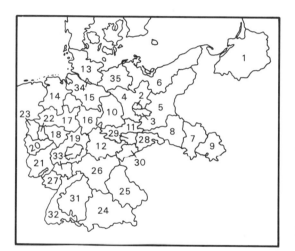

Electoral districts

1. East Prussia
2. Berlin
3. Potsdam II
4. Potsdam I
5. Frankfurt a.d. Oder
6. Pomerania
7. Breslau
8. Liegnitz
9. Oppeln
10. Magdeburg
11. Merseburg
12. Thuringia
13. Schleswig-Holstein
14. Weser-Ems
15. East Hanover
16. South Hanover-Brunswick
17. Westphalia-North
18. Westphalia South
19. Hesse-Nassau
20. Cologne-Aachen
21. Koblenz-Trier
22. Düsseldorf-East
23. Düsseldorf-West
24. Upper Bavaria-Swabia
25. Lower Bavaria
26. Franconia
27. Palatinate
28. Dresden-Bautzen
29. Leipzig
30. Chemnitz-Zwickau
31. Württemberg
32. Baden
33. Hesse-Darmstadt
34. Hamburg
35. Mecklenburg

support which Hitler had received from the 'establishment' was quickly dissipated following the events of November 1923 and right-wing opinion there became even more sharply polarised than in the earlier years of the Nazi Party.

The grand lesson of the failed *putsch* was that any Nazi revolution would have to be organised through the existing machinery of government and politics. To many of the party faithful, a campaign for parliamentary representation appeared anathema, but Hitler and several of his closest advisers quickly recognised that there was little alternative and thus the party made its first foray into nation-wide legal representation with the Reichstag elections of May 1924. Given the events of the preceding November, the results were surprisingly favourable. The radical right in combination achieved 32 Reichstag seats and 6.5 per cent of the national vote. In Mecklenburg and Franconia they registered results of over 20 per cent. There were further Reichstag elections in December 1924. This time, however, the radical right fared badly. Their seats fell to 14 and their percentage national vote to 3. Regionally, only Mecklenburg survived as a significant focus of support. This was the beginning of almost six years in the political wilderness. In the Reichstag elections of May 1928, for example, the party's percentage share of the national vote fell to 2.6 and there was not a single electoral district in which it polled above 10 per cent. The victors of the election were the Social Democrats, who were able to form a majority coalition government. The communists also gained ground, taking just over 10 per cent of the national vote.

LANDTAG ELECTIONS, 1928-30: NSDAP/VÖLK-NAT.
BLOC PERCENTAGE SHARE OF VOTE

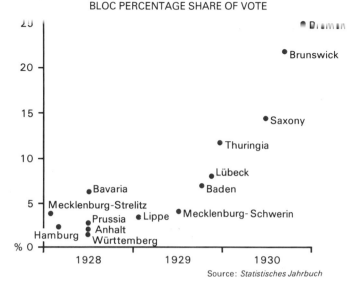

Source: *Statistisches Jahrbuch*

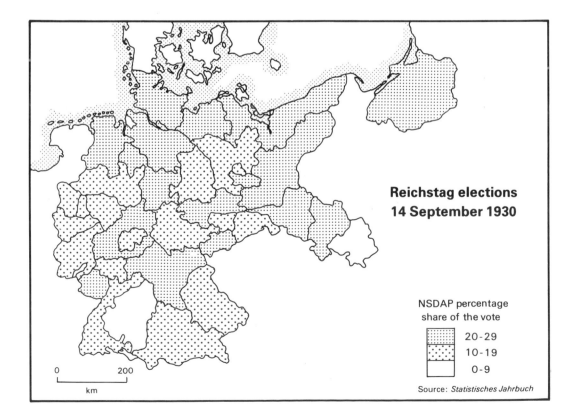

**Reichstag elections
14 September 1930**

NSDAP percentage
share of the vote

20-29
10-19
0-9

Source: *Statistisches Jahrbuch*

Electoral breakthrough

The relative impotence of the Nazi Party as an electoral force in the later 1920s was largely explained by the growing stability of Weimar Germany. The apparent success of Foreign Minister Streseman in handling the reparations issue, for example, and increasing economic vitality at home ran counter to the appeal of National Socialism and radical right-wing sentiments generally. However, the pattern did not last. By early 1929 signs of weakness in the world economy were becoming plain and the crash of the New York stock market in October finally set the seal on an unprecedented worldwide slump. Germany, with its postwar economy so dependent on foreign investment, suffered very badly. Parallel to this, a separate political ferment had been growing at home over Streseman's negotiations for a final agreement over reparations. The right-wing parties had combined to campaign for a national

plebiscite on the question. The Nazis joined in this and quickly found their access to the political arena much enlarged. Although the plebiscite, when it came in December 1929, resulted in a decisive defeat for the right, this was incidental to the more general remobilisation of rightwing sympathies which the campaign set in train. The pattern was clearly expressed in the various state elections of 1929 where the Nazis again began to register poll shares of the order of 10 and 20 per cent. It showed itself still more clearly in the Reichstag elections of September 1930 when the party secured 18.3 per cent of the national vote and 107 seats. Party support had become generalised at 20 to 30 per cent across much of the North German Plain and the south-east, except for cities and industrial foci. Representation was weaker in the Catholic south and the west, including Bavaria, but no district failed to register gains in Nazi support alongside the corresponding votes of May 1928 and December 1924.

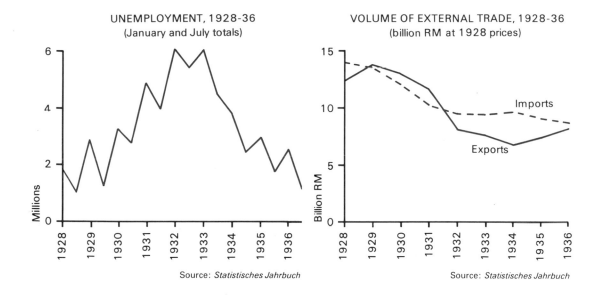

UNEMPLOYMENT, 1928-36
(January and July totals)

Source: *Statistisches Jahrbuch*

VOLUME OF EXTERNAL TRADE, 1928-36
(billion RM at 1928 prices)

Source: *Statistisches Jahrbuch*

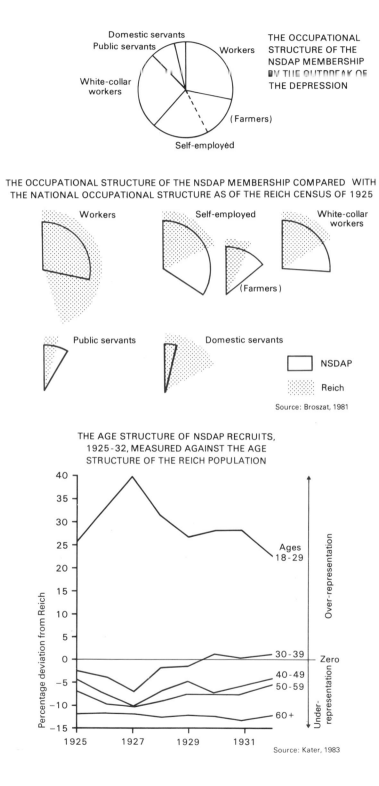

THE OCCUPATIONAL STRUCTURE OF THE NSDAP MEMBERSHIP BY THE OUTBREAK OF THE DEPRESSION

THE OCCUPATIONAL STRUCTURE OF THE NSDAP MEMBERSHIP COMPARED WITH THE NATIONAL OCCUPATIONAL STRUCTURE AS OF THE REICH CENSUS OF 1925

Source: Broszat, 1981

THE AGE STRUCTURE OF NSDAP RECRUITS, 1925-32, MEASURED AGAINST THE AGE STRUCTURE OF THE REICH POPULATION

Source: Kater, 1983

The Nazi Party

Few political parties attract representation from all sections of the community in uniform measure. As an extremist party, the NSDAP predictably found far stronger support in some than in others, although few of these sections conformed to the familiarly accepted breeding grounds of political radicalism. The NSDAP found most of its members from among the diverse ranks of the middle class, especially among the petit bourgeoisie. For example, self-employed farmers, artisans and tradesmen were represented in almost double the proportion suggested by the national breakdown of occupational groups. Much the same was true of the free professions, the civil service and white-collar workers generally. Working-class groups, however, were equivalently under-represented. The middle class were attracted to join the Party not for the vision of society that it embraced (most were probably ignorant of this, anyway), but for its stand against various elements of the established order.

Aside from its class bias, the other striking feature of the 'adolescent' NSDAP was the youth of its membership. In part this was the result of deliberate party policy: young, immature minds were correctly perceived as more receptive to propaganda techniques; it would have been much more difficult to achieve the same levels of persuasion among those with longer political and constitutional perspectives. However, the whole style of the Nazi Party was one that was likely to appeal to the physical and social energies of youth. The rite of the mass meeting, the adventurism of the paramilitary SA, the camaraderie of the Hitler Youth with its emphasis on physical training, and the *naïveté* and violent apocalyptic romanticism of the movement — all these features (and many others) set the NSDAP apart from the traditional political parties, except the communists. As unemployment rose in the Depression, therefore, as the hatreds and fears of the NSDAP spread like a contagious disease, the youthful following acquired a secular momentum from which the party organs fed easily as much as they manipulated.

The NSDAP's anti-capitalist, anti-Marxist and anti-semitic fervour struck distinctive chords within the wider electoral community, as did its more general antagonism towards republicanism and those who instituted and subsequently supported the Weimar regime. Long-standing disquiet amongst rural communities over the burgeoning growth and pervasive influence of industrialism was catalysed first by the Inflation and then the Depression; almost any political party which stood even remotely against the modern industrial ethos would have found a ripe body of support. Somewhat paradoxically, socialists and communists were viewed by Hitler as agents of modern capitalist industry. In this sense, alternative political parties were appraised less for their professed ideologies than for the socio-economic dispositions of their primary supporters. Hatred of 'Marxism' thus unified the most disparate interests behind Nazism.

NSDAP MEMBERSHIP, 1919-30

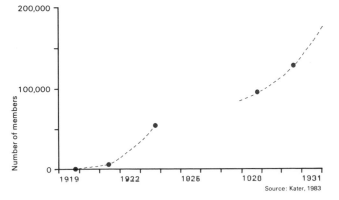

Source: Kater, 1983

25

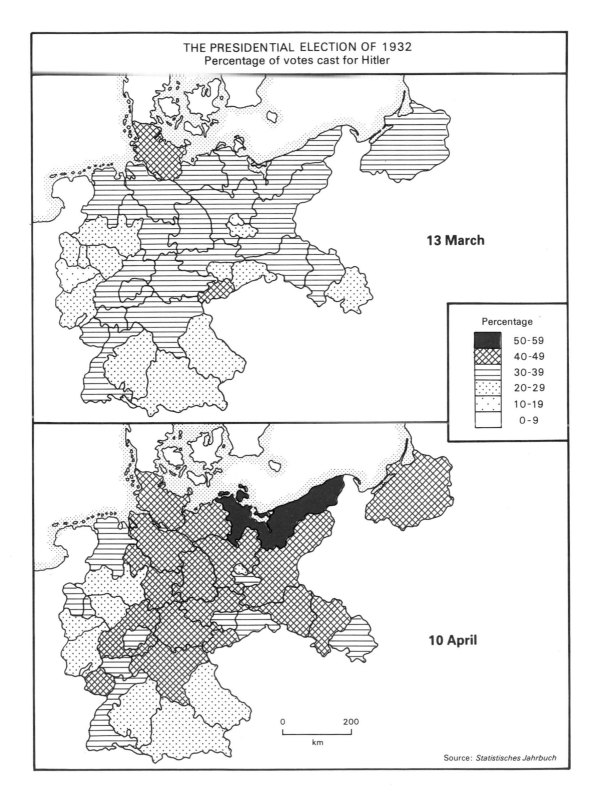

THE PRESIDENTIAL ELECTION OF 1932
Percentage of votes cast for Hitler

13 March

Percentage

50-59
40-49
30-39
20-29
10-19
0-9

10 April

0   200
km

Source: *Statistisches Jahrbuch*

Hitler's candidature for the presidency: spring 1932

Hindenburg's term of office as Reich President expired in the spring of 1932 and the prospect quickly became the focus for a round of intense political manoeuvring among the different forces of opposition and Brüning's emergency government. Hitler looked towards leadership in government if his party was to agree to support Brüning's scheme to re-elect Hindenburg. This proved too bitter a pill for Hindenburg and his allies to swallow. The outcome was thus a contested election in which Hitler soon emerged as Hindenburg's major rival, readily eclipsing the Nationalists' candidate, Düsterberg. The result of the first contest on 13 March revealed a staggering advance in the National Socialist vote against the September 1930 Reichstag elections. It rose from just under 6.5 million to just under 11.5 million, forming 30.1 per cent of the total. Moreover, this level of support was general throughout northern, eastern and central Germany. Hindenburg polled some 18.6 million votes but just failed to secure an absolute majority. Thus a second election resulted in which the ageing President obtained the necessary majority, but where Hitler increased his share of the vote to 36.8 per cent. The additional Nazi support came almost entirely from the areas which showed most strongly in favour of Hitler in the first election contest. A key to understanding the scale of Nazi success was the frenetic nature of the election campaign, which was masterminded by Goebbels. The party machine sought to penetrate every quarter of Germany and, in a novel propaganda *coup*, Hitler travelled by aeroplane from one election rally to another.

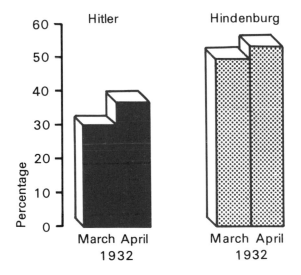

VOTES CAST FOR THE TWO MAIN
PRESIDENTIAL CONTENDERS

Source: *Statistisches Jahrbuch*

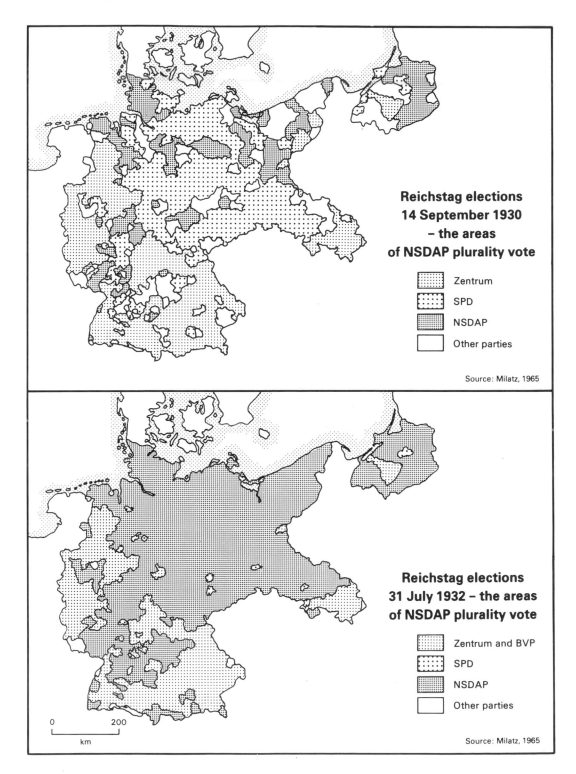

**Reichstag elections
14 September 1930
– the areas
of NSDAP plurality vote**

Zentrum

SPD

NSDAP

Other parties

Source: Milatz, 1965

**Reichstag elections
31 July 1932 – the areas
of NSDAP plurality vote**

Zentrum and BVP

SPD

NSDAP

Other parties

0   200

km

Source: Milatz, 1965

Electoral domination

The crowning point of the Nazis' electoral success came in the Reichstag elections of 31 July 1932. They increased their Reichstag seats from 107 to 230 and acquired 13.7 million popular votes. From the accompanying maps, it can be seen that party support had become yet more clearly generalised throughout northern, eastern and central Germany. Whereas in September 1930 its strongest support was spread disparately across the face of the country, by July 1932 it was continuous over extensive land areas. Only the predominantly Catholic south and west had resisted the appeals of National Socialism. With 37 per cent of the popular vote, the Nazis easily outstripped their former winning rival, the Social Democrats. Theoretically, Hitler was in a position to lead a coalition government. It was also possible that he might be drawn into a coalition under the then Chancellor, von Papen. Neither scheme materialised, however. The President held Hitler and his party in distaste and would not countenance Hitler as Chancellor or in any other prominent cabinet position. The prospect of a Hitler coalition, meanwhile, evaporated when Chancellor von Papen obtained a presidential decree for dissolving the Reichstag before it had even sat.

SHARE OF POPULAR VOTE OF MAIN POLITICAL PARTIES, 1924-32

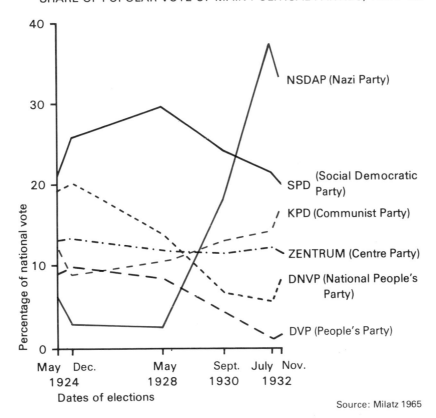

Source: Milatz 1965

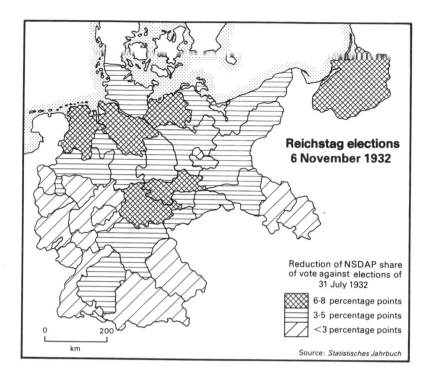

**Reichstag elections
6 November 1932**

Reduction of NSDAP share
of vote against elections of
31 July 1932

6-8 percentage points
3-5 percentage points
<3 percentage points

Source: *Statistisches Jahrbuch*

0   200
km

The new Reichstag elections on 6 November 1932 saw the Nazis lose ground on a significant scale. Their seats fell from 230 to 196 and their share of the popular vote from 37 to 33 per cent. Accompanying this, divisions were appearing in the party as a result of the frustrations experienced in achieving power by popular consent. Paradoxically, however, the waning Nazi vote and the internal unrest were two of the very factors which propelled Hitler to the chancellorship. By the end of January 1933, President Hindenburg had agreed to a government led by Hitler, the cabinet consisting of eight conservatives and only three Nazis.

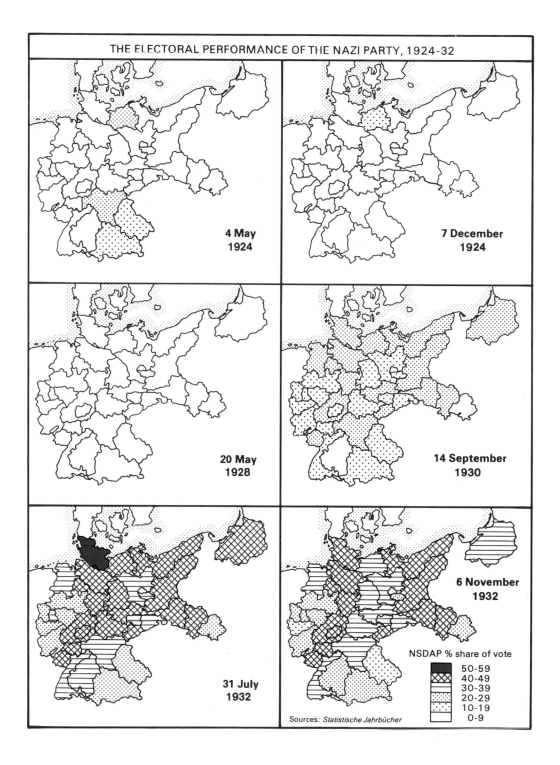

THE ELECTORAL PERFORMANCE OF THE NAZI PARTY, 1924-32

4 May 1924

7 December 1924

20 May 1928

14 September 1930

31 July 1932

6 November 1932

NSDAP % share of vote

50-59
40-49
30-39
20-29
10-19
0-9

Sources: *Statistische Jahrbücher*

The Road to Dictatorship

Although the Nazis failed to obtain a majority share of the popular vote in each of the elections of 1932, they undoubtedly held a fairly strong mandate to govern given the complex system of proportional representation of the Weimar constitution. But Hitler's chancellorship, together with the two supporting Nazi members of cabinet, did not really derive from this mandate. It sprang first from the presidency but, behind the façade of that office, from a variety of power blocs which had long been active in German political life and which had been gathering momentum in the economic and political turmoil which characterised Weimar Germany from 1929. Since March 1930, in fact, the authority of the Reichstag as the institutional embodiment of popular political opinion and as the forum of national government had been in a state of semi-abeyance. The collapse of the Social Democrat Coalition in spring 1930 marked the beginning of an era of extra parliamentary government under Article 48 of the Weimar constitution. The original purpose of this constitutional provision was to give the presidency special powers in times of national emergency. By mid-1930, however, the provision was being used to bypass the authority of the Reichstag. The Reichstag itself could repeal all legislation under such emergency rule, but since the presidency had power to dissolve the Reichstag, this was a poor safeguard. The pattern was set in motion when President Hindenburg appointed Heinrich Brüning to the chancellorship without the Reichstag's consent and threatened to invoke emergency rule if Brüning's policies were blocked. In July 1930, the Reichstag duly threw out Brüning's plans and a dissolution decree followed. The position was by no means irretrievable, since a newly elected Reichstag might have been more amenable to the new Chancellor's plans. However, the September Reichstag elections saw strong gains for the extremist parties. The result was a polarisation of the pattern. Between 1930 and 1932, the German President ratified 109 emergency decrees while the Reichstag passed just 29 bills, nearly all of them minor. By June 1932, the Reichstag's status had been reduced to that of a rump, its views neither listened to nor sought.

This was the framework of power relations in which Hitler first acceded to government. The framework is important in making clear that the Nazis did not come to power with the consent of the Reichstag, the parliamentary road, however far along that way it progressed. But it is even more vitally important in understanding the speed with which Hitler was able to move towards the creation of a more authoritarian and totalitarian regime. In the latter aspect, Hitler's actions were presaged by one of his immediate predecessors as Chancellor: Franz von Papen. In mid-July 1932 von Papen instituted a peaceful *coup d'état* over the Prussian Land administration in an attempt to consolidate his shaky power base. The government there readily capitulated and the result was the undermining of a critical element of German federalism. The incorporation of Prussia was achieved through an emergency presidential decree. Hitler enjoyed the same facility upon his assumption of office in late January 1933.

Extraparliamentary government presents a route to dictatorship which can be readily elucidated. It hardly explains why the route ended in a Nazi take-over. The party's electoral successes were undoubtedly substantial; and to an extent

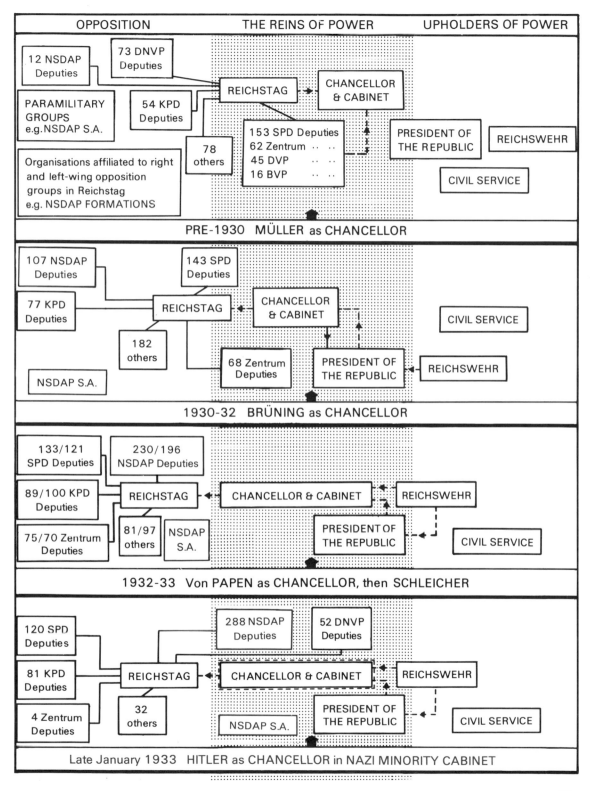

OPPOSITION   THE REINS OF POWER   UPHOLDERS OF POWER

PRE-1930 MÜLLER as CHANCELLOR

1930-32 BRÜNING as CHANCELLOR

1932-33 Von PAPEN as CHANCELLOR, then SCHLEICHER

Late January 1933 HITLER as CHANCELLOR in NAZI MINORITY CABINET

THE FUEHRERPRINZIP

Party organisation (circa 1926)

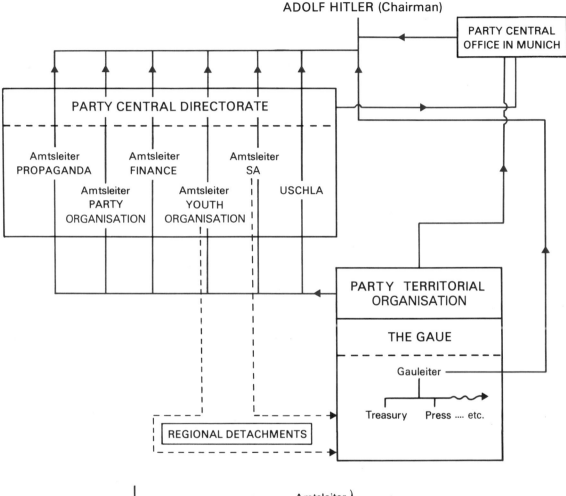

ADOLF HITLER (Chairman)

PARTY CENTRAL OFFICE IN MUNICH

PARTY CENTRAL DIRECTORATE

Amtsleiter PROPAGANDA

Amtsleiter FINANCE

Amtsleiter SA

Amtsleiter PARTY ORGANISATION

Amtsleiter YOUTH ORGANISATION

USCHLA

PARTY TERRITORIAL ORGANISATION

THE GAUE

Gauleiter

Treasury   Press .... etc.

REGIONAL DETACHMENTS

Lines of subordination

Amtsleiter ⎫
Gauleiter ⎬ Delegate leaders

which transcended the impotence of the Reichstag. But the final clues to Nazi accession lie in simple historical eventuation. The Nazis' mild reverse in the November 1932 polls which gave their opponents a false sense of confidence; army responsiveness to Nazi schemes of rearmament; the authoritarian designs of Hindenburg and von Papen; and the acquiescence of big business were some of the elements which in complex combination eventually placed Hitler in power. With a backcloth composed of the economic and social cataclysms of the Depression, the Nazi entourage entered upon a predisposed stage-set, its choreography determined largely by the actions of others, to emerge with lightning speed into the most infamous police state of the twentieth century.

The Fuehrerprinzip

When examining the growth and organisation of the Nazi Party and, after 1933, the workings of the Nazi state, it is difficult to erase from the mind such common organisational principles as delegation and hierarchy. But one has to do this in order to understand fully the operation of the Nazi machine. Despite their advancing scale and intricacy, the institutions of Nazism bore no shred of comparison with the orthodox systems of administrative bureaucracy. The Fuehrerprinzip placed individual personages above bureaucratic structures as the final authority. The result was that Nazi leaders could interfere at every level, at will or whim. The only power relationship recognised within the Fuehrerprinzip was the responsibility of subordinates to their superiors. This relationship was undefined and yet total. The pattern was already well established in the mid-1920s, as the accompanying chart of party organisation reveals. Despite the façade of an administrative hierarchy involving delegation of authority, the reality was otherwise. The Gauleiters, for instance, could exploit their regional bases to a degree quite inconsistent with the position of their offices in an orthodox administrative system. They were directly subservient to Hitler (by whom they were appointed), and saw themselves as his direct agents in the field. However, other Nazi leaders viewed the Gauleiters as their own subordinates. One of these was the Chief of Central Party Office, another the Amtsleiter for Party Finance. The inevitable result was a remarkable confusion of responsibility, one that became a hallmark of Nazism. The Fuehrerprinzip became a pervasive feature of the party and, later, of the state. While Hitler represented its ultimate embodiment, surrogate leadership became widespread in the Third Reich. It was a crucial symptom of the style of Hitler's dictatorship: improvised, remote from details, and built on patronage, not principle.

Berlin military parade under the Third Reich

The Third Reich is Born

In the eyes of many outside the Nazi Party, Hitler's chancellorship was a temporary expedient in a time of difficult political and constitutional transition. Few opponents of the National Socialists were unaware of the extra-legal activities of organisations such as the SA, but most saw this as a necessary evil given Hitler's mass following and most were complacent about the opposition's ability to control the Nazis' course, whether through the federal structure or via one of the major institutions of state. That an institution like the Reichswehr should give token backing to Hitler reinforced this state of mind, for here was the ultimate guardian (historically) of Reich security. These features combined to give a muted character to the forces of opposition as the authoritarian and totalitarian goals of the Nazis were rapidly revealed. And before more concerted efforts could be set in train, the Nazis had all but destroyed the legitimate means of dissent. One of the critical difficulties faced by opposition groups was the astonishing speed with which Hitler was able to consolidate the Nazis' power. In part this was a result of preceding developments: the suspension of parliamentary government and its replacement by government by emergency decree; and the absorption of Prussia into the Reich. Hitler capitalised fully on the emergency powers at his disposal as Chancellor and, by managing to invest his two cabinet members as Ministers of the Interior in the Reich and in Prussia, the Nazis held a trump card in their ability to manipulate the rule of law very quickly. However, none of this can detract from the simple fact that the Nazis had a powerful grass-roots party organisation, highly effective coercive forces (the SA and the SS) with which their will could be reinforced and, above all, a leader and central party apparatus with a clearly defined goal which was to be pursued with unremitting zeal and sometimes acute political acumen.

MINISTERIAL CONTINUITY, 1932-3		
Von PAPEN Cabinet 1932	SCHLEICHER Cabinet 1932/3	HITLER Cabinet 30 Jan. 1933
		Hitler
Von Papen		Von Papen (Vice-Chancellor)
Von Neurath	Von Neurath	Von Neurath (Foreign Office)
Krosigk	Krosigk	Krosigk (Finance)
	Von Rübenach	Von Rübenach (Communications)
Gürtner	Gürtner	Gürtner (Justice)
		Seldte
		Hugenberg
		Frick
		Goering
		Von Blomberg

THE ARENA FOR THE MAKING OF AN AUTHORITARIAN NAZI STATE

The forces against authoritarianism	The forces in favour of authoritarianism in some form

Political parties :
  KPD (including Communists'
    Combat League)
  SPD (including Reichsbanner
    organisation)
 	
Free Trade Unions
 	
Reichstag officers
 	
Legal system and the Weimar
constitution
	President
	
	Reichswehr
	
	Non-Nazi cabinet members
	
	Political parties:
	  DNVP
	  Zentrum
	  DVP
	Civil service, especially ministerial
	bureaucracy in Reich, in Prussia, and in
	some Länder
	{ 'Big Business'
	  Reich Association of German Industry
	Reich Land League
	
	Stahlhelm

Hitler's first move as Chancellor was to obtain a decree for the dissolution of the Reichstag and the calling of new elections on 5 March 1933. If the Nazis could be seen to win a parliamentary mandate, the task of political and constitutional manipulation would be that much easier. The dissolution was quickly followed by one giving power to ban public meetings and the press where they were deemed to undermine the security of the Reich. In effect this became a blanket facility for silencing opposition in the run-up to the election and was most successfully applied in Prussia under Goering's interior ministryship and in those remaining Länder where National Socialist governments prevailed. Von Papen's Prussian *coup* in July 1932 had not entirely taken over the reins of administration and control, but this was completed in a presidential decree of 6 February 1933, whereupon police chiefs and other officials unsympathetic to the Nazi cause were replaced. The spreading tentacles of Nazi control in Prussia gathered further momentum when on 22 February Goering set up an auxil-

iary police force drawn from the ranks of the SA, the SS and the Stahlhelm, ostensibly to combat the excesses of political opposition. The relative moderation which characterised the Nazis' approach to their opponents in Hitler's first month of power was brought to a dramatic close when the Dutch communist van der Lubbe set fire to the Reichstag building on 27 February 1933. It was the act of an individual, but the Nazis seized upon it as indicating a general communist uprising and draconian measures were demanded. By the Reichstag Fire Decree of the following day, all basic democratic rights enjoyed under the Weimar constitution were terminated and the Reich government was accorded special powers to override the Land governments in the event of their failing to observe the decree adequately. In Prussia Goering did not hesitate to use the decree to make large-scale arrests of communists and any persons who co-operated with or supported them. Outside Prussia, arrests were more selective, but all Communist Party activities became illegal.

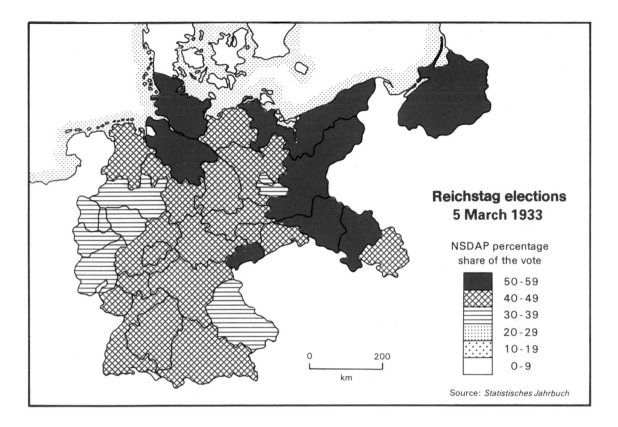

Reichstag elections
5 March 1933

NSDAP percentage
share of the vote

50 - 59
40 - 49
30 - 39
20 - 29
10 - 19
0 - 9

0   200
km

Source: *Statistisches Jahrbuch*

In the Reichstag elections of 5 March 1933, the Nazi Party polled 43.9 per cent of the national vote, an increase of almost eleven percentage points over the previous November election. Even given the impediments to a free election posed by the various emergency decrees of February 1933, this result constituted one of the strongest mandates in the electoral history of the Weimar Republic. And the degree to which a free election was impeded is counterbalanced by the extraordinary 88.7 per cent turnout, the more so given that the election was the third inside a year. In the preceding votes of July and November 1932, the turnouts had been 84 and 80 per cent respectively. Previous nonvoters were clearly being mobilised and, judging from the increase in Nazi support, Hitler's appeal was a decisive influence in their political activation. The Nazi election performance was not, however, sufficient to achieve a parliamentary majority. Hitler achieved this only through the indulgence of the DNVP, which gave him 51.9 per cent of the popular vote in total.

It is clear from the electoral map that the Nazis did not enjoy overwhelming support anywhere. They remained strongest in East Prussia, in the eastern border lands and in the north, but in none of the Reichstag electoral districts did they record more than 56 per cent of the vote. In the industrial west, meanwhile, the Nazis were supported by less than 40 per cent of voters.

Hitler interpreted the election results as a grand success, as a mandate for 'national revolution'. And as the following weeks and months of 1933 unfolded, this view was put vigorously into practice. Now Hitler began to make full use of the elaborate party organisation on the ground, including the SA and the SS. The paramilitary wings moved swiftly into action in those Länder where the party still had no majority, namely in Bavaria, Baden, Hesse, Saxony and Württemberg, and in the city states of Hamburg, Bremen and Lübeck. In many cases, their precipitateness was self-appointed, Hitler playing no direct executive role. To this extent Germany was seeing the beginnings of a revolution from below. Town halls, courts, banks, trade union, party and newspaper offices were occupied. There were summary arrests of opponents of the regime. The setting up of auxiliary police forces, as had occurred earlier in Prussia, proliferated and the subordination of these party police groupings to the regular state police (and hence to the Reich government) became increasingly suspect. What Goering had already achieved in Prussia was now repeated even more rigorously in what remained of the Federal Republic. In a matter of days, in fact, effective government of the Länder was in the hands of Reich commissioners, many of them prominent Nazi officials. The strongest resistance came in Bavaria, but the Nazis won the day when appeals for the

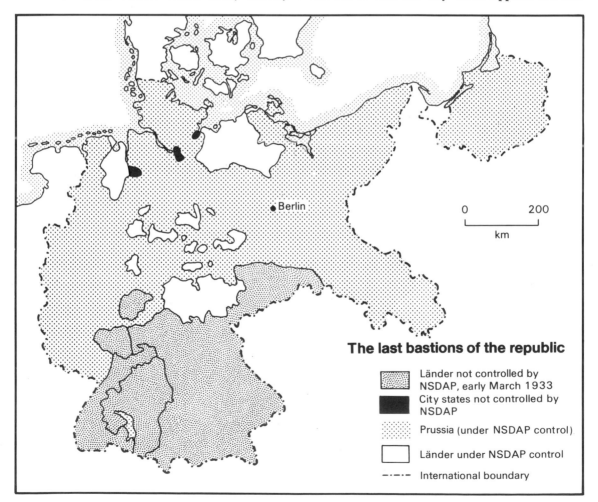

The last bastions of the republic

- Länder not controlled by NSDAP, early March 1933
- City states not controlled by NSDAP
- Prussia (under NSDAP control)
- Länder under NSDAP control
- – - – International boundary

intervention of the Reichswehr were rebuffed by Hindenberg, the ageing President.

With the reins of government at regional as well as national level in his hands, Hitler set about strengthening his control as Chancellor. He did this first by persuading the new Reichstag to grant him (as Chancellor) full executive and legislative powers for a period of four years. This the Reichstag did on 23 March, after the Nazis had locked up the 81 KPD deputies and won over the Catholic Centre Party with vague promises in order to get the required two-thirds majority. The second stage was the progressive elimination of the parties. The parties of the left, the communists especially, were already well on the way to extinction as a result of the Reichstag Fire Decree. By late May all communist assets had been seized by law. A month later the same fate met the SPD and the party was also prohibited from further political activity. The remaining political parties all gradually dissolved themselves. Some of their members saw alliance with the Nazis as the only way ahead; some gave in after persistent political manoeuvring and intimidation by the Nazis; others, like those making up the mainly Catholic Centre Party, were won over by clever propaganda moves — in this instance largely by the conclusion of a concordat between the Nazi government and Rome, the Catholic Church having previously set its face against Nazism. The Centre Party was the last to go, and within days of its dissolution, ironically on 14 July, a law was enacted prohibiting the establishment of political parties. The NSDAP became the only legal party. The one-party state was born, with Hitler as its leader.

The monopoly of political power and the subjugation of Prussian autonomy and that of the remaining Länder could not, of course, deliver an authoritarian, totalitarian Nazi state overnight. To wipe out one's competitors for power was one thing, but to dismantle all the elements and vestiges of a pluralist republic, a federal republic at that, was further away. The

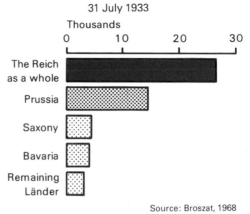

NUMBERS DETAINED IN CONCENTRATION CAMPS
31 July 1933

Source: Broszat, 1968

civil service was purged of Jews and political unreliables under an Act of April 1933, but steps had at the same time to be taken to preserve the civil service from over-zealous Nazi infiltration for fear of general administrative impotence. The working classes remained a potential threat to Nazism, particularly through their trade union organisations. Thus Hitler was driven again into clever propaganda frays which led to the banning of free unions on 2 May 1933 and the enrolment of all employees in the German Labour Front (DAF), a kind of single national union. Any ideas that the DAF would have real independent bargaining power quickly proved illusory, however; Hitler, in alliance with the leaders of big business, ensured against this. In most cases of this kind it was largely a matter of political will and expediency, and time, before the bulk of the substructures of Weimar and Wilhelmine Germany had been swept away. Much more problematic, however, were the conflicts which were emerging within the National Socialist camp, in large part deriving from the Fuehrerprinzip. The most serious came to a head in 1934. It concerned the position of the SA and Röhm in the new National Socialist state.

The Stormtroopers

The SA (Sturmabteilungen: Stormtroopers) were the strong-arm squad of the Nazi Party and they grew very much in line with it. Ernst Röhm, later to become SA leader, joined the German Workers' Party even before Hitler and was soon recruiting ex-Freikorps and ex-servicemen to swell the ranks of the new Nazi Party, by then under Hitler's tutelage. From its very beginnings, the SA became an instigator of political violence. It was a protection squad for party members and their activities, but, much more than this, it actively sought confrontation with other political groupings, especially of the left. In this way the party was propelled into the centre of the public arena whether the public was interested or not. And because the Bavarian authorities harboured strong right-wing sympathies, acts of political violence perpetrated by the SA were viewed with remarkable complacency.

With the failure of the Munich *putsch*, the SA followed the party into relative obscurity, although not without a festering dispute concerning the SA as a militaristic organisation. SA leaders saw their organisation as revolutionary and insurgent. Hitler wished for subservience to the political leadership, eschewing the idea of a military role.

As the Nazi Party regrouped in the later 1920s, so too did the SA. Recruitment increased among young people, notably in urban areas where marches and demonstrations, invariably ending in street brawls, soon became almost nightly events. From being largely an old fighters' organisation, the SA was becoming an outlet for the frustrated energies of youth, a pattern that intensified as unemployment climbed during the Depression years. As an exclusively male organisation, the mob violence of the SA became a kind of virility test. And whatever else, SA membership gave a uniform, food and a sense of belonging where before there had often been none.

Statistics about SA membership are problematic. The turnover rate of membership was high. Some members were extraordinarily active, but many were not. Most people joined for opportunistic reasons rather than from any deep political commitment to the Nazi movement. Before Röhm took over as SA chief in January 1931, membership was roughly 100,000. Under his organising energy, there was a striking expansion of membership and a consolidation of the SA territorial organisation. By early 1932 there were nearly 300,000 members and the SA had been transformed into the most efficient of party armies, with an elaborate central command organisation and 21 regional groups.

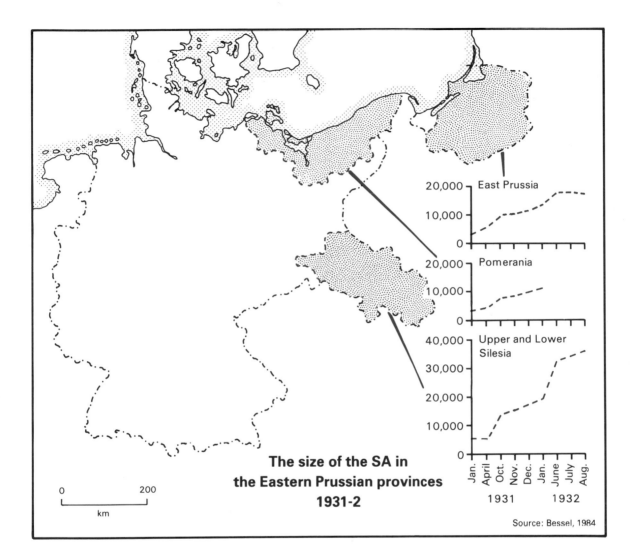

**The size of the SA in
the Eastern Prussian provinces
1931-2**

East Prussia

Pomerania

Upper and Lower Silesia

Source: Bessel, 1984

As the Nazi Party's fortunes at the polls improved over 1930 to 1932, SA leaders increasingly perceived their organisation as poised for a new Nazi *putsch* and, more widely, as the imminent purveyors of a social revolution. For Hitler, this proved both a blessing and a threat. The latent force represented by the SA and the more immediate street violence were obvious bargaining levers in the disinte- grating face of the Weimar Republic. But the danger was in over-hasty action which could summarily prejudice the party's goals. By a combination of luck and judgement, Hitler and the party leadership successfully walked this tightrope, even with a temporary ban on the SA in mid-1932 as a consequence of government anxiety over a *coup*.

43

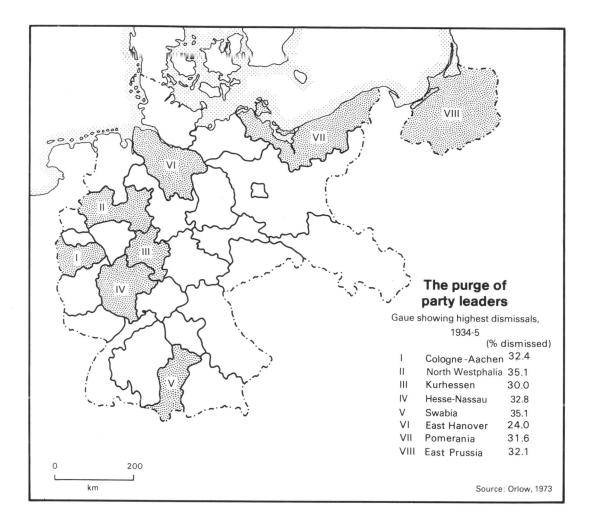

The purge of party leaders

Gaue showing highest dismissals, 1934-5

		(% dismissed)
I	Cologne-Aachen	32.4
II	North Westphalia	35.1
III	Kurhessen	30.0
IV	Hesse-Nassau	32.8
V	Swabia	35.1
VI	East Hanover	24.0
VII	Pomerania	31.6
VIII	East Prussia	32.1

Source: Orlow, 1973

Hitler's accession to the chancellorship saw people flocking to join the SA and by 1934 membership may have been approaching 3 million. SA intimidation and street violence reached a new pitch throughout the spring and summer of 1933 and were instrumental in deterring the limited forces of opposition to Nazism that remained. The SA officer corps lived in feverish expectation of taking a leading part in Nazi government and in a revolutionary dismantling of the existing state. However, reality proved otherwise. Hitler consolidated Nazi power with the co-operation and connivance of the traditional German elites. Official positions went not to old stalwarts but to converts from the German establishment. The resulting tension was inevitable and culminated in a bloody purge of SA leaders in mid-summer 1934, including the murder of Röhm. Subsequently, the SA was entirely restructured to make it into a kind of training ground for the Wehrmacht. It became a subservient organisation, stripped of its former trappings of power. The SA had performed a vital task in the political warfare leading up to January 1933. Thereafter it became dispensable. Nazi Party leaders who were active in the SA, or in close sympathy with it, were removed in a series of purges over 1934-5, as the map above demonstrates.

SA men escorting suspects to prison, 1934

Leaders of the German government in Spring 1935, Hitler flanked by Goering and von Blomberg.

Part Two
Administrative and Political Structure

Reich Organisation and Administration
Party Organisation and Administration
The Army
The Police State

THE MINISTRIES OF THE NAZI STATE CIRCA 1936

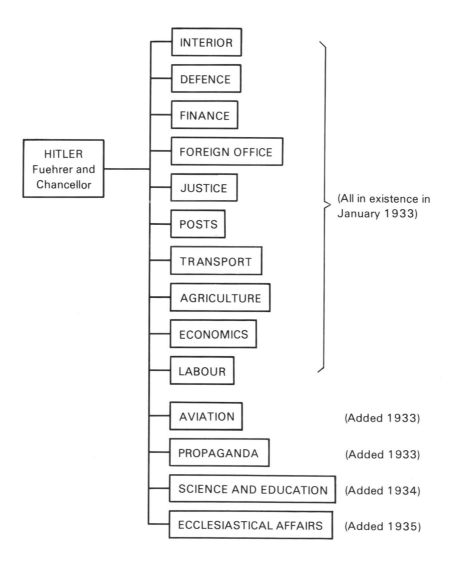

Reich Organisation and Administration

The Nazi state defies most conventions of understanding and explanation. It embraced no clear constitution; indeed the constitution of Weimar was never formally abolished. Its relationship with the party was never clearly defined. The process whereby all legislative and executive power came to rest in Hitler's hands displays no thread of legality. The most meaningful label for the Third Reich is the *Hitler state*. If it had a constitution, it was represented in the will of the Fuehrer, Adolf Hitler. This will formed a supreme authority which was inalienable and unlimited. If one seeks to rationalise the Nazi state, it is thus to Hitler that one turns. But this presupposes that rationality was a prevailing feature of the Hitler mind: it was not. One has also to confront the facility with which Hitler delegated his power, as well as the ability of delegate leaders to make laws under the guise of carrying out the Fuehrer's will.

In the early days of the Third Reich, government was by a collegiate body, the cabinet, and the continued existence of the presidency (still occupied by the ageing Hindenburg) maintained a basic element of the constitutional state. But this pattern did not last long. Within months of his accession as Chancellor, Hitler had achieved a position of absolute authority in cabinet, by deviousness and personal popularity. Subsequently, meetings of the cabinet became fewer and fewer, its role reduced to that of an advisory council; after February 1938 it ceased to function altogether. The office of President effectively disappeared when Hindenburg died in August 1934; Hitler united it with the chancellorship, but nevertheless assumed all the presidency's powers, including supreme command of the armed forces. Henceforward,

Hitler was designated Fuehrer and Reich Chancellor. The Reichstag, the other major organ of legal authority, had witnessed a progressive erosion of its power even before Hitler's chancellorship. The action against communists of late February 1933, following the Reichstag fire, weakened it further. Then, under the Enabling Law of 23 March, it was largely emasculated. It remained as an institution, but simply to acclaim the laws and practices of National Socialism.

At the beginning of the Nazi era, Reich government was divided among 10 ministries, and by 1935 the number had grown to 14. All ministry chiefs were cabinet members and their ranks were augmented by the granting of cabinet status to such Nazi leaders as Hess and Himmler. By these means, and also by the dismissal of DNVP leader Hugenberg, Hitler was able to increase the number of National Socialists in government from three to eight within a matter of months, although such numerical domination was insignificant alongside the creation of a Nazi-led Propaganda Ministry; under Goebbels' direction this became one of the most vital props of National Socialist dominion. Because cabinet government had a short existence in the Nazi state there was soon a serious vacuum of ministerial co-ordination and a certain trend towards ministerial and ministry polyocracy. Had Hitler consorted with ministers regularly and shown a broad interest in Reich administration and government, the problems would have been less. As it was, Hitler became increasingly remote from ministers and their offices, a number of whom grew quite skilled at exploiting the resulting silences and confusions.

THE SUPREMACY OF THE FOUR-YEAR-PLAN ORGANISATION
IN THE TRADITIONAL STATE BUREAUCRACY

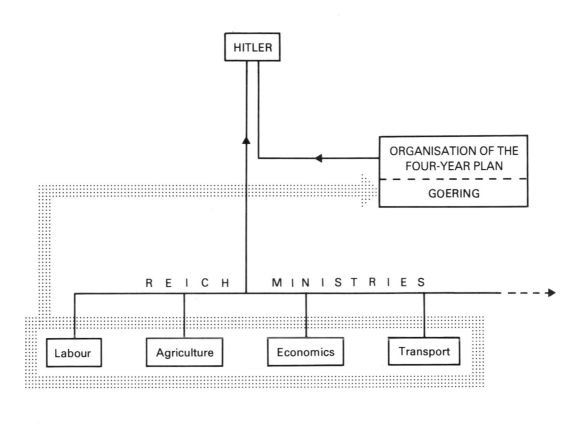

Ministries effectively within
the orbit of the Four-Year-
Plan Organisation

DEPARTMENTS OF THE ORGANISATION OF THE FOUR-YEAR PLAN
1. Production of German raw materials
2. Distribution of raw materials
3. The labour force
4. Agricultural production
5. Price supervision
6. Foreign exchange matters

The department for the production of German raw materials was the most important sector of the Four-Year Plan. In June 1938, it was transformed into the Reich Agency for Economic Consolidation, becoming an entirely separate Reich authority on a level with the Four-Year-Plan Organisation. The department was staffed by officials from Goering's Air Ministry and by private industrialists. It was to become a vital 'engine' of Hitler's rearmament programme.

Supreme Reich Authorities

The comparative independence of the various Reich ministries and their uncoordinated actions were not, however, the sum of administrative chaos in the Nazi state. Yet greater problems stemmed from the practice of creating specialist government agencies which transgressed areas of ministerial jurisdiction but were never formally under them. The first agency of this kind was the General Inspectorate of the German road system, headed by Todt. The Reich Labour Service and the Office of the Four-Year Plan were further examples. All these agencies were subservient only to Hitler. They were designated Supreme Reich Authorities and had powers to issue extraordinary decrees. They could operate without reference to each other or to the availability of resources. The administrative and organisational chaos created by these autonomous government agencies almost defies description, the more so because they seldom remained unchanged. And when coupled with the similar cleavages of jurisdiction among the party Reichsleiters, some of whom also held Reich offices, the picture is even more confused. At some stage it is logical to ask how far such a state of affairs was consciously created by Hitler or whether it grew through its own momentum. The answer probably lies somewhere between the two. Ill-defined, shifting and overlapping competencies were certainly an innate and inevitable feature of the operation of the Fuehrerprinzip, especially given the way Hitler linked it with a considerable delegation of authority. However, there is no mistaking Hitler's 'divide and rule' tactics. Ever conscious of the potential for erosion of his ultimate control, he played off one institution against another — party, Reich ministries, civil service, army — rarely failing to capitalise on the strengths and weaknesses of their various leaders. Needless to say, so complex did the internal structure of the Third Reich become, particularly from 1939, that it would have required a superhuman leader to be aware of its real nature and construction: to this extent Hitler became a victim of his own creation; and it is here that the Nazi state displayed a volition of its own.

Whatever the degree to which the Supreme Reich Authorities were alien to the traditions of administrative bureaucracy, it remains the case that some accumulated an impressive record of achievement in the shorter term. Fritz Todt, for example, was able to set up a state construction business which grew from being initially concerned with building the autobahn system to servicing the construction needs of the military and, later, the Nazi war machine at large. Because he had independent powers of legislation, Todt could conscript firms as well as workers, set prices and wages, and in general engineer an administrative apparatus which enabled his goals to be realised with maximum efficiency and speed. In this way Hitler's Reich was capable of remarkable dynamism; the difficulty lay in sustaining such dynamism in the face of war and an entrenching polyocracy.

Economic regions (1943)

——	WIRTSCHAFTSBEZIRKE (Economic regions)
●	Landeswirtschaftsamt (Regional economic office)
•	Gau economic chamber

Königsberg
Danzig
Kiel
Schwerin
Stettin
Hamburg
Bremen
Berlin
Poznan
Hanover
Münster
Magdeburg
Düsseldorf
Kassel
Dresden
Breslau
Cologne
Weimar
Liberec
Koblenz
Katowice
Wiesbaden
Saarbrücken
Fürth
Karlsruhe
Stuttgart
Vienna
Munich
Salzburg

0   200
km

Source: Bodleian

The administrative regions of the Economics Ministry with their regional offices circa 1943. The Gau Economic Chambers illustrate the creeping jurisdiction of the Nazi Party. They were established in 1942 to replace the 111 former Chambers of Industry. By this date, also, the Wehrkreise had taken on an increasing economic importance, notably in association with Speer's Armaments Ministry. Thus the power and jurisdiction of the Economics Ministry were becoming shadowy and ill-defined by the middle years of the war.

The administration of territory

The chaos of authority and administration which characterised the central organs of state under Hitler invariably conveyed itself to the system of territorial organisation by which those organs were able to discharge their functions 'on the ground'. The party had its territorial organisation in the Gaue; the Reich Ministries, the Supreme Reich agencies, the civil service and the army all had theirs. Predictably, there was little spatial correlation among these various territorial organisations. Most had very distinctive systems of geographical division. Within the territories incorporated to form the Greater German Reich, moreover, the basic organisational systems often followed a different model altogether. By 1938 the so-called 'field system' of the Finance Ministry split the Reich into 28 administrative districts, whereas the Propaganda Ministry had 38. Likewise, the Ministry of Posts used a system of 46 subdivisions, while under the Transport Ministry there were 29 regions for railway administration. The Supreme Reich agencies generated

their own sets of field systems, as did the armed forces. Few of these systems matched, nor did they bear much relation to the Reich Ministry regions with which they were logically linked. The field system of the civil service was represented in what remained of the administrative organs of federal Germany, namely the Länder, including Prussia and its separate provinces. The civil service was under the Interior Ministry, but given the former sovereign rights of the Länder and the powerful tradition of the Prussian civil service organisation, it formed a power base of its own which its Minister, Frick, sought to exploit in pursuit of his own designs on the Nazi dictatorship.

Gau Thuringia, showing a few of the instances of low spatial correlation in administrative field systems. There was some coincidence of boundaries. Those for the Gau Thuringia were the same as for the corresponding economic region (see 'Economic regions' map). But neither of these matched the altogether larger territorial divisions of the army (Wehrkreise) or of the Reich Labour Ministry (Landesarbeitsamtsbezirken). The Land Thuringia was actually smaller in area than the Gau, while the borders of the local administrative region for railways (Reichsbahndirektionen) formed a pattern entirely their own.

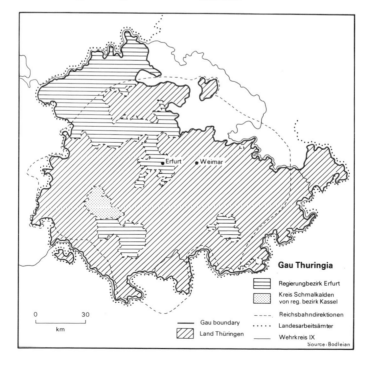

Gau Thuringia

Regierungbezirk Erfurt
Kreis Schmalkalden von reg. bezirk Kassel
Reichsbahndirektionen
Landesarbeitsämter
Wehrkreis IX

Gau boundary
Land Thüringen

Source: Bodleian

53

Aborted administrative reform

At several stages in the early history of the Nazi state efforts were made to effect administrative reform. Territorial reform had been in the minds of many Gauleiters for some years; most sought to consolidate and enhance their geographical power bases. But the specific task of planning such a reform fell to Hess and his Office of the Deputy Fuehrer. A draft document for the reconstruction of the Reich submitted in February 1935 envisaged a system of Reichsgaue grouped in a series of economic-strategic circles around the German heartland following directly from the ideas of the geo-politician Haushofer. Reform of the machinery of central government became a major objective of Frick and his Interior Ministry. In 1936 and again in 1937 he sought a regularisation of procedures and jurisdictions to combat the mounting chaos of ministerial and departmental polyocracy. However, neither of these reforms became a reality. There were too many conflicting views and Hitler constantly vacillated over their pursuance.

The areas of civil administration in the expanded Third Reich, circa 1942. They functioned as organs for the discharge of such services as health and education. Although many of the areas were direct descendants of the old sovereign states (free states under Weimar), they enjoyed little or no autonomy under Nazism. Power and decision-making rested fundamentally with the central Reich organisations.

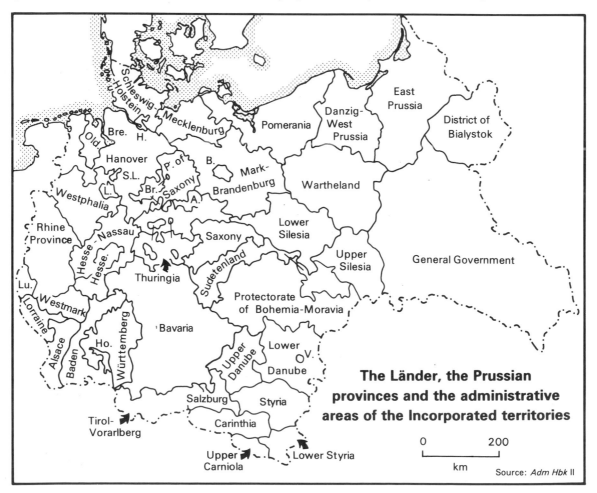

The Länder, the Prussian provinces and the administrative areas of the Incorporated territories

0   200
km

Source: *Adm Hbk* II

SCHEMATIC PRESENTATION OF CONFLICTING TERRITORIAL DIVISIONS CIRCA 1936
(Altreich only)

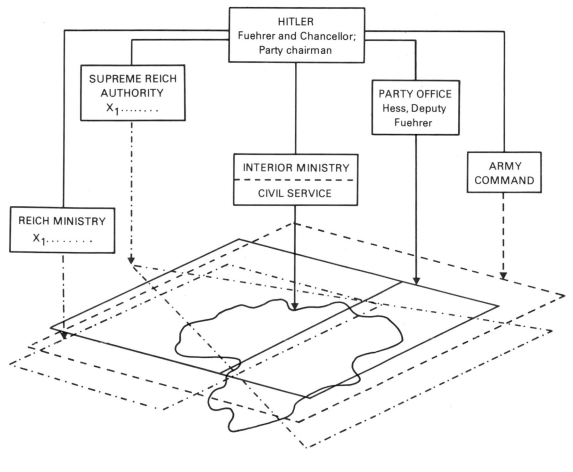

——— Land/Province boundary

——— Gau boundary

– – – Wehrkreis boundary

–·– Ministry region boundary

–··– Supreme Reich Authority region boundary

CONFLICTING AND OVERLAPPING ADMINISTRATIVE COMPETENCIES : THE LÄNDER
CIRCA 1935

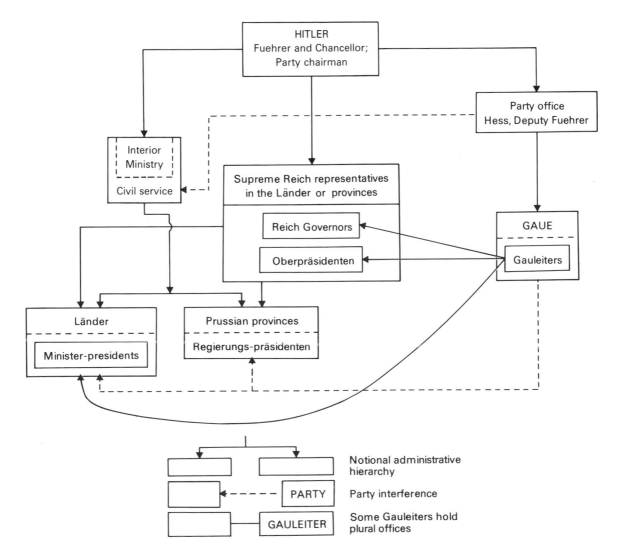

Administrative pluralism

A final distinguishing feature of Nazi government, which at times simplified but more often intensified its structural and jurisdictional chaos, was plurality of office-holding. This probably found most widespread expression in relation to the party. The offices of Reich Governor for the former Länder and their equivalent in the Prussian provinces, the Oberpräsidenten, were largely filled by existing Gauleiters. Thus there was a fusion of personnel authority even if the territorial boundaries of the respective domains did not agree. The outcome was not necessarily harmonious, though. Because there were more Gaue in Prussia than there were provinces, some Gauleiters failed to obtain posts of Oberpräsident. This encouraged friction in regional party–state relations and merely served to underline the depth of dualism which incongruent territorial systems forged. With the Reich Governors as well as the Oberpräsidenten, there was an added problem over the precise nature of their authority. Whether they were subordinate to Hitler or to Frick, the Reich Minister of the Interior, was never properly clarified, for example. And their powers in relation to the various regional state officials — the Regierungspräsidenten in Prussia and the Minister-Presidents in the Länder — were likewise ambiguous.

Pluralism was also a characteristic of the Nazi elite. Indeed, the list of offices accumulated by leaders such as Hermann Goering was reminiscent of the pluralism of the medieval church. At various times he ruled over the Reichstag and over Prussia, over the police and the Gestapo, and over aviation policy and rearmament. He was also Air Force Chief and in charge of the Organisation of the Four-Year Plan. Goebbels enjoyed a power base of lesser breadth, but as Party Propaganda Chief, as head of the Propaganda Ministry and as Gauleiter of Berlin, he held a formidable springboard from which to influence German and Nazi alike. In this respect, Goebbels was a most effective exploiter of his pluralist holding, whereas Goering had far greater difficulty in reaping as efficient a return from his more disparate and unwieldy empire. The most successful Nazi leaders were undoubtedly those who held key party and key government offices. And in Hitler, of course, one found the apotheosis of the breed.

Party Organisation and Administration

The Nazi Party and its organisation represent a key to the understanding of the Third Reich. The party's complex central apparatus, its regional and local constituents, the Hitler Youth, the SA and the elite corps of the SS — all of these fulfilled roles and exercised influence which bore directly on the face of the Third Reich as it evolved over time and as it extended across Europe. It is important, though, to register that the Nazi Party remained separate from the Nazi state. There were elements of fusion, particularly of personnel. Beyond this, however, there were as many instances of dualism, sometimes reflecting basic differences of policy and action.

The party itself was far from a model of consistency. The structure of its organisation was in an almost constant state of flux. And even where a seemingly stable organisational system can be identified, the operation of the Fuehrerprinzip much restricted its real significance. Thus Gregor Strasser's wide-ranging reform of central party organisation in 1932 provides only limited help in comprehending the sequence of policy decision and action. The newly created economic division IV, for instance, was quickly superseded by the NSDAP Reich Economic Council, which Hitler established in September 1932, while the relative strengths of the various party offices were largely a function of the closeness of their appointed leaders to the person of the Fuehrer. The pattern was one which prevailed right up to the collapse of the Third Reich in the spring of 1945.

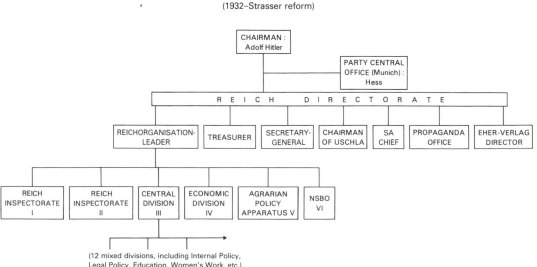

NAZI PARTY CENTRAL ORGANISATION
(1932–Strasser reform)

(12 mixed divisions, including Internal Policy,
Legal Policy, Education, Women's Work, etc.)

Source: Broszat, 1981

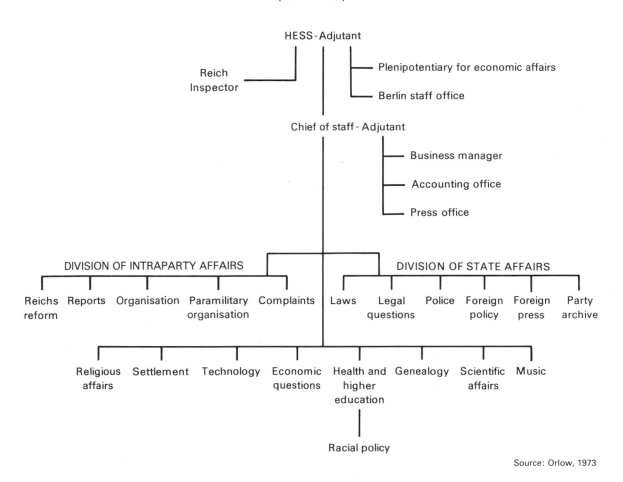

OFFICE OF DEPUTY FUEHRER
(Late 1935)

Source: Orlow, 1973

The relative inconstancy of the party organisation was yet more profoundly reinforced by the persistent rivalries between certain of its leading offices. Just as the importance of a particular office at any one time varied in accordance with the closeness of its leader to the Fuehrer, so it also changed according to the success with which a leader was able to infiltrate the domains of others and so assemble a stronger power base. One of the most remarkable examples of this was found in the Office of the Deputy Fuehrer, headed by Rudolf Hess until 1941 and then by Hess's former deputy, Martin Bormann. In the mid-1930s, the scale of this office grew phenomenally. By 1936 it had established a foothold in the operating spheres of most Reichsleiters. At the same time it began to try to exploit its position as supreme territorial party authority, that is over and above the Gauleiters. From this potential power base, Hess and Bormann attempted to enhance the rule of Central Party Office at the expense of the other party leaders (of policy areas or of territorial areas) who, predictably, resented and resisted such interference with their role as Hitler's derivative agents.

The party as protector of the common people

The founding of the Nazi state presented some very real problems for the future of the party movement; in some respects it signalled a watershed. In the decade to 1933, the party machine became progressively geared to the task of acquiring power. It was seen in the way the Gaue coincided with the Reichstag electoral districts; it was apparent in the regional growth of the SA as a potential instrument of political coercion. But once the reins of power were in Nazi hands, such functions lost much of their purpose. The SA presented the most serious problem in this respect; the murder of its leadership and its downgrading as a general organ of power were predictable events. For the party machine, the task was one of redefinition of role and purpose. With the NSDAP established as the only political party, many of the standard functions of a political party became superfluous. Instead, the NSDAP became more and more a reservoir of ideology and an educator of the masses in the fundamental tenets of the Nazi political faith. The party spawned a growing array of associate organisations designed to supplant ones already in existence: such bodies as the Nazi associations of women, of students, of youth, of teachers, of technicians, and so on. In this way German society became progressively honeycombed with Nazi ideas and practices. In its relations with the state, the party increasingly assumed the role of ideological guardian and protector of the material interests of the masses. And the pattern became even more clearly crystallised in the case of the SS: the party elite which became the specific guardian of Nazi racial ideology and which developed so that it almost formed a state within a state.

The Adolf Hitler Jugendherberge (youth hostel) in Berchtesgaden

Hitler's aeroplane over Nuremberg, just prior to arriving at the Party Day celebrations in 1934. This annual rally became a ritual focus for many Germans.

THE NAZI PARTY

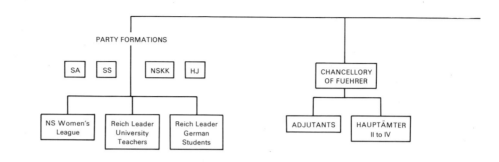

PARTY FORMATIONS

| SA | SS | | NSKK | HJ |

| NS Women's League | Reich Leader University Teachers | Reich Leader German Students |

CHANCELLORY OF FUEHRER

| ADJUTANTS | HAUPTÄMTER II to IV |

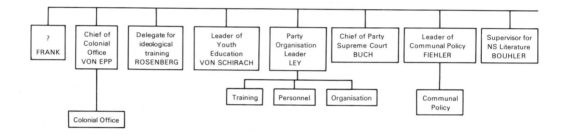

| ? FRANK | Chief of Colonial Office VON EPP | Delegate for ideological training ROSENBERG | Leader of Youth Education VON SCHIRACH | Party Organisation Leader LEY | Chief of Party Supreme Court BUCH | Leader of Communal Policy FIEHLER | Supervisor for NS Literature BOUHLER |

Colonial Office

| Training | Personnel | Organisation |

Communal Policy

INSIDE GERMANY

(by March 1945)

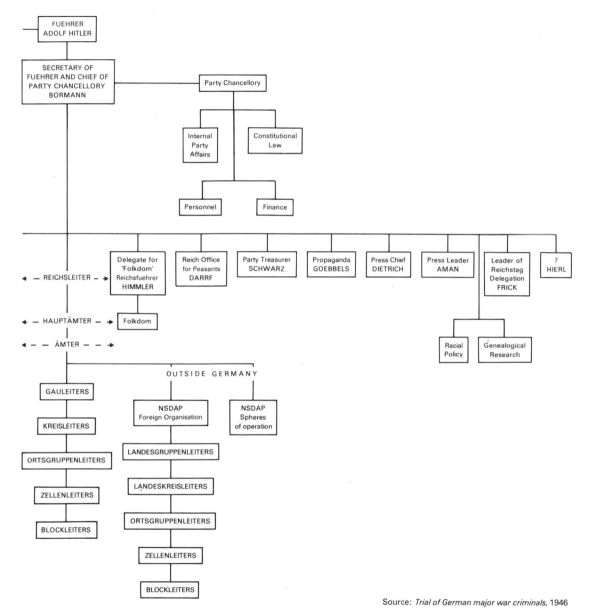

Source: *Trial of German major war criminals*, 1946

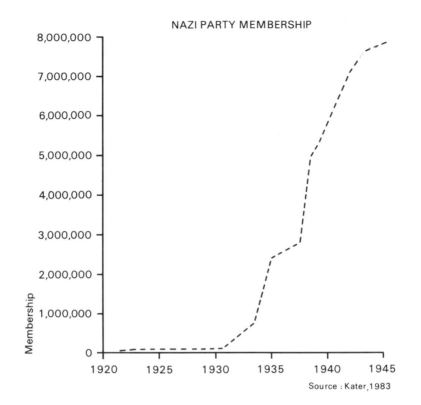

NAZI PARTY MEMBERSHIP

Source : Kater,1983

Party membership

At Hitler's accession, membership of the Nazi Party numbered around 850,000. By the middle of the war this had risen to about 7 million. Areas which before 1933 had shown only very limited acceptance of Nazism became some of the most buoyant in new recruitment, although industrial regions continued to lag behind agricultural ones in the degree of party penetration. The dominance of the lower middle class remained a persistent feature of party membership during the Third Reich's short existence, but from 1933 there was a secular upward trend in the proportion of the working class joining the party.

In January 1935, 65.5 per cent of the party's members were under the age of 41 and 37.6 per cent under 30, perpetuating the youthful character of its earlier growth. The pattern was facilitated by the SA purge of 1934, which removed many older party stalwarts, and by the progressive elimination of the populist tradition in the party led by Gregor Strasser before his dismissal in 1932.

In a country with a population of some 70 million by 1940, it may seem surprising that party membership amounted to only about 10 per cent. In fact, this was part of a deliberate policy, dating back to 1933, to confine party membership so as to form an elite. It would not be correct to infer from the relatively small scale of party membership that this reflected the general status of Nazi influence in German society. Firstly, this would be to underestimate the party's powers of intimidation and persuasion; secondly, it would gloss over the force represented by the many organisations affiliated to the party: in this way a majority of Germans became exposed or connected to the party in some shape or form; lastly, it would neglect the influence on the masses exerted by Goebbels' new Propaganda Ministry, itself largely staffed by party loyalists.

NEW PARTY MEMBERS, 1930-44

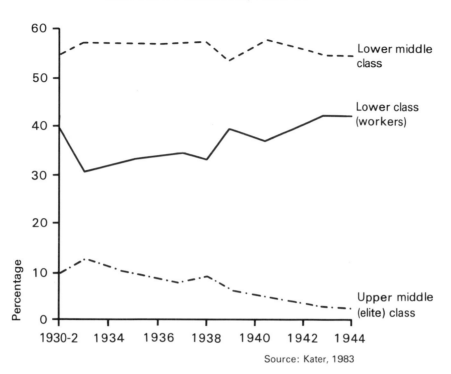

Source: Kater, 1983

AGE DISTRIBUTION OF PARTY MEMBERS: 1 Jan. 1935
Numerical total of members : 2,493,890

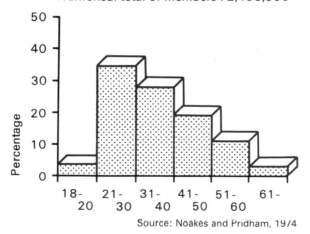

Source: Noakes and Pridham, 1974

The party's territorial organisation

One of the most important agencies of the strength of Nazi influence was found in its regional organisation. This was headed by the Gaue, a series of administrative regions which were adjusted and augmented as Hitler's goal of a Greater Germany was approached. By 1944 the Gaue were 42 in number and embraced the former Austrian state, the former Czech Sudetenland, parts of what was formerly western and northern Poland, and Alsace-Lorraine. The Gaue varied considerably in size and population; and those in the west were generally smaller than those in the east. The older Gaue closely resembled the Reichstag electoral districts, consistent with the party's search for a parliamentary road to power from 1924; they bore little relation to regular administrative divisions, either under Weimar or in the Third Reich. The newer Gaue, however, made party and civil administration as one. Thus Austria was divided into seven *Reichsgaue*, while parts of Poland annexed to make up Greater Germany were similarly treated, for example the Reichsgaue of Danzig-West Prussia and Wartheland. The office of Gauleiter was of special importance in the Third Reich. After such prominent Nazis as Goering, Himmler and Goebbels, the Gauleiters represented some of the most powerful party officers; they were Hitler's direct representatives in the regions. Their influence was reinforced, moreover, by Hitler's practice of appointing some Gauleiters to offices of civil administration in the regions. Thus, although the boundaries of civil and party administration were rarely coincident, the offices of their leadership sometimes were, even if the real power of those offices remained confused and subject to constant dispute.

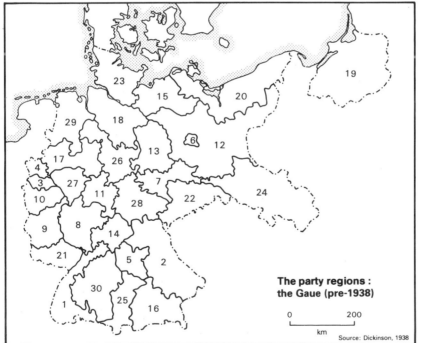

1. Baden
2. Bavarian Ostmark
3. Düsseldorf
4. Essen
5. Franconia
6. Greater Berlin
7. Halle-Merseburg
8. Hesse-Nassau
9. Koblenz-Trier
10. Cologne-Aachen
11. Kurhessen
12. Kurmark
13. Magdeburg-Anhalt
14. Main-Franconia
15. Mecklenburg-Lübeck
16. Munich-Upper Bavaria
17. North Westphalia
18. East Hanover
19. East Prussia
20. Pomerania
21. Saarpfalz
22. Saxony
23. Schleswig-Holstein
24. Silesia
25. Swabia
26. South Hanover
27. South Westphalia
28. Thuringia
29. Weser-Ems
30. Württemberg-Hohenzollern

The party regions: the Gaue (pre-1938)

0   200

km

Source: Dickinson, 1938

The Gaue (1944)

Source: *Adm Hbk* II

This map should be compared closely with that on the opposite page. Within the area of the Altreich, it shows how Gau organisation remained largely unchanged, despite its increasing anachronism in the face of war and wartime exigencies.

1. Baden
2. Bayreuth
3. Berlin
4. Danzig-West Prussia
5. Düsseldorf
6. Essen
7. Franconia
8. Halle-Merseburg
9. Hamburg
10. Hesse-Nassau
11. Karnten
12. Cologne-Aachen
13. Kurhessen
14. Magdeburg-Anhalt
15. Main-Franconia
16. Mark Brandenburg
17. Mecklenburg
18. Moselland
19. Munich-Upper Bavaria
20. Lower Danube
21. Lower Silesia
22. Upper Danube
23. Upper Silesia
24. East Hanover
25. East Prussia
26. Pomerania
27. Saxony
28. Salzburg
29. Schleswig-Holstein
30. Swabia
31. Steiermark
32. Sudetenland
33. South Hanover-Brunswick
34. Thuringia
35. Tirol-Vorarlberg
36. Wartheland
37. Weser-Ems
38. North Westphalia
39. South Westphalia
40. Westmark
41. Vienna
42. Württemberg-Hohenzollern

The Gaue were at the head of four further subdivisions of the party's regional and local administration: the Kreise, the Ortsgruppen, the Zellen and the Blocke — in descending order. In 1939 there were 822 party Kreise (each with its own Kreisleiter), nearly 28,000 Ortsgruppen (covering sections of cities, small towns or country areas), nearly 93,000 Zellen (cells, consisting of assemblages of streets or other units), and some 480,000 Blocke (street blocks). Leadership and organisation in the local groups, cells and blocks were carried out largely by voluntary party workers. But the Gauleiters and Kreisleiters had permanent offices and staffs. To a large degree the Gau offices mimicked the functions and affiliations of Central Party Office.

67

The Army

The armed forces and the German Army in particular were comparatively unaffected by the Nazi take-over of power and remained so until early 1938. Historically, the army represented a formidable power bloc, resting on a long line of Prussian victories. The defeat of 1918 by no means destroyed its prestige and the highly coherent officer corps of the army remained intact. The provisions of Versailles, which restricted the army's size to 100,000 men were not insignificant, of course. But rearmament plans were being laid as early as 1928, five years before Hitler's accession, and from March 1935 conscription was reintroduced.

Opinions differ as to the part played by the army in the Nazi take-over. That Hitler enjoyed army support is undoubted. The question is over the forces which propelled the army to this position. The Nazis' plans for rearming Germany and their vigorous denials of Versailles were undoubtedly attractive in many quarters of the officer corps. It is also clear that many army officers favoured a more authoritarian regime. Had the army wished to block the Nazi succession it is clear that they would have succeeded, even in the face of the 400,000-strong SA. But its leaders were determined not to be drawn into a civil war. Thus Hitler's rise went unchallenged.

Between 1933 and 1939 the manpower of the German Army expanded almost twenty fold. The number of active divisions rose from 10 to 51; by 1939 there were also 51 reserve divisions. For much of this expansionary phase the army retained its traditional autonomy in relation to the German state. The technical head of the army was the President, but under Hindenburg this amounted to nothing more than making the most senior appointments and observing ceremonial. Hitler did comparatively little to alter the position after his assumption of the presidency. In fact, he protected the army leadership from SS smear campaigns and allowed the army, generally, to stay aloof from the supervision of the party. Under the Reich Defence Law, no soldier was permitted to be a party member. From early 1938, however, the pattern was altered radically. On 4 February Hitler assumed direct command of all the armed forces and established the *Oberkommando der Wehrmacht*, OKW (Armed Forces High Command), which was effectively a military bureau for Hitler as Head of State and War Minister. The comparative independence of the armed forces was immediately reduced. And the army, although it represented over three-quarters of the armed forces, suddenly found itself placed on equal footing with the navy and the air force. Joint authority and responsibility under the War Ministry gave way to the Fuehrer's will. The OKW became the tool of a warlord.

Military regions (1943)

——— WEHRKREISE (military regions, with regional military HQ)

——— Boundary of Greater Germany

0   200
km

Source: Bodleian

The German Army had its own administrative areas (Wehrkreise), which served as bases for administration, recruitment and training of troops. Each area formed the home of an Army Corps, with the Corps HQ located in one of the major towns. The Wehrkreis boundaries were unrelated to any other administrative boundaries in the Third Reich, with the exception of the SS organisation after 1938.

The Police State

One of the peculiar features of the Third Reich was the degree to which it continued to use existing institutions. There was no wholesale revolution of the state administrative structure, for example, nor any thorough purge of its officialdom; and the army remained a largely autonomous organisation during the regime's first five years. In large measure, this pattern reflected the simple fact that the Nazis had no detailed plans for fundamental revolution. Indeed, the foundation and evolution of the Nazi state were characterised by a long succession of improvisations. Without a state monolith in the Stalinist mould, the Nazis relied for the maintenance of their authority on the spreading tentacles of party organisation and, above all, the police. The label 'police state' is a singularly appropriate one for the Third Reich. It was not only that the police were used to sustain the Nazi hold on power; they were also used to pursue the regime's special policies, including those on settlement and race.

The architect of the Nazi police state was Himmler, and its institutional bases the GESTAPO and the SS. The Geheime Staatspolizei (Gestapo — Secret State Police) was established by Goering in 1933 out of the old political police of Prussia. Goering was then Prussian Minister of the Interior. Subsequently the term Gestapo was applied to the political police of all the old Länder who by 1933/4 had come under the control of the SS and its leaders, Himmler and Heydrich. When Goering's Prussian Gestapo chief retired in spring 1934, Himmler succeeded him, bringing the entire political police organisation under SS tutelage. Seizure of control over the political police had been revolutionary rather than constitutional and the result was that the Gestapo became an organisation outside state jurisdiction, including the courts. This gave relatively free rein to totalitarian terror and the position was finally consolidated in June 1936 when Himmler was invested with the newly created office of Chief of German Police, which he exercised in conjunction with his office as Reichsfuehrer SS. The entire police force was subjected to centralised SS control and, although Himmler remained responsible to Frick, the Reich Minister of the Interior, this turned out in practice to be purely nominal. By 1943, Himmler was himself Reich Minister of the Interior, thereby ending the confusion altogether.

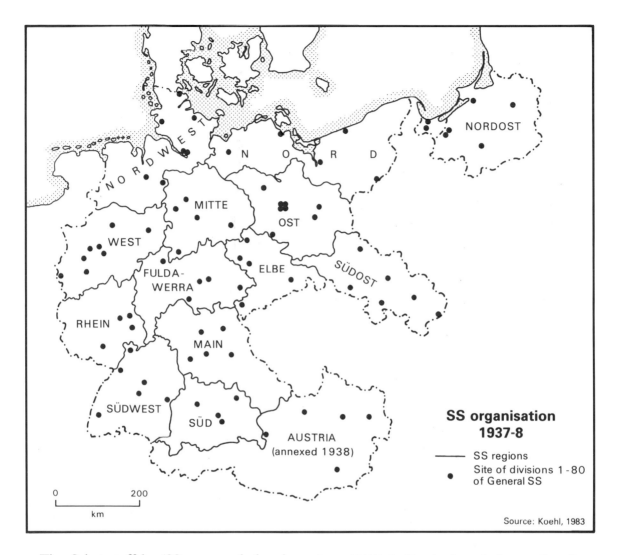

SS organisation 1937-8

— SS regions

• Site of divisions 1-80 of General SS

Source: Koehl, 1983

NORDOST

NORDWEST

NORD

MITTE

OST

WEST

FULDA-WERRA

ELBE

SÜDOST

RHEIN

MAIN

SÜDWEST

SÜD

AUSTRIA (annexed 1938)

0   200

km

The Schutzstaffeln (SS — guard detachments) originated in 1925 as Hitler's personal guard, but over the ensuing two decades developed into an inner elite of the Nazi Party, with the SS organisation itself forming what was almost a state within a state. Himmler was installed as leader of the SS in 1929 when the organisation numbered some 250 men. Thereafter, however, it expanded rapidly. By 1931 membership was around 10,000. This rose to some 50,000 in early 1933 and 200,000 in early 1935. There was a parallel development of SS organisations. In 1931, Himmler established an

From mid-1938, the SS regional organisation was adjusted to coincide with the army Wehrkreise.

internal security service for the SS under Heydrich (SD — Sicherheitsdienst). The aim was to protect SS ideology and to safeguard its leadership. The SS guards who had formed Hitler's bodyguard were expanded to form SS special duty troops and SS special guard groups for concentration camps. The former grew into the famous Waffen-SS (armed SS troops). The guard groups became the hated SS Death-Head units.

71

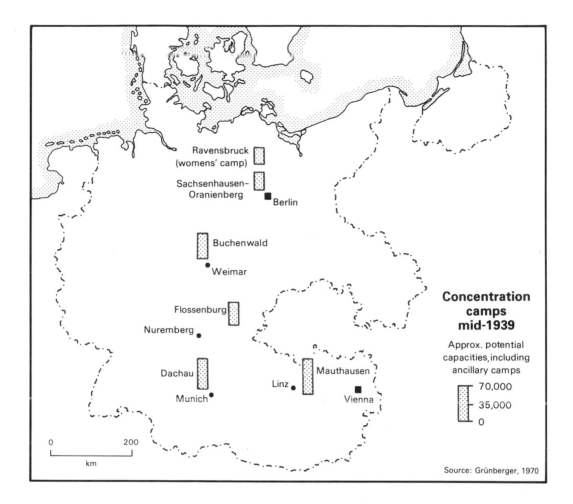

Ravensbruck
(womens' camp)

Sachsenhausen-
Oranienberg
■ Berlin

Buchenwald
• Weimar

**Concentration
camps
mid-1939**

Flossenburg

Nuremberg •

Approx. potential
capacities, including
ancillary camps

70,000

35,000

0

Dachau

Linz •
Munich •

Mauthausen

■ Vienna

0   200

km

Source: Grünberger, 1970

The actual number of camp detainees fluctuated wildly. For example, there were only about 3,000 prisoners at Buchenwald in May 1938, but by December of the same year this figure had risen to 17,000, only to fall again to 5,000-6,000 six months later. The total number detained at the time of the outbreak of war was just 25,000, only slightly less than the number in custody in mid-summer 1933. All this was a far cry from the 714,000 detainees registered by January 1945.

The role of the concentration camp system in the early years of the Nazi state must necessarily be seen in conjunction with an increasingly repressive criminal law which gave rise to a rapid increase in regular imprisonment. There was a point in 1937, before Hitler's run of territorial annexations and the political repression that followed them, when the camps were actually beginning to appear redundant. Ultimately, though, the concentration camps became a linchpin of SS existence. And they provided penal colonies not only for political undesirables, but also for racial and social outcasts. They also formed sources of labour for SS enterprises. By 1938, camp labour was being used for quarrying, road construction, market-gardening and handicrafts, not to mention the building of the concentration camps themselves. Thus was laid the framework for the SS slave empire which grew to yield an annual turnover in excess of 50 million Reichmarks by 1943.

The size and power of the SS grew like a cancer as the short life of the Third Reich ran its course. The steady acquisition of police power was a primary stage. But by the middle of the war the Waffen-SS vied in authority with the army, the occupied territories were to all intents and purposes under SS domination, SS racist ideology was being put into practice in the mass killing of millions of Jews, and Himmler sat at the head of an economic empire which underpinned the diverse activities of his SS organisation, thereby contributing to the notion that the Third Reich was an SS state. By the last years of the war, the SS enjoyed an existence largely separate from the state administration and the Nazi Party. It had its own complex bureaucracy, some of which shadowed the bureaucracy of the state, some of which reflected its role as ideological champion of National Socialism. It was in the nature of a special Fuehrer executive, subordinate only to Hitler. But it also developed a leader-retinue structure of its own which contributed to the separateness of its existence and the distinctiveness of its authority. Alongside the apparatus of the party, the state and the military, the SS formed yet another ingredient in the maze of incongruent jurisdictions which characterised the *Hitler state.*

One may well ask how a state which was so riven by internal rivalries and confusions could possibly develop the political and military power which enabled it to subjugate most of Europe. The question is much debated and cannot be easily resolved. Part of the answer lies in the fact that the bitter competition for power among the various ministries and agencies within the Third Reich tended to make these institutions individually more efficient, at least in the short term: thus the army became more ruthless as an occupying force in part in order to defend its position against the SS. The internal rivalries also helped to produce an explosive dynamism which was directed outwards — conquest provided the space in which the sectional appetites for power could be partly satisfied. But the Nazi political system never developed a plausible conception of a *status quo,* in which its various component parts were co-ordinated in a stable manner. It throve only on war, in which the parts were in continual motion, against each other as well as against real and imagined enemies.

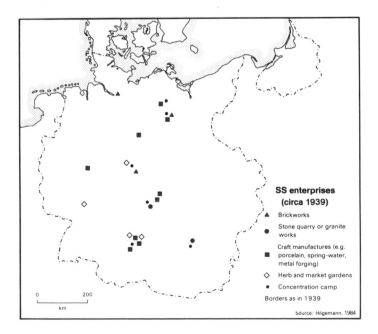

SS enterprises (circa 1939)

▲ Brickworks

● Stone quarry or granite works

■ Craft manufactures (e.g. porcelain, spring-water, metal forging)

◇ Herb and market gardens

• Concentration camp

Borders as in 1939

Source: Hilgemann, 1984

0   200
km

Speer's monumental design for the Nuremberg Zeppelinfeld, the scene of the annual Nazi Party rallies.

Part Three
Society

Nazi Racialism

The racist doctrines of Hitler and his leaders were at the core of National Socialist ideology. They formed a vital propaganda tool in the seizure of power and in the consolidation of support among Nazi activists. They provided justification for the regime's acts of aggression, notably in the east. And they offer insight into the self-destructive face of the Third Reich as its fortunes in war faded and popular assent became less secure.

As in so many of the Nazi regime's acts, it was the negative, destructive aspects of its racial doctrine which were pursued with most force. This was revealed most clearly in Nazi anti-semitism and found horrifying conclusion in the extermination camps of Himmler's SS. There was no clear consensus among National Socialists concerning the Jewish population, however. Some Nazis saw the Jews in economic, not biological, terms, whereas the biological anti-semitism of Hitler and Himmler, in which Jews were seen as parasites, was uncompromising and often manic in its force. It was from this latter view, of course, that the policy of physical extermination sprang. To this extent, the Holocaust was a Hitler, not a Nazi, creation.

The campaign against the Jews underwent a distinctive progression. It began with expulsions from defined professions: in April 1933, for instance, Jews were expelled from the civil service and universities. By September 1935, though, Hitler's own brand of anti-semitism had found formal expression with the Nuremberg Laws. These made marriage and intercourse between Germans and Jews punishable by imprisonment. Three years later, in 1938, there began a mass expropriation of Jewish business concerns. And by November of that year Nazi activists were engaged in mob violence against Jews and Jewish property. As the tide of anti-semitism grew, many Jews emigrated. Some 320,000 had left by 1939.

For the Jews that remained, there was first a scheme for transporting them to Madagascar and later a plan to make East Poland or Siberia the reception area. However, this soon gave way to the so-called 'final solution': the mass killing not only of Germany's Jews, but those of occupied Europe.

JEWS AS A PERCENTAGE OF THE GERMAN POPULATION, 1871-1933

Source: Kwiet and Eschwege, 1984

76

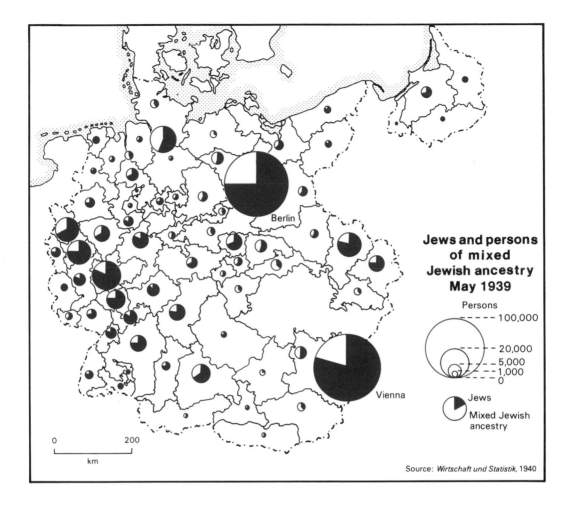

**Jews and persons
of mixed
Jewish ancestry
May 1939**

Persons

- - - - 100,000

- - - 20,000
- - - 5,000
- - - 1,000
- - - 0

Jews

Mixed Jewish
ancestry

Source: *Wirtschaft und Statistik,* 1940

Part Jews (Mischlinge) were divided into two grades: those with two Jewish grandparents and those with one. Each category was subject to varying degrees of discrimination.

A second plank of Nazi racial doctrine was the pursuit of racial purity. This prompted laws encouraging marriage between healthy 'Aryan' Germans, granting financial bonuses for children of such marriages, and state assistance for illegitimates with 'Aryan' parenthood. A law for the protection of hereditary health became a basis of campaigns to sterilise the unfit and to liquidate, under the guise of 'mercy killing', the infirm, mentally defective and chronically diseased. Far less is known about the operation and effects of these eugenic plans than is of the campaign against the Jews. Owing to public disquiet, the regime was forced in 1941 to abandon the mercy-killing scheme. Similarly, Himmler's own ideas for a Nordic polygamy, spearheaded in the SS, were never realised.

Underpinning these two primary facets of Nazi racialism were the dual beliefs of Nordic supremacy and Social Darwinism. The first asserted that the Aryan Nordic race, of which the German people incorporated representatives of varying purity, was the highest of all the races and the dynamic force behind modern civilisation. The second claimed that human history was the history of racial struggle, between higher and lower groups, with the Jews forming the basest and most dangerous of them.

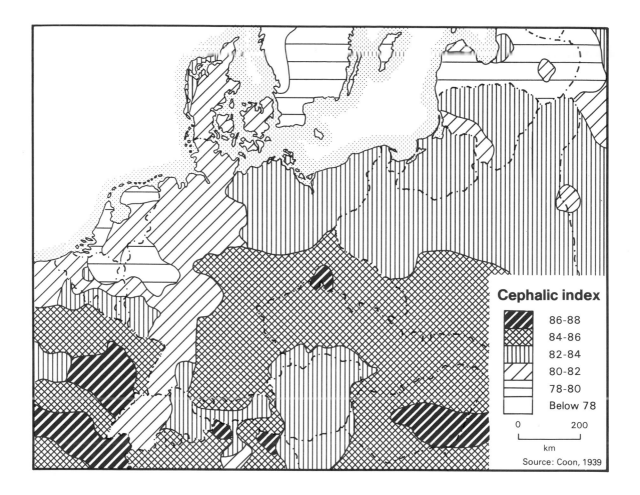

The cephalic index expresses the maximum breadth of the head as a percentage of its maximum length.

The various doctrines making up Nazi racialism have long been discredited. The idea that Germany contained within it a biologically distinctive population is confounded by the evidence of physical anthropology. Germans of the Rhineland, for instance, show far greater affinities with their neighbours in the Low Countries than with their fellow Prussians to the east. The idea, too, that there were to be found in Germany descendants of a pure race (in this case Nordic) is also unsupported by the evidence. Physical characteristics like the colour of hair and eyes are not inherited in groups but independently. The gene factors responsible for pigmentation, cephalic form, etc. are differently sorted in each succeeding generation. Hence the Nazis' picture of racial supremacy as being presented in the tall, blonde, blue-eyed and narrow-headed German was a myth.

Equivalent objections can be made concerning the Nazi view that modern civilisation was spearheaded by Nordic or Aryan racial types. For example, the fundamental shift from hunting and gathering to settled agriculture from about the eighth millennium BC occurred first in the river basins east of the Mediterranean, the practice spreading to Northern Europe later. Similarly, there is little to the view that Nordic or Aryan types are superior in intelligence. In sum, one can state unequivocally that Nazi racialism had no scientific basis and was, to quote one early distinguished historian of the regime, 'a vast system of bestial, Nordic nonsense'. However, it is vital to appreciate that, whatever its untruths, Nazi racial dogma must be carefully examined if a proper understanding of the regime is to be formed. It represented a critical 'engine' of the *Hitler state*, one which changed progressively in pitch and power as the years passed. And the process was augmented and intensified by the way Nazi racialism was dressed up so that it *appeared* scientific. New university professorships were established in racial science, for example, and race studies became a subject for the state professional examinations. In schools, racial education became interlocked with the various pronouncements of the Nazi state in pursuit of racial purity, such that dicta learned in the classroom in one month could be observed being carried through in another. In propaganda terms, the 'science of race' had yet another dimension. The scientific label lent mystery as well as respectability in the popular mind. Thus legislation encouraging marriage between 'Aryan' Germans could be interpreted as essential social hygiene in the face of ill-understood or vague threats.

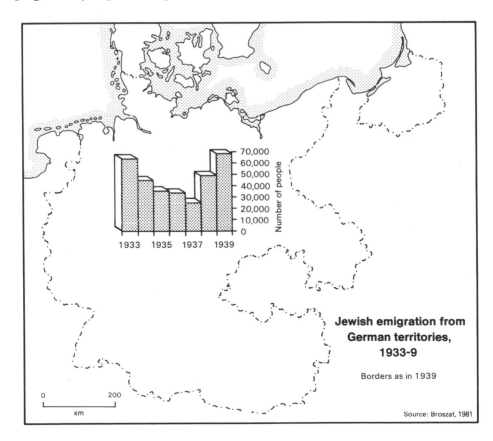

Jewish emigration from German territories, 1933-9

Borders as in 1939

Source: Broszat, 1981

Women

Women enjoyed little status in Nazi Germany. They were excluded from office other than in those organisations concerned solely with women. Their tasks in life were confined largely to the family and, above all, to procreation in pursuit of Nazi racialism. Even when labour shortages became acute during wartime, there was never any comprehensive mobilisation of women as occurred in Britain. But contrary to Nazi propaganda, attitudes and policies towards women were not determined by ideology alone. Women were retained in their customary unskilled and low-paid workplaces, in agriculture especially. To have done otherwise would have exacerbated further the shortage of unskilled labour, in farming in particular, which was to grow to serious proportions by 1939. The stress on procreation was not popular, either; and the accompanying persecution of abortionists was widely resented. Prior to the

return of relatively full employment in 1936/7, there was obvious merit in blocking women's access to the labour market in the eyes of men, but this clearly ceased to apply once shortage of labour became apparent in the final years of peace.

In pursuance of a higher birth rate, the regime instituted a policy which has been viewed as among its most ingenious pieces of social engineering. From the summer of 1933 marriage loans were made available for couples satisfying certain tests of economic, political and eugenic eligibility. For industrial workers, the loans represented four to five months' wages and the time-scale for repayment was a long one. More significant, the loan was reduced by a quarter upon the birth of each child. The immediate effect upon the marriage rate was dramatic. In 1932 there were around 516,000 recorded marriages; two years later the figure

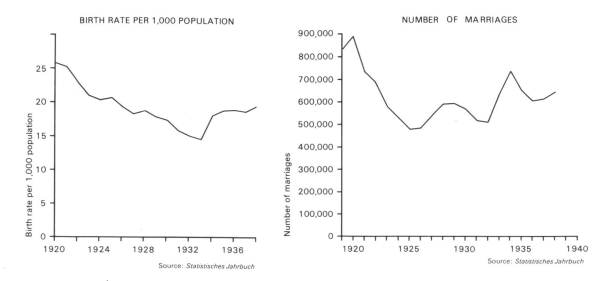

BIRTH RATE PER 1,000 POPULATION

NUMBER OF MARRIAGES

Source: *Statistisches Jahrbuch*

Source: *Statistisches Jahrbuch*

had risen to 740,000. The rate was not sustained, however. The 1934 total was not exceeded until 1939, even if the aggregate picture for the 1930s was measurably greater than that for the preceding decade. The immediate repercussions for the birth rate were equally striking. The number of live births per thousand population rose from 14.7 in 1933 to 18.0 in 1934. In this case, moreover, the increased rate was sustained, although it still failed to match the levels of the early 1920s.

The marriage loan policy was complemented by various measures which were supportive of the maternal role: Mothers' Schools, improved maternity and welfare benefits, and better tax allowances. In many of these, propaganda loomed large. Whatever economic and eugenic reasons lay behind the campaign to increase births, it has also to be seen as a political measure. The Nazis were creating an alternative to female emancipation. They were playing on the latent joys and stabilities of family life for men: soldiers and industrial workers were more malleable when they knew their immediate kin were viewed as an object of care and reward by the state.

Franz Eichhorst, *Mutter und Kind*

Public Welfare

Germany under the Weimar regime pursued an enlightened and progressive welfare policy; and in Prussia the postwar period witnessed the establishment of a new Ministry of Public Welfare. One of the most notable features of Weimar welfare legislation was the emphasis on the individual rights of the child, in particular that each German child should have the facility to be brought up physically, mentally and socially fit.

Under National Socialism there were important changes in the goals of public welfare and in its underlying ideology. The individual became much less important than the community or body of the nation. Nazi racist dogma was then applied to this community with a view to 'breeding' a pure human stock in the Nordic/Aryan mould. Public welfare thus became racially discriminatory, especially with reference to Jews. And public welfare personnel were themselves subject to racial discrimination which resulted in a considerable loss of trained professionals, including some 5,500 Jewish doctors. The Nazi Party had evolved an interest in public welfare long before January 1933. In the National Socialist state, this party machinery to some extent overlapped and duplicated that of the Reich Interior Ministry, which was responsible for public health, so that the familiar administrative cleavages of the *Hitler state* soon emerged to encourage inefficiency and waste. In terms of absolute numbers, there was a marked increase in registered doctors over the first ten years of Nazi rule, aided by a two-year reduction in the length of training. But any expected benefits to the community at large were compromised by the medical demands of the Wehrmacht, the SS and various party organisations, together with the need to service a steadily extending land area. As a result, there was in some areas a dramatic decline in the ratio of practitioners per head of population, especially in the east. During the peacetime years alone, the ratio in the Reich as a whole is estimated to have fallen by 6 per cent.

The local party organisation (Ortsgruppe) as the guardian of the family.

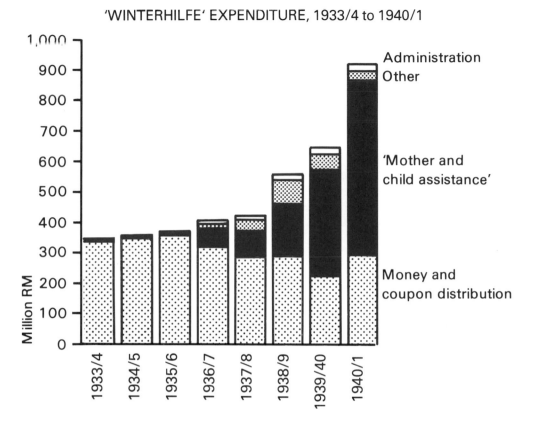

'WINTERHILFE' EXPENDITURE, 1933/4 to 1940/1

Source: *Wirtschaft und Statistik*, 1941

The vigour of any distinctly National Socialist approach to public health was clearly circumscribed in some degree by the number and nature of trained professionals, but in less specialised branches of public welfare, involving financial and material benefits for groups like young mothers and children, or the very poor, the scope was considerably more open. The most striking Nazi welfare activity in this field was *Winterhilfe* or Winter Relief, first instituted in 1933. This was a system of party-sponsored poor relief in which the party itself contributed only the propaganda. It relied on public charity, on door-to-door collections of money, food, bedding, clothing and other household items. In early years, the system was a logical, humane response to the plight of the unemployed millions. Once full employment had been achieved, the needs were ostensibly less evident

or immediate, yet the system continued to be expanded, especially during the war. In fact, Winterhilfe ultimately became a massive 'gratuitous ritual', aimed at raising popular feeling and inculcating self-sacrifice. It operated from October to March, was elaborately and ingeniously thought out, was invariably inaugurated in a wave of publicity, and, for the dedicated Nazis, became a test of political faith for the masses. Failure to give to Winterhilfe at all was strongly condemned, as was failure to give enough. Thus what was made out to be a voluntary charity was effectively a compulsory tax which ate into workers' wages, making some of them in turn liable to be recipients of relief. The system became self-fulfilling. In 1937/8, for instance, at a time when the unemployment problem had largely been solved, some 8.9 million people received relief.

Education

The ultimate goal of Nazi education policy was the creation of 'the political, National Socialist, human being'. Education was not to be a training towards free, independent activity, but to develop the abilities of young Germans so that they fulfilled the aims and desires of the Nazi state. The reorganisation of the education system on Nazi lines had a number of distinctive dimensions. It involved an extensive revision of the curriculum. It involved the progressive removal of political and racial undesirables from the profession of teachers. It embraced the establishment of a stream of specialist schools where the future Nazi elite was to be trained. Finally, it applied the Fuehrerprinzip to the whole structure of educational administration and brought the professional teaching organisations firmly within the Nazi orbit. Certain of these aims were more quickly achieved than others: the purge of teachers, as well as the co-ordination of administration in accordance with the Fuehrerprinzip. The nazification of the curriculum was more protracted and initially fell prey to some of the rivalries of the *Hitler state*, notably between the Education Ministry and Hess's Central Party Office. Curriculum consolidation was hampered, anyway, by a declining supply of teachers and money, a feature which grew more serious after the outbreak of war. The enormous stress that the Nazis laid on physical education also slowed the learning process, regardless of the burdens that may have been imposed by a novel ideology. Pupils could spend up to five hours a day engaged in sports. There was also a latent conflict with the Hitler Youth, which set a rival focus for children's energies and loyalties.

TECHNICAL COLLEGES

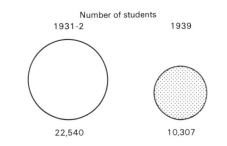

Number of students

1931-2	1939
22,540	10,307

COLLEGES OF ECONOMICS AND POLITICAL SCIENCE

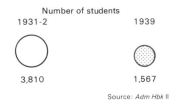

Number of students

1931-2	1939
3,810	1,567

Source: *Adm Hbk* II

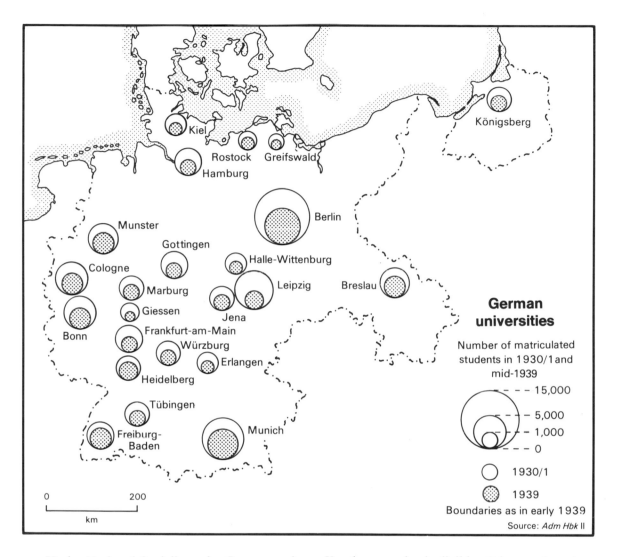

German universities

Number of matriculated students in 1930/1 and mid-1939

- - - 15,000
- - - 5,000
- - - 1,000
- - - 0

○ 1930/1

◉ 1939

Boundaries as in early 1939

Source: *Adm Hbk* II

Under National Socialism, the German universities saw a substantial decline in the numbers of both students and teachers, as well as a steady diminution in the range and quality of scholarship. Between the winter of 1930-1 and the summer of the outbreak of war, the number of matriculated students fell from just under 96,000 to a little over 39,000. The nazification of curricula and the concomitant restrictions upon academic freedom made university life increasingly unattractive. Non-Aryans were excluded from university; and those who could not show a satisfactory record in the Hitler Youth were also ineligible. Other explanations were found in the increasing career opportunities in business and in the armed forces as the Third Reich moved towards a war footing. Earlier, in 1933, the number of students had actually been cut by law, on account of very high graduate unemployment.

During the great phase of Nazi *Gleichschaltung* (1933-4), the universities lost some 16 per cent of their staff in a wave of ejections. The technical institutes lost around 10 per cent, the law schools some 21 per cent. Many of the more distinguished scholars took to emigration.

85

NATIONAL SOCIALIST SCHOOLS

SECONDARY SCHOOLS

NAPOLAS
(National Political Educational Institutes)

Ages : 10-18; established 1933 onwards, partly modelled on old Prussian cadet schools. Formally under Education Ministry, but senior personnel from SA and SS. There were 23 Napolas by 1940, containing almost 5,000 pupils, nearly all of them male. Majority of graduates entered armed forces.

AHS
(Adolf Hitler Schools)

Ages : 12-18; established 1937 onwards; operated and financed exclusively by the Nazi Party. Intended as training schools for future Nazi leaders. Selected graduates eventually enter the ORDENSBURGEN. Of the first group of graduates (1942), 67 per cent chose political leadership for their careers.

ORDENSBURGEN
(Order Castles)

Curriculum

1. Racial, biological and ideological education

2. Sport and physical training

3. Political education

LANGEMARCK SCHOOLS

Designed to aid pupils of poor parents to gain the necessary qualifications for university entry. Selection made in mid-teens. Successful entrants underwent eighteen months' training.

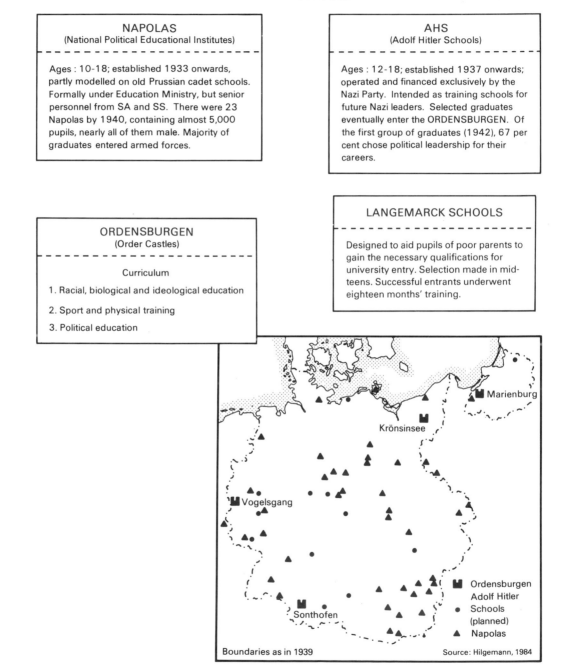

Boundaries as in 1939

Source: Hilgemann, 1984

Marienburg, Krönsinsee, Vogelsgang, Sonthofen

Ordensburgen / Adolf Hitler Schools (planned) / Napolas

86

Nazification of the curriculum

Curriculum development in the service of National Socialism presented a formidable task for party and state officials. That progress was haphazard and the actual results often dubious is a reflection of this, especially given the regime's relatively short life-span. The censorship of school text-books was one of the first and perhaps most readily implemented strategies, and yet this was not directed centrally until the spring of 1938; up to that time teachers performed the task of censoring. The institution of guidelines for elementary and secondary school curricula was similarly slow, even given that the task was no simple one. The brakes to more rapid progress were the desires of the various power groups within the Third Reich to influence education for their own ends. Subjects such as history and geography were variously recast to reflect Nazi racial doctrines. *German* history was studied largely to the exclusion of all other, and focused on Hitler and the rise of National Socialism. Vain attempts were made to interpret the Third Reich as the apotheosis of specified developments and trends in German history. German literature was sifted and categorised so that blood ties and sense of community were thrown into greater relief, and explicitly *völkisch* literature was emphasised as part of this. Religious instruction was increasingly replaced by a motley collection of anti-Christian nationalist ideas, the change enhanced by the steady abolition of confessional schools. In the natural sciences, biology (predictably) was revised in accordance with Nazi racial theories, and *racial science* was granted an academic status which justified the establishment of new professorships in the universities. Many of the more mature among the German people held undeniable misgivings about the distortion of historical perspectives and the ascientific nature of some of the regime's teachings. In German youth, however, Nazism found an understandably more receptive constituency, one which was cultivated as much outside the schoolroom as in it. The ideological campaign in the schoolroom was complemented in the machinery of the Hitler Youth.

Cartoon from a Nazi children's book purporting to show the immorality of Jews compared to Aryans

The Hitler Youth

By early 1939 the Hitler Youth had a little over 7.25 million members, age ten to eighteen, including girls. From December 1936, membership was compulsory for all Germans. But even before that, it counted a significant proportion of German youth amongst its members through absorption of existing youth organisations and dissolution of others. The Catholic organisations remained separate until 1938, whereupon they too were dissolved. A particular novelty of the Hitler Youth was that it was run largely by the adolescents themselves. This held a wide appeal, although it also led to much indiscipline and denunciation.

The title *Hitler Youth* is of particular significance. Although the movement started life under SA control and hence within party jurisdiction, by late 1936 it held the status of a Supreme Reich Authority, largely outside party and ministry jurisdiction, and answerable solely to Hitler. In other words, the Hitler Youth represented a further outflanking of orderly command structures within the Third Reich.

The public face of the Hitler Youth was one which emphasised *community* and *partnership* in the service of the entire German people. Nazi propaganda techniques subsequently channelled this community awareness towards a specific destiny: the birth of a new German Empire. And as the prospects for this empire grew, the Hitler Youth was increasingly drawn in to its realisation. Training sessions became more and more military in character. In effect, the Hitler Youth became an armed force in the making, a seedbed for militarist aggression. Thus resulted the ultimate paradox: a movement which enshrined the partnership of youth and encouraged self-reliance and co-operation became increasingly co-ordinated in the service of a regime seeking to divide society under ruthless authoritarianism; and there were groups of young people who actively opposed it for this reason.

Detachment of the Hitler Youth on parade

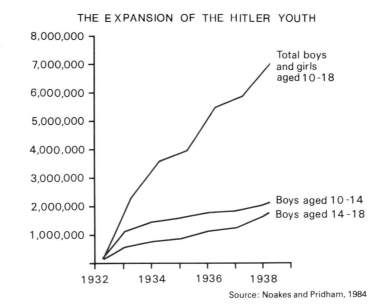

THE EXPANSION OF THE HITLER YOUTH

Total boys
and girls
aged 10-18

Boys aged 10-14
Boys aged 14-18

Source: Noakes and Pridham, 1984

The training scheme set out for use in the Hitler Youth's 'toughening-up' camps for war service, 1944

1. The war
2. The enemies of Germany
3. Our Volk
4. The Fuehrer and the movement
5. The fundaments of our ideology
6. Volk and race
7. Our socialism
8. The Reich

Source: *Glauben und Kämpfen* (Berlin, 1944)

The section 'the enemies of Germany' included the following examination of Jews:

1. Is this also a German?
2. The Jew, creator of the Marxist heresy
3. Every German is an anti-semite
4. The Jew is condemned to destroy humanity
5. The unheroic fundaments of Jewry
6. What does the Jew, Rawage, say?
7. Is there a Jewish riddle of the universe?
8. They stand the law of nature on its head
9. The Jew is uncreative
10. Our war against the Jewish parasites

Culture

Under National Socialism, cultural life in its true sense disappeared. The setting up of the Reich Chamber of Culture in November 1933, under the masterly propagandist eye of Goebbels, co-ordinated all German cultural life in the service of Nazism. The chamber covered art, literature, music, theatre, broadcasting and the press. Former professional associations were rapidly moulded into corporate professional groups, membership of which became compulsory. And every part of the cultural apparatus, ranging from the creative artist to the art dealer, the commercial photographer to the postcard seller, was subjected to central control.

The most populist facet of National Socialist culture was its anti-modernist stance, particularly in the visual arts and in architecture. Beyond this, the Nazis cultivated a pattern which reflected and supported their ideology, satisfied the cultural pretensions and social separateness of their elite, and countered or masked deteriorating fortunes in war. Thus the works of Jews were summarily banned. Farmer, factory worker and soldier were cast as idyllic partners of social production. Allegorical themes saw a resurgence. And historic wars and conflicts were resurrected and mythologised. Among the most pervasive themes of National Socialist culture was the 'heroic'. It was seen, for instance, in Hitler's passion for Wagnerian opera. It found most lasting and perhaps most vivid expression in the monumental architecture of the Third Reich. The massive granite and marble-faced edifices created by Hitler and his architect, Albert Speer, were intended as 'Parthenons' of later millennia.

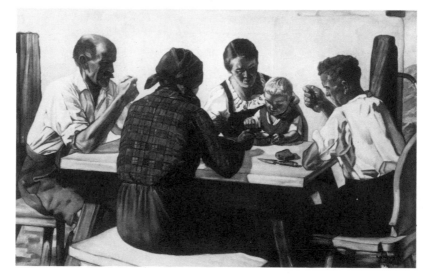

Otto Hoyer, *Bauernmahl*

Carl Baüm, *Pflüger am Oberrhein*.

Franz Eichhorst, *Maschinen Gewehrnest*.

Religion

The geography of religion in Nazi Germany was distinctive in several ways. Protestants dominated in northern and central Germany, but to the west and south there was a progressive preponderance of Roman Catholics, some 70 per cent in Bavaria. In 1933 the ratio of Protestants to Roman Catholics was roughly two to one, but with the reincorporation of the Catholic Saar territory in 1935 and, later, the annexation of Austria and the Sudetenland, both Catholic, that figure altered to almost one to one, Protestants retaining a very slight majority.

German Protestantism had long been a political force. Prussian hegemony in Germany after 1871 drew extensive support from the conservative/Protestant stratum and Lutheranism became a pro-state creed. The Nazis enjoyed much the same basis of support, as the geographical pattern of the July 1932 Reichstag elections bears witness. Roman Catholicism formed a long-standing rival to Prussian authority, not least within the borders of Germany itself. And the determined reluctance of Roman Catholics to support National Socialism before 1933 clearly illustrates this. In fact, Roman Catholicism in Germany was yet more politically identified in that it had its own party political base: the Centre. But, somewhat paradoxically, it was this unity, coupled with the authoritarian structure of the Roman Catholic Church, which saw Catholic opposition to Nazism largely localised upon the conclusion of the Papal Concordat. The contrast was with the Protestant Church, which, under the co-ordinating pressures of Nazism, began to display its diverse origins and structure. There had never been a united Protestant Church in Germany. The Nazis sought one, under their own political banner, but failed decisively.

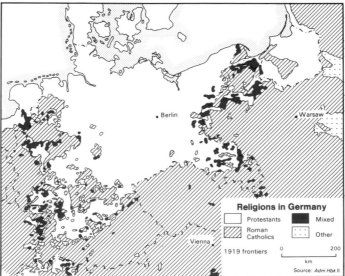

Religions in Germany

Protestants	Mixed
Roman Catholics	Other

1919 frontiers

0 — 200 km

Source: *Adm Hbk* II

Berlin

Warsaw

Vienna

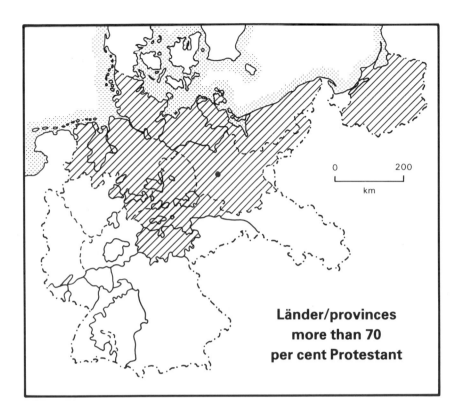

**Länder/provinces
more than 70
per cent Protestant**

The relationship between National Socialism and the churches was an ambiguous one. Many Nazi leaders were atheists and wished to erode the influence of Christianity, but most of their supporters thought of themselves as Christians. The result was confusion and compromise. The ecclesiastical realm was subjected to a campaign of co-ordination (*Gleichschaltung*) in the way of almost every other sector of society under Nazism. Included in this was the exclusion of 'racial undesirables' from the clergy, a measure which at once split the Lutheran Church. At a very early stage the Nazis also succeeded in depoliticising the Catholic Church with its prominent party political representation. The clergy, too, fell increasingly prey to the persecution and terror of the SA, the Gestapo and SS organisations. However, a cautious quality permeated many of these activities. At the higher levels of authority there was a reluctance to impress the Nazi mould where religious feeling revealed unease towards it. Hitler was especially sensitive on religious issues and the campaign of *Gleichschaltung* was characterised by persistent reversals, often at Hitler's will, as forces of opposition, even within the conservative establishment, showed their face. A separate Reich Ministry of Ecclesiastical Affairs was established in 1935, partly as a response to the difficulties of co-ordination in the service of National Socialism. But even by the war years, despite the atheism of most sections of the Nazi leadership, the relationship of the churches, the Protestant Church especially, remained largely unresolved. The Church Minister, Kerrl, took the view that National Socialism needed Christianity because it had nothing with which to replace it. Thus religious faith became a passive support, almost an unwelcome surrogate for faith in National Socialism, impossible to attack frontally during the war.

Farm Entailment

Among the various sectors of German economic production, agriculture was one of the most rapidly co-ordinated in the service of National Socialism. In part this was due to Nazi penetration of many agrarian organisations prior to 1933. It reflected, too, the relative strength of Nazi support in the agricultural sector, which was reinforced by substantial measures of economic relief for farmers in 1933. But it was also linked to the ideological significance attached to agriculture in the goals of National Socialism. Hitler, in alliance with his agrarian policy chief, Darré, saw the agricultural peasantry as the core of future German nationhood and a prime vehicle in the consolidation of the Greater German Reich. The communion of blood and soil became a pervasive image, to be echoed in art and in literature. The outcome was that among the policy measures of National Socialist agriculture were laws on the entailment of peasant holdings. These were deliberately aimed to preserve the bonds of blood and soil in perpetuity. Agricultural holdings of between 7.5 and 125 hectares were tied to active farmers of German blood and to their direct descendants in perpetuity. The entailed farms became known as *Erbhöfe* and the proprietor-farmers were designated *Bauer*. The latter term was subsequently used exclusively with reference to entailed farms. Local Erbhof courts became the exclusive organs of entailment. In regions where partible inheritance systems prevailed, the practice had been for farmholdings to be granted to the eldest male heirs and for remaining children to be given money payments. Under the entailment laws, such payments were restricted to farmholdings' current receipts in an attempt to curb indebtedness. In Prussia, entailment was established in May 1933. The Reich Entailment Law followed in September 1933.

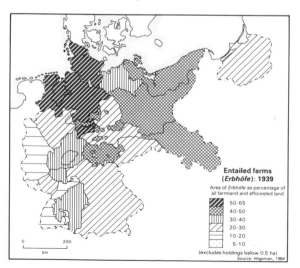

Entailed farms (*Erbhöfe*): 1939

Area of *Erbhöfe* as percentage of all farmland and afforested land

- 50-65
- 40-50
- 30-40
- 20-30
- 10-20
- 5-10

(excludes holdings below 0.5 ha)

Source: Hilgeman., 1984

0   200
km

94

ENTAILED HOLDINGS BY SIZE

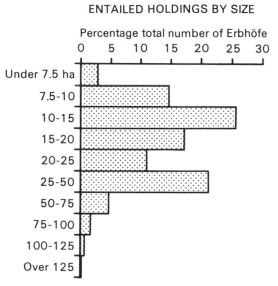

Source: Farquharson, 1976

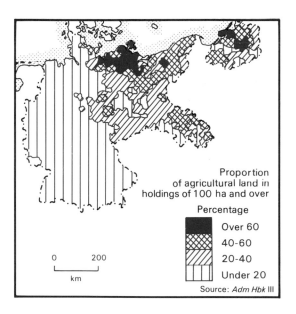

The *Erbhöfe* never covered more than about one-third of all farms, and they contributed little to the improvement of agricultural efficiency. The farming community itself was not enamoured with entailment. Many viewed the legislation as a restriction on freedom and on the new guarantees against sequestration in cases of farm indebtedness, even with the compensations of guaranteed prices which were introduced almost simultaneously under the newly formed Reich Food Estate. Outside the entailment legislation were the mass of smallholdings, as obvious an arena for land reform as any, and then at the further extreme the vast Junker estates east of the Elbe. In 1938, 2.5 million of the smallest farmholdings had less land area than the top tenth of the top 1 per cent of holdings. Had entailment been part of a comprehensive land reform programme, some improvement in efficiency might have been obtained. Such a reform had certainly long been in the party programme. But as became so typical of National Socialism in practice, party commitments were implemented haphazardly, the more immediate needs of the regime readily holding precedence. Radical land reform would have compromised the regime's drive for agricultural self-sufficiency in preparation for war. Entailment, therefore, was hardly a political measure and even less an economic one. Most of all it was part of the great myth propagated by the Nazis about the rebirth of German nationhood — the anticipated *völkisch* empire.

The Labour Front

The working classes were never fertile ground for the National Socialists. Attempts to win their support in the late 1920s through a Nazi Party factory cell organisation (NSBO) made little headway. And by the time Hitler held the reins of power, the working-class organisations, notably the trade unions, remained as an independent power block. However, in a classic *coup d'état*, the Nazis smashed trade union power on 2 May 1933, having only a day previously courted union goodwill by declaring 1 May (International Labour Day) a national holiday. In place of the unions, the Nazis established the German Labour Front (Deutsche Arbeitsfront — DAF), led by Robert Ley. The DAF was a highly improvised and ill-defined organisation, qualities which were to bear forth a long succession of disputes and rivalries within the polycratic structure represented by the Third Reich. The DAF was not a state organ but an auxiliary arm of the Nazi Party. However, its links with the party were close enough, given that Ley was staff leader of the party's political organisation at the same time as being DAF leader. The DAF in fact mimicked in general terms the organisational structure of the party with its large central office and with its 13 territorial divisions, the latter subdivided into Kreise and the Kreise split into local groups. But this neighbourhood organisation was ultimately overshadowed, in practical terms, by the factory-centred organisation, or *Betriebs-Gemeinschaften.*

The overwhelming paradox of the German Labour Front was that although it ultimately had some 25 million compulsory members and received vast sums in membership dues, it never represented them in any material sense. Despite repeated efforts by Ley, the DAF never won power to negotiate wages, for example. This rested with the Trustees of Labour, state officials, whom Hitler appointed in mid-June 1933. It was this absence of wage-bargaining power that persuaded employers to adopt a positive attitude when moves were made for their incorporation into the DAF later in 1933.

The underlying ethos of the DAF was one which sought to create a 'people's community' in place of the class conflict embodied in the familiar employer/employee relationship. The factory was to become a partnership which would raise productivity and generate pride in the collective achievement. Bereft of any direct power over worker conditions, the DAF launched a campaign under the label 'Strength through Joy' (*Kraft durch Freude*). This sought to compensate for the strains of industrial labour by sponsoring cheap holidays and entertainments on a national scale. At the same time, a Department of the Beauty of Work was created within the DAF, the object being to enhance the aesthetic appearance of the workplace. The ultimate measure, however, was the programme for a 'People's Car', the *Volkswagen*. In outward appearance the DAF was clearly taking on the mould of a propaganda organisation, but in an indirect way it was also gaining an economic power base. Its holiday schemes, for instance, became crucial to the prosperity of the German holiday industry at large and provided enormous revenues for the railways. The initiation of the Volkswagen programme signalled a foothold in the motor-vehicle industry. The DAF sought more direct increments to its power with its entry into vocational training in 1936-7 and, increasingly, Ley proceeded to capitalise on his dual positions as a party Reichsleiter and as leader of the

Organisation diagram for Strength through Joy, from *Der nationalsozialistische Schulungsbrief*, 1934

DAF. The power echelons of the party were exploited by the Front's massive organisational apparatus such that its regional leaders to some extent vied in authority with the party's Gauleiters and Kreisleiters. In fact, the DAF grew to become the largest organisation in the Third Reich, readily eclipsing the Nazi Party, in funds as well as membership.

In the final years of peace, it was the singular pursuit of power rather than the condition of labour which guided the German Labour Front's activities. And this was against a background of growing labour crisis, notably a shortage of skilled labour, from 1936 onwards. Whatever propaganda means were devised to wed the working classes more firmly to the goals of National Socialism, circumstances conspired to make the power of labour largely independent of them. As shortages of labour in the booming metal, engineering and construction trades became more acute, wage spirals and the pirating of workers by employers became widespread. The regime made movements towards a comprehensive direction of the labour market, but the measures were piecemeal and often indecisive, and the population slow to conform. The Labour Front actually got in the way of such efforts and continued to make populist propaganda. It was the inmates of the concentration and work camps who were to become the real labouring class of National Socialism: at once impressed, servile and unremunerated, where 'Kraft durch Freude' was anathema.

Law and Justice

From the very outset, National Socialism perverted the legal system in its own service. The prosecution of the Reichstag 'arsonists' in 1933 on the basis of a law passed after the event transgressed a fundamental legal principle. Special courts (*Sondergerichte*) were established following the Reichstag Fire Decree to try those committing offences under its provisions. They were political courts as such, and the judicial procedures were streamlined in ways which contravened primary legal conventions. The number of *Sondergerichte* grew from 13 in 1933 to over 70 by 1945. The People's Court (*Volksgericht*) in Berlin, also established in 1933, functioned to try acts of treason.

The German judiciary was only slowly subjected to large-scale Nazi interference. Its relationship with National Socialism was much the same as that of the civil service and the army; all were institutions which had to be maintained for the efficient working of the state machine, Nazi or otherwise. The judiciary engaged in tacit co-operation with the regime, many seeing political interference in terms of longer-term national good. Some jurists also looked towards the creation of a distinctly National Socialist body of law in a broadly *völkisch* authoritarian tradition. However, such a body of law was fundamentally inconsistent with the precepts of National Socialism. The existence of a rigid and defined body of rules and precedents was inimical to a regime in which improvisation, arbitrariness and summary action were hallmarks.

Although the Nazis maintained a legal front in that there was no mass purge of the judiciary and much legal apparatus (e.g. in civil law) remained unchanged, they progressively undermined legality by the propagation of endless new laws which were often ill-defined, by interfering in judicial matters, and, above all, by permitting and encouraging the growth of extra-legal organs like the Gestapo and the SS. The war signalled the watershed in this process. By 1943 there were over forty crimes for which the death penalty was prescribed, whereas in 1933 there had been three. By the closing years of the war, Hitler was personally altering court sentences and judges were receiving regular guidelines from the Justice Ministry, making mockery of any remaining judicial independence. But it was in the Nazi police state that the destruction of justice was most rapid. Summary arrests, the removal to concentration camps of prisoners decreed innocent in the courts, and SS execution squads were all features of a growing alternative basis of law in which the judiciary and its organs had less and less influence. In some ways the courts became servants of the police, but in other respects they played no part at all, particularly as the racial ideology of Himmler's SS was pursued with ever-increasing zeal.

ARRESTS BY STATE POLICE, OCTOBER 1941

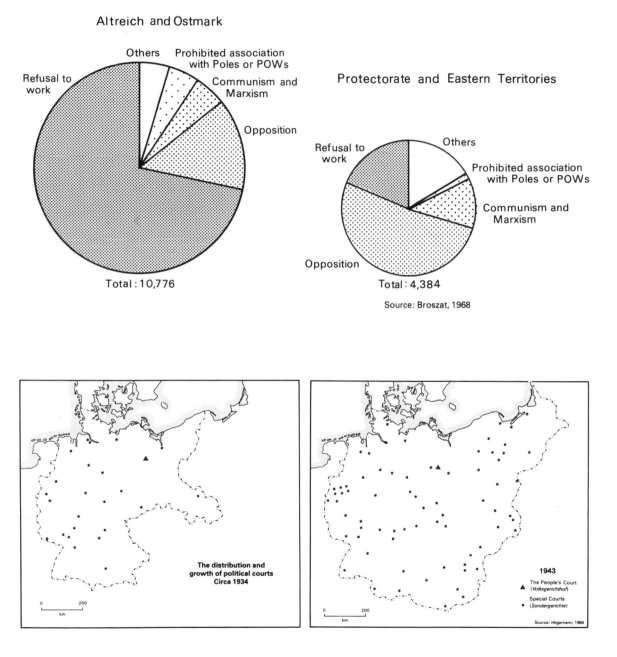

Altreich and Ostmark

Others

Prohibited association
with Poles or POWs

Refusal to
work

Communism and
Marxism

Opposition

Total: 10,776

Protectorate and Eastern Territories

Refusal to
work

Others

Prohibited association
with Poles or POWs

Communism and
Marxism

Opposition

Total: 4,384

Source: Broszat, 1968

The distribution and
growth of political courts
Circa 1934

0   200
km

1943

The People's Court
(*Volksgerichtshof*)

▲

Special Courts
(*Sondergerichte*)

●

Source: Hilgemann, 1984

0   200
km

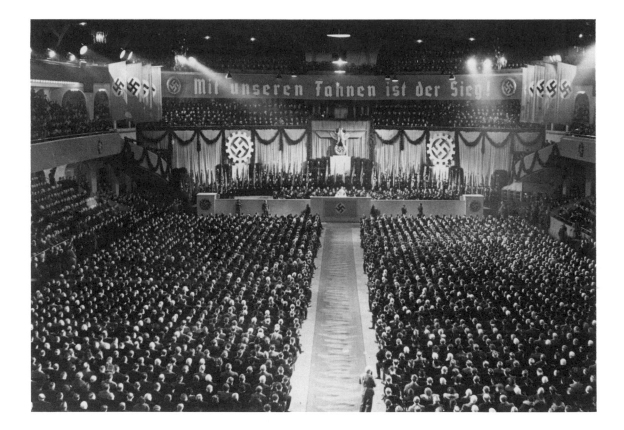

Hitler addressing the Nazi Party at the Berlin Sportpalast. The venue was used often by Hitler for making major new policy pronouncements.

Part Four
Population and Economy

Population
Agriculture and Food Supply
Raw Materials and Industry
Transport and Communications
Trade and Trade Policy

Population

A persistent theme of Nazi propaganda was that Germany was a nation with an inadequate land area relative to the size of its population. Most commonly this was conveyed by reciting the progressive shrinkage in the land area of Germany and its historical predecessors as far back as the Holy Roman Empire. Another misleading device was to compare the population densities of world states with their colonial territories incorporated. In this manner, Germany came close to Japan and far ahead of any European state in the degree of its 'overcrowding'. However, the reality was quite otherwise. Germany's 69.6 million people of 1939 resided on a larger per capita land area than either the British, Dutch or Belgian peoples; only against France was the comparison in any measure valid. What is more, the Nazi state took deliberate steps to raise the reproductive rate of its population. And by the later 1930s it was suffering a chronic shortage of able-bodied manpower. Thus have commentators been led to claim that Nazi Germany was a 'space without people', rather than a 'people without space'.

Except for the upward trend in the net reproduction rate, Nazi Germany exhibited most of the demographic features common to countries of Europe during the interwar years, namely a rising level of urbanisation, continuing rural–urban migration, a higher level of fertility in the countryside than in the towns, and a transfer within city regions from inner to outer suburbs. As is apparent from the accompanying map, extensive areas of Germany (with Austria and the Sudetenland) lost population between 1933 and 1939, notably in the rural east and south. The areas gaining population reflected the decisive programme of industrial expansion and resource development undertaken by the Nazi regime: for example, ship-building and all its ancillary industries at coastal centres on the North Sea and the Baltic; mining, metals, engineering, chemicals and agricultural processing in the belts centred on Hanover and Brunswick, and Leipzig and Dessau. Munich, Silesia and the Saar afford further examples. Most of these areas grew considerably from internal migration, as the adjacent map of migration balance reveals.

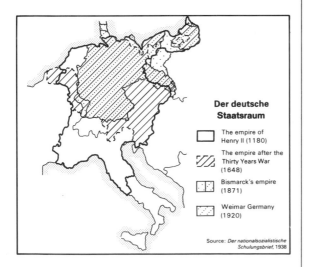

Der deutsche Staatsraum

- The empire of Henry II (1180)
- The empire after the Thirty Years War (1648)
- Bismarck's empire (1871)
- Weimar Germany (1920)

Source: *Der nationalsozialistische Schulungsbrief*, 1938

Contractions of the German state in history

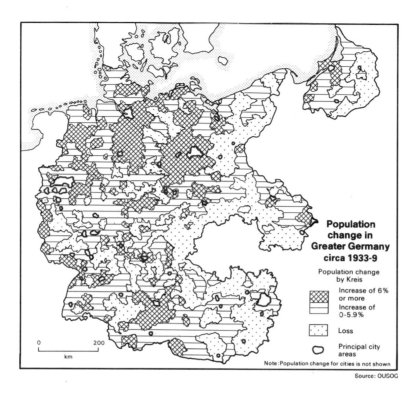

**Population
change in
Greater Germany
circa 1933-9**

Population change
by Kreis

⊠ Increase of 6%
or more

▤ Increase of
0-5.9%

⋯ Loss

◯ Principal city
areas

Note:Population change for cities is not shown

Source: OUSOG

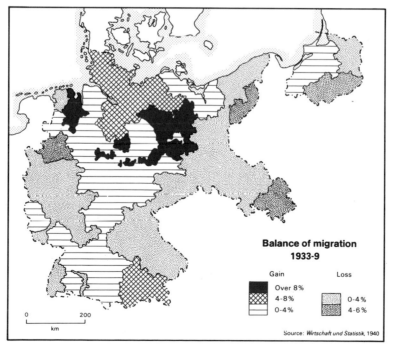

**Balance of migration
1933-9**

Gain

■ Over 8%

⊠ 4-8%

□ 0-4%

Loss

▤ 0-4%

▦ 4-6%

Source: *Wirtschaft und Statistik*, 1940

103

The pattern of city growth between 1933 and 1939 echoes in many ways the general picture of population change, even if some gains were attributable to boundary extensions. A selection of cities declined in population over the period, notably in the Ruhr (Gelsenkirchen, Duisburg-Hamborn, Dortmund, Oberhausen, Bochum) and in the former state of Saxony (Leipzig, Dresden, Chemnitz). Nowhere was the margin of decline greater than 6 per cent and it arose partly from out-of-town population movements. But in the case of the Ruhr, the pattern reflected a conscious policy to concentrate new industrial capacity away from the vulnerable border regions, and also the depressed state of the coal industry up to 1936.

The majority of these demographic trends, though consistent with those of much of Europe, were quite contrary to Nazi policy goals. This applied particularly to the role cast for the farming peasantry in the future Nazi state and to the importance of the eastern lands in realising that objective.

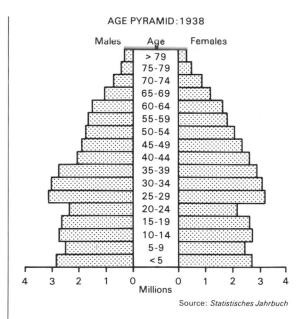

AGE PYRAMID: 1938

Source: *Statistisches Jahrbuch*

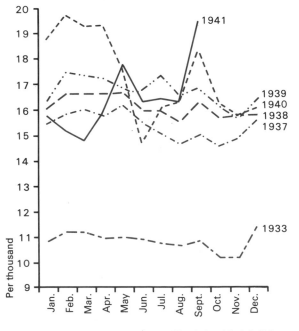

BIRTH RATE IN MAJOR GERMAN TOWNS (Großstädten)
1933 and 1937-41

Source: *Wirtschaft und Statistik*, 1941

N

The war naturally brought with it radical and sometimes abrupt changes in Germany's demographic characteristics. The birth rate held up in the first eighteen months of war, but thereafter it fell. In 1942 the total was 14.9 per thousand, almost back to the level of 1933. As the war progressed, there was a rising number of deaths among civilians due to enemy bombardment. By May 1945 the cumulative total was 650,000, not far short of the average for the annual number of deaths in Germany in the 1930s. In geographical terms, however, the most significant demographic changes occurred in migration. Civilian workers were compulsorily transferred to meet specific labour shortages. Territorial expansion involved vast movements in the military population and all their supporting civilian personnel. German minorities totalling over half a million in the Baltic states (Lithuania, Latvia and Estonia), Poland, eastern Rumania and South Tyrol were resettled in Greater Germany. Europe's Jews were progressively rooted out and forcibly transported to the concentration and death camps in the eastern territories. Then, as Hitler's empire was forced to contract in the face of Allied advance, the scale and intensity of migration advanced further. By early 1945, it was dominated by the westward flight of Germans in the path of the advancing Red Army.

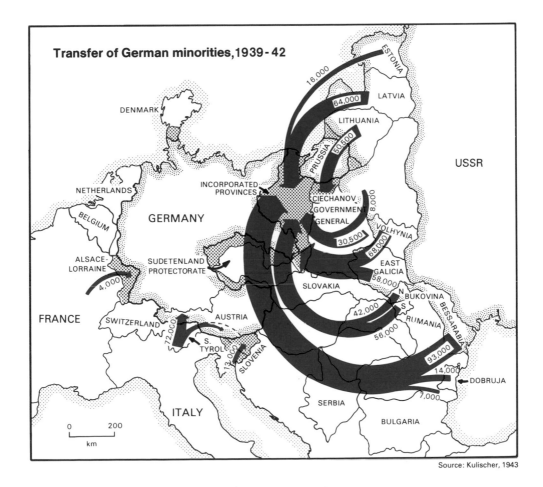

Source: Kulischer, 1943

Agriculture and Food Supply

Any examination of agriculture and, more specifically, food supply in Nazi Germany has to accommodate the special problems posed by world markets under the forces of depression and also the variability of climate over northern and central Europe. The room for manoeuvre in setting out a determinedly National Socialist agrarian policy and the problem of meeting production targets were both considerably circumscribed by these two features. For several decades before Hitler's accession, protectionism in agriculture had been a familiar cry, for a host of different reasons. The world depression pushed Germany further along the path of agricultural autarky as the country's exporting potential was curtailed and the capacity for food imports was reduced in turn. Throughout the 1930s Germany suffered a persistent shortage of foreign currency, making large-scale foreign food imports impossible. And to complicate the position, Nazi rearmament policies made increasing demands on the meagre foreign currency reserves in the purchase of industrial raw materials like quality iron ore not found within the Reich's borders. Thus, when the National Socialists declared their intentions towards a more self-sufficient agriculture, particularly in the long-standing deficit area of fats, they were responding as much to force of circumstance and traditional predisposition as to any preferred policy, for all that policy was consistent with their war aims. Moreover, the force of circumstance took a new twist in 1934 following a disastrous harvest season. This prompted the setting up of the 'Battle of Production' in which the acreage under grain was to be reduced, but the quantity of grain maintained and the released land then made over to fodder cultivation. However, the scheme soon ran into difficulties, most of them triggered by another poor harvest in 1935.

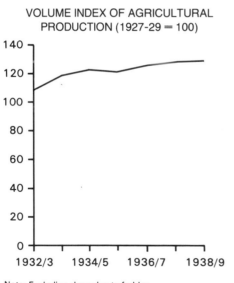

VOLUME INDEX OF AGRICULTURAL
PRODUCTION (1927-29 = 100)

Note: Excluding share due to fodder

Source: Klein, 1959

Farm incomes, by contrast, did not tell so grim a story in the first years of the Nazi regime. Much of the agrarian sector saw a growing surplus. In 1932-3 the excess of sales over expenses had fallen to 0.5 billion RM. By 1934-5 it had risen to 2.3 billion RM with the aid of higher prices, debt relief measures and tax cuts. Unfortunately, the pattern was not maintained for long.

AGRICULTURAL PRODUCTION AND STOCK HOLDING:1932-8

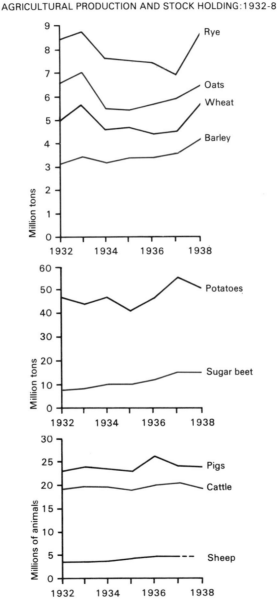

Source: Farquharson, 1976

107

New measures for agricultural production were introduced in 1936 under Goering's Four-Year-Plan Organisation. These included reductions in fertiliser prices, mechanisation subsidies and grants for bringing new land under cultivation. The results were measurably favourable, assisted by a good harvest year in 1938 and again in 1939. By 1938/9, farm production was some 20 per cent up on the figure for 1928/9. Fodder areas had grown substantially. There was also an increase in food consumption per head of population of about 4 to 5 per cent. But still by 1938/9 the country was able to meet only 57 per cent of its fats demand. This was only a four-point rise on 1933/4. Indeed, it was half the corresponding rise between 1927/8 and 1933/4 (nine points). The explanation was that the provisions of the Four-Year Plan had been heavily biased towards arable rather than livestock farming. In 1938/9, 43 per cent of livestock feed was still imported, the unit costs of which had been steadily rising on the world market. Thus compared with their arable counterparts, livestock farmers benefited from few subsidies and faced rising costs for items such as farm housing and machinery at a time when agricultural prices were effectively frozen by the Reich Food Estate. This was not the sum total of the policy failures, though. For behind improvements in the other food sectors there lay a basic growing weakness: the flight from the land. Between 1933 and 1939 agriculture may have lost up to half a million people, and most of the measures that the Nazis introduced to stem the flow actually intensified it in the longer term.

LAND SOWN WITH FODDER AND FIBRE-BEARING PLANTS (thousand ha)

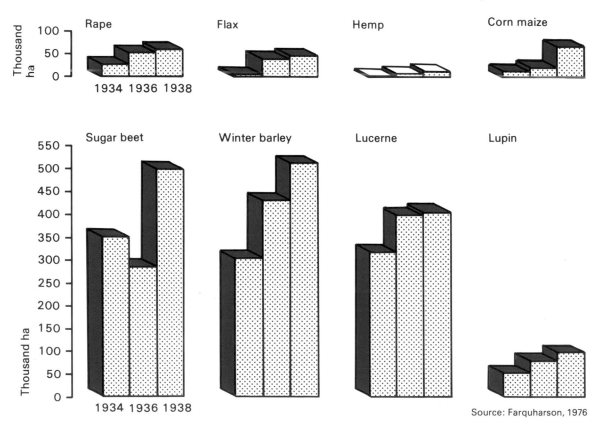

Source: Farquharson, 1976

The onset of war conditions magnified the many problems of National Socialist agriculture. Trade blockade brought a drastic decline in fodder imports and in essential fertilisers like potash. Labour loss intensified such that women, juveniles and foreign workers were being engaged in increasing numbers by the middle of the war. And despite the pre-existence of a central co-ordination and planning body in the form of the Reich Food Estate, a variety of factors (not least the conflicting power blocs in the Third Reich) impeded a full-scale direction of agriculture.

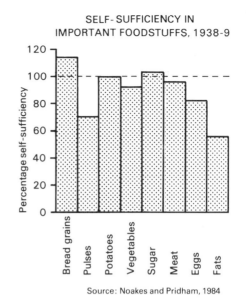

SELF- SUFFICIENCY IN
IMPORTANT FOODSTUFFS, 1938-9

Source: Noakes and Pridham, 1984

AGRICULTURAL YIELDS IN 1933, 1939 AND 1944
(per hectare; in double zentner)

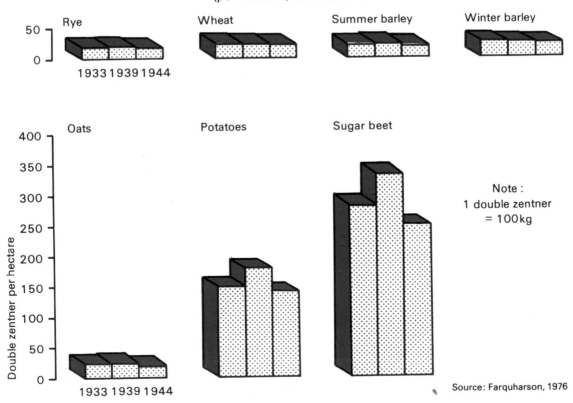

Note :
1 double zentner
= 100 kg

Source: Farquharson, 1976

Raw Materials and Industry

Germany's industrial machine underwent a traumatic decline during the Depression years. In some sectors, production fell by around 70 per cent over the years 1929 to 1931. Thus the immediate preoccupation under National Socialist rule was simple regeneration of industrial capacity and industrial investment. In fact, it took until around 1935/6 to achieve the levels of production of the pre-Depression years. This was not the sum total of the Depression's effects, though. As in agriculture, the deficient state of the country's export earnings capacity placed severe limits on imports of industrial raw materials and goods. Foreign currency reserves were small and had to be strictly rationed. Again in common with agriculture, therefore, a policy of autarky was set. The primary vehicle was Goering's Four-Year-Plan Organisation with its exceptional room for intervention in economic administration. Three materials were singled out in particular: iron ore, oil and rubber.

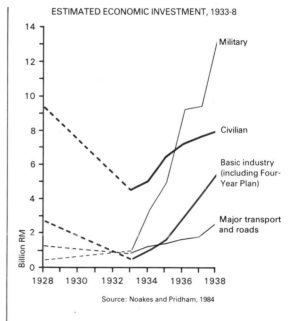

ESTIMATED ECONOMIC INVESTMENT, 1933-8

Military

Civilian

Basic industry (including Four-Year Plan)

Major transport and roads

Source: Noakes and Pridham, 1984

INDUSTRIAL PRODUCTION
Index (1928=100)

Iron and steel

Coal

Engineering

Chemicals

Source: *Adm Hbk* III

In the later 1930s, Germany was second only to the USA as a world producer of iron and steel. However, such dominance was not based on German ores. The country had extensive ore deposits but these were mostly poor in quality, some with iron contents of only 20 to 30 per cent. Thus the bulk of Germany's ore came from outside, particularly from Sweden where iron content was typically around 60 per cent. Goering's scheme was to expand substantially the exploitation of home ores, notably those in the Salzgitter field in Hanover. For this purpose, an industrial corporation, the Hermann Goering Ore and Foundry Company, was established. Ore production was scheduled to rise to 24 million tons by 1944, whereas at the time of the corporation's establishment the Salzgitter field yielded less than a million tons. There was to be a parallel though lesser-scale development of ore-fields in Franconia in the south, and in both mining areas iron and steel plants were to be erected on site, bringing in coking coal from the Ruhr. The whole scheme was patently uneconomic, but the Nazi leadership saw this as immaterial given the reduced reliance on foreign ores and the strategic gain of a dispersion in iron and steel capacity. In practice, ore extraction and iron and steel capacity never matched anything like that envisaged in the scheme. Ore production from the Salzgitter field, for instance, was only 4.2 million tons in 1942, while the Franconian iron and steel plant never materialised at all. The reasons for this were various, some highly specific but others more ill-defined. The territorial expansion of the Third Reich, beginning with Austrian annexation in 1938, brought with it ore supplies of better quality and augmented iron and steel capacity on a very substantial scale, especially with the conquest of France and Benelux in 1940. The speed of success of Hitler's Blitzkrieg operations rapidly undermined the rationale behind domestic exploitation and development. Similarly significant, though, was the manner in which the Goering industrial enterprise grew. Like so many organisations of the *Hitler state*, it developed a force and momentum of its own, becoming a massive, almost capitalistic, industrial conglomerate through new development, partnership and amalgamation, particularly in occupied territories, and bearing increasingly little relation to the aims of the Four-Year-Plan Organisation under which it was born.

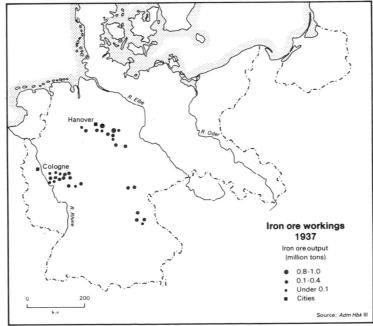

Iron ore workings 1937

Iron ore output (million tons)

● 0.8-1.0
● 0.1-0.4
· Under 0.1
■ Cities

Source: *Adm Hbk* III

NET PROFITS OF THE IG-FARBEN COMBINE, 1933-9

Source: Noakes and Pridham, 1984

A somewhat similar story was presented in oil production. The Four-Year Plan instituted a battery of measures to advance the production of mineral oil, including high tariffs on imported oil. In parallel, the production of synthetic oil (from coal and lignite) was to be radically expanded. However, the Plan targets were not met. In 1939 production of mineral and synthetic oil was around 40 per cent below the level intended. In 1940 it was 20 per cent below. Production performance was better in mineral than in synthetic oil, where the enormous manpower and transport requirements for a process using 5 to 6 tons of coal to produce one ton of oil made real difficulties.

Rubber production, by contrast, was one area of the Four-Year Plan where the target was more nearly approached. In the mid-1930s, Germany had the largest rubber industry of continental Europe, based on imported natural rubber. The Plan aimed to reduce this import dependency by developing the manufacture of synthetic rubber (Buna) from acetylene. A pilot plant already existed at Leverkusen. The Plan envisaged the establishment of three major production plants, the first of them at Schkopau near Leipzig. By the outbreak of war, synthetic rubber production was 22,000 tons per annum, as against a natural output approaching 100,000 tons. By late 1943, nine synthetic plants were producing almost 100,000 tons annually, which met consumption needs in broad terms.

The programme of synthetic production was spearheaded by the giant chemicals firm IG-Farben. Carl Krauch, a senior member of its board, had been appointed to the Four-Year-Plan Organisation from its inception in 1936 and from 1938 became General Plenipotentiary for Chemicals. This meant that he exercised full control over the planning and production of synthetics, a position of inestimable value to IG-Farben as a near-monopolist in the German chemical sector. This form of alliance between an organisation of the Nazi state and a leading empire of private industrial capital became typical as the regime moved to a war footing. It was the most expedient way of achieving a given production objective. 'Big business' was thus drawn yet further into the 'unholy alliance' for which it was to be so bitterly chastised after Germany's defeat. IG-Farben saw its business profits describe a quantum leap, although its direct contributions to Nazi Party funds did not rise as impressively. The records of other firms were less spectacular, but in 1939 undistributed profits of limited liability companies were four times higher than in 1928.

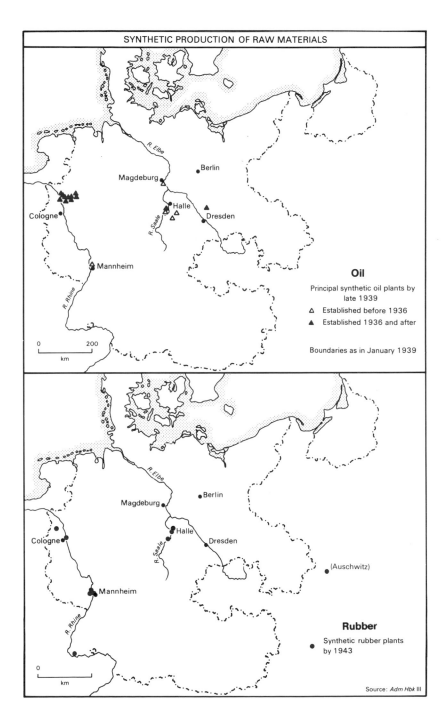

SYNTHETIC PRODUCTION OF RAW MATERIALS

Oil

Principal synthetic oil plants by late 1939

△ Established before 1936

▲ Established 1936 and after

Boundaries as in January 1939

Rubber

● Synthetic rubber plants by 1943

Source: *Adm Hbk* III

The largely unavoidable concentration of the Fischer-Tropsch oil capacity (using coal and coke) in the Ruhr was to prove a serious liability in the face of the Allied bombing campaign from 1943.

Alongside the drive for self-sufficiency in raw materials, the key feature of industrial manufacture in Nazi Germany was rearmament, embracing a whole range of production sectors. In 1932 Germany spent only 1 per cent of its GNP on defence and armament. By 1939 the figure had risen to nearly a quarter. Measured against public investment alone, military spending reached 74 per cent of the total in 1938. The making of armoured vehicles, weaponry and munitions, together with naval building, defensive fortification and the development of the Luftwaffe, all placed heavy demands upon Germany's productive capacity. It is estimated that investment in this sector grew from 1 billion RM in 1933 to 13.6 billion in 1938, with much of it concentrated in the north and west. From 1934 the Reichsbank was issuing extensive credits to assist production expansion in those firms engaged in armaments contracts. Industrial investment, much of which was directly and indirectly tied to military demands, grew from 0.5 billion RM in 1933 to 5.6 billion RM in 1938. This included the synthetic programmes of the Four-Year Plan and the mining of low-grade metals. The manufacturing sector that proved most inadequate in meeting the requirements placed on it was steel. The problem was that, aside from the Hermann Goering enterprises, little new steel-making capacity was added under Nazi rule. There was also a persistent weakness in the priority allocation of steels, demands from sectors entirely extraneous to rearmament often absorbing valuable output. Labour for all this expanded industrial production was drawn largely from the ranks of the unemployed, their number falling from around 6 million in early 1933 to around 1 million by late 1936. This meant that there was no fundamental redirection of labour within the German economy. There was some out-movement from agricultural occupations, but the production of consumer goods, for example, was not greatly affected by rearmament. Consumer goods production showed consistent growth throughout the peacetime years of National Socialism. In fact, there was a determination on the part of Nazi leaders not to force civilian sacrifices. To reiterate a common contemporary expression: many, not all, Germans under Hitler had both guns and butter, though at the cost of a rapidly rising public debt.

The map shows plants with a capacity of 20,000 tons p.a. and over. Sulphuric acid was vital to the production of explosives and forms a fundamental base to chemical industries generally. In 1937 the Lower Rhine area contributed nearly 43 per cent of sulphuric acid production.

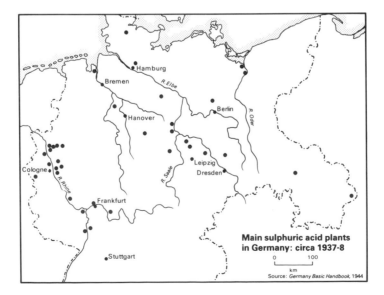

Main sulphuric acid plants in Germany: circa 1937-8

0   100

km

Source: *Germany Basic Handbook*, 1944

National Socialism's impact on the organisation and control of industry has to be seen against the background of a relatively highly organised pattern of economic life well before 1933. And aside from the creation of such bodies as the Four-Year-Plan Organisation, the Nazi accession mostly witnessed a consolidation of this pattern. Membership of the former widely representative trade associations became compulsory, for instance, and the Fuehrerprinzip was established within them. The largest of these was that for industry and this remained so from 1933. The *Reichsgruppe for Industry* had seven functional subdivisions and each subdivision was further subdivided. The general label the Nazis used to describe this form of organisation was 'self-administration'. But the only real sense in which this applied was in terms of personnel. Industrial administration was carried out by industrialists, not civil servants, but nevertheless under direct state supervision.

Before 1933, Germany also had a comprehensive industrial and business organisation in the field, i.e. a distinctive geographical organisation. Indeed, membership of a local *Chamber of Industry and Commerce* had been compulsory for all firms. The Chambers were staffed through democratic election among their members, and there were statutory regulations providing for consultation between the Chambers and central government departments. The Nazis largely confirmed this organisational pattern, except that the Fuehrerprinzip, that is control from the top, was substituted for the previous democratic arrangement. There were 111 separate Chambers and this remained so until 1942 when their number was reduced to 42 to bring them into line with the party Gaue.

DISTRIBUTION OF INVESTMENT IN ORGANISATION OF THE FOUR-YEAR PLAN, 1937

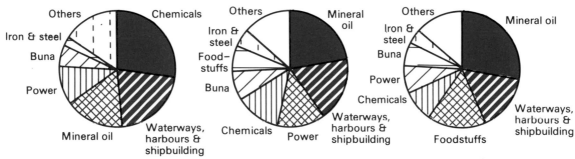

Source: Petzina, 1968

Transport and Communications

The autobahn programme

Of all the measures instituted by the National Socialists, the autobahn programme must have been among the most positive. Indeed, the autobahn system remains today as one of the few lasting reminders of Hitler's Germany. The concept of the high-speed motor-road with separate carriageways and limited access points had already been employed in Berlin and, on a larger scale, in Italy and the USA. In Nazi Germany, however, the concept was carried forward on an even more comprehensive scale and at a more rapid rate. Within five years of the programme's inception, some 3,000 km of road were open, another 1,500 km were under construction, and a further 2,400 km were authorised. For its time the autobahn programme represented a highly advanced engineering venture in which many of the latest techniques of civil engineering were applied, particularly in surface construction and finish, and in the large-scale use of concrete. It provides one of the many cases in Nazi Germany where the use of advanced scientific technology rested side by side with pseudo-science as practised in the regime's racial and eugenic policies.

The objectives of the autobahn programme were at once political, economic and strategic. In January 1933 the total number of unemployed had topped 6 million. A major road-building programme offered a way of absorbing some of that figure. By late 1934, some 350,000 people were directly and indirectly employed in it. The geographical configuration of the autobahn system in part reflected the internal trade demands of a well-developed industrial economy, witnessed in the early completion of the links between the major ports of Bremen, Hamburg and Lübeck, and those joining the north-west industrial region based on the Ruhr with the central industrial belt extending from Hanover through Leipzig to Dresden. As the map reveals, however, the planned network looked outward from the country's border regions as much as it sought to bind internal elements of it: for instance, in the south-eastward extensions from Nuremberg and Munich and in the eastward thrusts from Breslau and Bayreuth. All these had strategic significance in a military sense, although army leaders favoured railway rather than road transport. Nuremberg's position in the network was also justified in terms of it being the site of the annual Nazi Party rally.

The rapid progress of the autobahn programme owed much to the Supreme Reich Authority under the direction of Dr Fritz Todt. Outside of ministerial jurisdictions, and yet with powers to initiate legislation and to issue administrative decrees, Todt was able to devise a form of organisation geared specially to his road-building task and to marshal private and public enterprise accordingly. Much as Goering in his capacity as chief of the Four-Year-Plan Organisation, Todt enjoyed an element of direct Fuehrer authority and exercised it widely. He went on to organise conscripted and slave labour for construction projects across occupied Europe. By November 1944, the *Organization Todt* had a workforce numbering over 1.25 million.

**Autobahns
early 1939**

——————	Open to traffic
– – – – –	Under construction
· · · · · · ·	Authorised

Boundaries as in early 1939

Source: OUSOG

INVESTMENT IN ROADS AND RAILWAYS, 1925-38

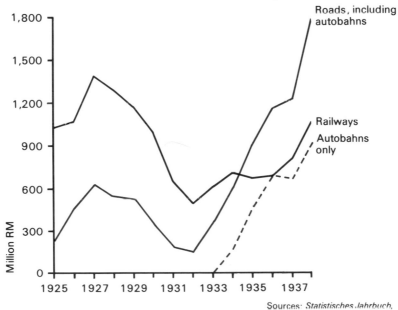

Roads, including autobahns

Railways

Autobahns only

Million RM

Sources: *Statistisches Jahrbuch,
Statistisches Handbuch*

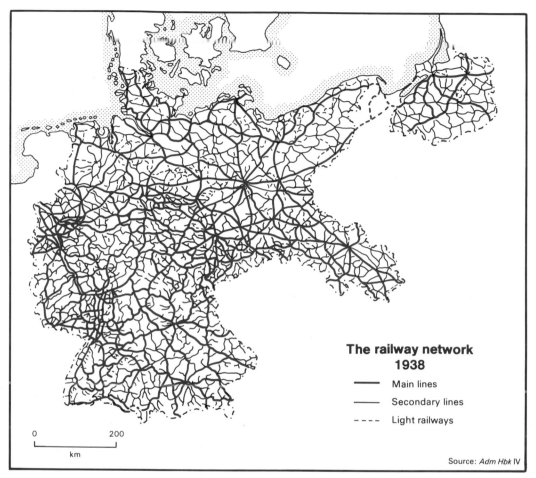

**The railway network
1938**

——— Main lines

——— Secondary lines

- - - - Light railways

Source: *Adm Hbk* IV

The Reichsbahn

Nazi Germany possessed one of the largest European railway systems. Its 54,000 kilometre length was exceeded only by the USSR. In terms of network density and mileage per head of population, it equated closely with the United Kingdom. The fairly wide availability of coal for locomotive fuel and the relatively wide spread of industrial and other economic foci made German railway operation a profitable business. Germany's geographical position at the centre of Europe reinforced this in terms of the opportunities for cross-border passenger and freight traffic.

The German state had a long tradition of involvement in the railways. By 1910, Prussia, for instance, owned some 98 per cent of its lines following a policy of state acquisition extending over thirty years. Under the Weimar constitution, the entire German railway system came under state control, but the subsequent collapse of the currency enforced a largely independent management structure for the railways, notably in budgetary terms. The working profits of the railways then became one of the principal sources of reparation payments. By the early 1930s, the German railways' revenues were again their own, and by 1937 the Nazis had co-ordinated the system in the service of the state by abolishing its independence through the fusion of the duties of railways chief and Minister of Transport.

Despite the formidable transport facility represented by the railway system, the story of its relations with National Socialism is one characterised by lagging investment, strategic oversight and jurisdictional inefficiencies. From the beginning the railway system was cast in the shadow of Todt's great autobahn programme. And in some Nazi quarters, railways were viewed as *passé*, to be superseded by the growth of motor and air transport. The vast scale of the railway administrative organisation also generated antipathy in Nazi officialdom. Much as the civil service was distrusted by Hitler and his leaders, so too was the railway administration. It had too wide and too deeply rooted a power base. Moreover, the almost complete lack of coincidence between the railway administrative regions (Reichsbahnsdirektionen) and the party Gaue intensified difficulties. The railway director at Frankfurt-am-Main, for instance, had to deal with six different Gauleiters.

The paradox was that by the late 1930s effective demand for rail transport was greater than it had ever been. Conditions of economic boom, the refortification schemes in the west and the army's growing requirements combined to intensify pressure on the system. In 1938 there were difficulties moving the coal mined. By 1939 passenger trains were increasingly subject to sudden cancellation. Electrification schemes in progress on some routes added to the problems.

The Nazi attitude to railways was reflected in their very limited use of them in the reoccupation of the Rhineland and in the annexation of Austria. In fact, the regime entered into war in 1939 with no proper plans for the railways, either in strategic or investment terms. The railway system was soon under intense strain. There were shortages of manpower and machines, and there was a minimum of centralised co-ordination in the service of war. Even greater strains were imposed as territorial conquests accumulated. By December 1941 some 15,000 km of broad-gauge track in Russia had been converted to standard gauge, but this had needed 70,000 men from the Reichsbahn organisation. No special locomotive production programme was introduced until late 1941. Only then, under the organising impetus of Armaments Minister Albert Speer, was a standard wartime locomotive class commissioned. Later, Speer set up a production organisation for motive power and stock which was separate from the Reichsbahn.

As the Reichsbahn attempted to meet the diverse demands of transporting men, materials and the victims of Himmler's death camps, as the various power groupings of the Third Reich fought bitterly over railway capacity, Hitler was busy planning a super broad-gauge railway consistent with his monumental dreams for the thousand-year Reich.

H	Hamburg	Op	Oppeln
Sw	Schwerin	C	Cologne
Sn	Stettin	W	Wuppertal
Ks	Königsberg	F	Frankfurt-
Ms	Münster		am-Main
Hn	Hanover	Er	Erfurt
B	Berlin	Sr	Saarbrücken
Fo	Frankfurt-an-	Mz	Mainz
	der-Oder	N	Nuremberg
E	Essen	Kr	Karlsruhe
Kl	Kassel	S	Stuttgart
Ha	Halle	A	Augsburg
Dr	Dresden	M	Munich
Bs	Breslau	Rn	Regensburg

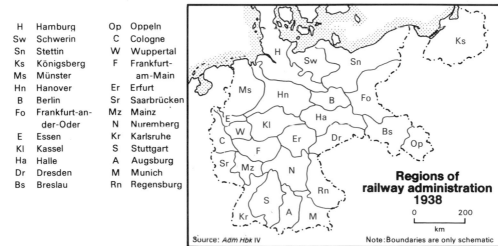

Regions of railway administration 1938

0   200
km

Source: *Adm Hbk* IV   Note: Boundaries are only schematic

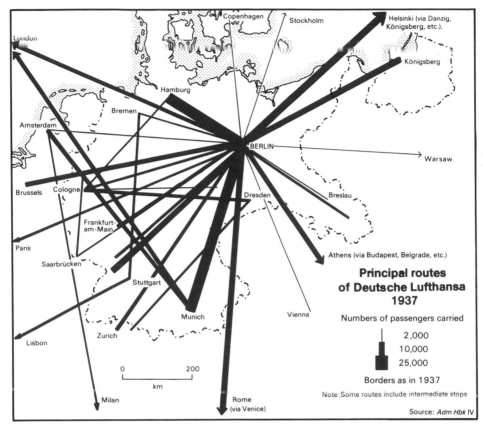

**Principal routes
of Deutsche Lufthansa
1937**

Numbers of passengers carried

2,000
10,000
25,000

Borders as in 1937

Note: Some routes include intermediate stops

Source: *Adm Hbk* IV

Aviation

The Versailles Treaty had forbidden the construction of aircraft for military purposes, but there was no slackening in the pace of German investment in civil aircraft development; this laid the foundation for a vigorous civil aviation industry by the early 1930s, heavily backed by successive German governments. National Socialist policy was to extend this pattern, as witnessed in the foundation of an Air Ministry headed by Goering within months of Hitler's chancellorship and by increasing levels of state subsidy, often in excess of regular commercial demands. The expansion of the civil sector, particularly the technical research and development that accompanied it, was an obvious springboard for the reinstatement of a combat air force. Thus, when Hitler announced the beginning of air rearmament in March 1935, a vigorous Luftwaffe was not long in creation.

From the mid-1920's, civil air services became the monopoly of one company, Deutsche Lufthansa, and by 1937 it operated directly some 76 routes and maintained interests in many others. In 1939 50 per cent of the company's revenue came from direct subsidy, 35 per cent from passengers and 15 per cent from cargo and mail.

The Nazis used aviation to boost their progressive image in much the same fashion as they used the autobahn programme. Hitler became a frequent air traveller, a pattern instituted by Goebbels as a symbolic means of reinforcing the Fuehrer's overarching appeal to the German nation. The supreme irony of this later on in the war was that Hitler forbade his senior military commanders to travel by air because of the enemy risk. Thus Rommel was a critical ten hours in getting from his home in Germany to command the Normandy defence against the Allied landings on 6 June 1944.

Radio broadcasting

The importance of radio to the Nazi dictatorship hardly needs to be emphasised. The German state held a broadcasting monopoly long before Hitler, as indeed was the case in Britain. There were sound operational reasons for national control of broadcasting, quite aside from matters of governmental stability. But in the hands of a regime seeking to radicalise or overturn existing practices and institutions of the state, of course, radio was a devastatingly effective medium. The Nazi Propaganda Ministry was quick to appreciate this and programming was soon rigorously systematised in the service of Nazism. In parallel, the mass production of cheap radio receivers became a priority, with the result that the number of households with access to a receiver rose from 4.5 million in early 1933 to 16 million by the middle of the war. Nazi Germany soon had the densest radio receiver coverage in the world.

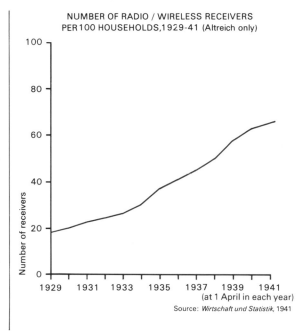

NUMBER OF RADIO / WIRELESS RECEIVERS
PER 100 HOUSEHOLDS, 1929-41 (Altreich only)

(at 1 April in each year)

Source: *Wirtschaft und Statistik*, 1941

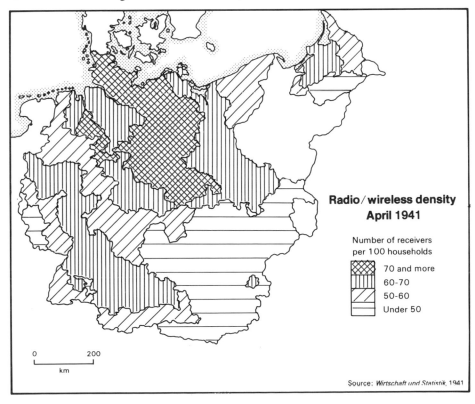

**Radio/wireless density
April 1941**

Number of receivers
per 100 households

70 and more
60-70
50-60
Under 50

Source: *Wirtschaft und Statistik*, 1941

121

Trade and Trade Policy

The nature and course of Nazi trade policy are not themes which lend themselves to simple interpretation. For example, there was no fundamental discontinuity between the policies of the later Weimar administrations and those of Hitler. In large part, this reflected basic facts of German economic life before, during and immediately after the Depression. A deeper problem, though, centres upon the longer-term goals of Nazi trade policy. Was the policy mainly a response to evolving economic expediencies? Or did it embrace dimensions of Nazi ideology, including the extension of German living space in eastern Europe?

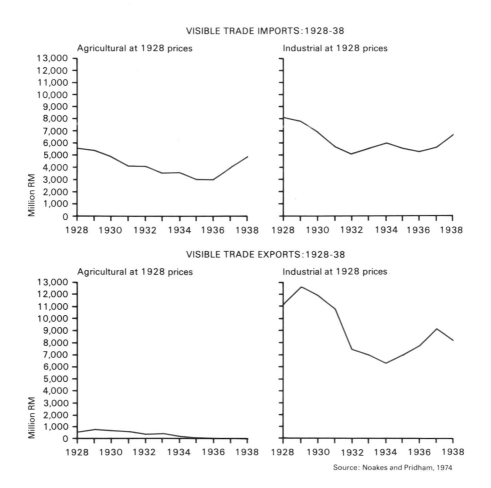

Source: Noakes and Pridham, 1974

122

German foreign trade declined dramatically over the years of the Depression and stagnated throughout the 1930s. The country was continually short of foreign exchange for the imports of food, textiles and industrial raw materials, and exports required subsidy in the face of declining world prices. However, up to 1936/7 the prices of most of the commodities imported fell much faster than the prices of Germany's characteristic exports. As the adjacent graphs show, the *volume* of imports (i.e. imports at fixed prices, 1928) held up relatively well, given the severity of the world depression. This was of vital importance for the foodstuffs sector and for the expansion of the armaments industry.

In the supply of industrial raw materials as well as of foodstuffs, National Socialism sought import substitution or autarky. But the scale of expansion in the armaments and related industries was well beyond the country's substitution capacity and thus the trend was for an increasing proportion of imports to be taken up by industrial raw materials. In 1932 they formed some 27 per cent of imports by value. By 1936 the figure had risen to just over 37. Food imports dropped from around 46 per cent to 35 per cent in the corresponding period. However, the trends were not sustained, for in the closing years of peace the gap narrowed once more. Even so, it is impossible to escape the way imports such as iron ore grew in magnitude. Between 1935 and 1937 the total rose from 14 to 21 million tons, roughly half coming from the rich Swedish fields.

The debate over the goals of Nazi Germany's 'autarkic' trade policy is a difficult one. The crisis of world capitalist organisation from 1929 to 1932 and the haunting lessons of food supply during the First World War undoubtedly struck their own path towards autarky, in agriculture as well as in industry. But some commentators have seen the policy in a far more positive light, as part of a deliberate plan by Hitler, aimed, among other things, at rearmament. A variant of this interpretation argues that rearmament was itself a primary driving force towards autarky in terms of the pressures that it placed on currency reserves and the severe political repercussions of any deceleration in the arms industry's expansion.

123

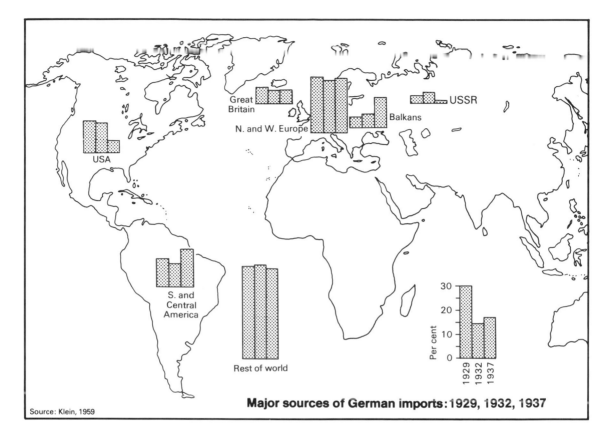

Major sources of German imports: 1929, 1932, 1937

Source: Klein, 1959

Under National Socialism, Germany also saw a reorientation of primary trading partners, involving an expansion of dealings with the Balkans and South and Central America, and a reduction of dealings with former partners such as the United States. The policy had its origins in the last administrations of the Weimar regime when foreign trade with Western Europe (including Great Britain) and America became difficult, largely due to the relative uncompetitiveness of German export goods as a consequence of an overvalued mark. The solution took the form of bilateral trading agreements with countries such as Yugoslavia, Rumania and Hungary (most of whom found themselves similarly placed to Germany), transactions essentially being carried out on a barter basis. Germany exported to these Balkan states a range of manufactured goods and imported vital raw materials like chrome, bauxite and oil. The National Socialists took up this foreign trade policy and reinforced it. Similar trade agreements were forged with countries of Latin America, and, with the added facility of an increasingly centralised regulation of the dealings of German importers and exporters, National Socialism was able to apply considerable leverage on its bilateral trade partners.

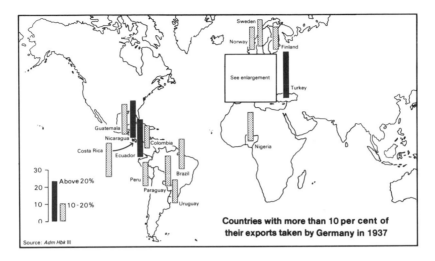

Countries with more than 10 per cent of
their exports taken by Germany in 1937

Source: *Adm Hbk* III

The accompanying diagrams illustrate the substance of these various changes. By 1937 the Balkans and Latin America were supplying some 28 per cent of German imports by value, whereas in 1929 they had supplied only 15. Bulgaria had 43 per cent of its exports (by value) taken by Germany, Turkey 36 per cent and Greece 31 per cent. In certain of these countries, Germany ran an import surplus, thereby underscoring the degree of dependence.

The strategic dimensions of this evolving trade policy require little elucidation. Trade sources in south-east Europe were not liable to blockade in the event of war, while the political allegiances of Latin American states were as likely to be neutral or pro-German as they were pro-Western. These various merits were soon to reveal themselves as Hitler embarked upon his plans for territorial annexation, ultimately taking Germany into world war.

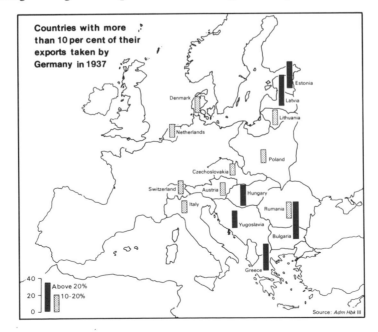

Countries with more
than 10 per cent of their
exports taken by
Germany in 1937

Source: *Adm Hbk* III

German tanks in Wenceslas Square, Prague, March 1939.

Part Five
The Search for Living Space: the Third Reich at War

Territorial Annexation
Territorial Conquest
Allied Bombing
The Allied Road to Berlin

Territorial Annexation

National Socialist foreign policy does not lend itself to simple explanation. The facts of territorial acquisition and aggression may be incontrovertible but the reasons behind them have long been a seat of argument. Some have seen Nazi foreign policy as continuing trends which characterised the Weimar and Wilhelmine eras, particularly in the desire for eastward territorial extension. Some consider that anti-communism was the central driving force behind Nazi policy; others that it was fired by racialism and the desire for Aryan hegemony in Europe and, later, in the world. But the most difficult controversy is that embracing the *functionalist* and *intentionalist* interpretations of events and actions. The latter sees Nazi foreign policy as the outcome of deliberate plans and ideas, not necessarily rigid but embodying certain defined goals and illustrating some internal logic. The functionalist interpretation sees Nazi policy as mainly articulated by forces acting upon the leadership. The stage for Hitler's actions was circumscribed by the evolving relations and political positions of the European states; in this way Hitler emerges as something of an opportunist. Events at home may be examined in a similar manner. It has been argued, for example, that the drive for additional territory in 1938-9 was powered by a growing internal economic crisis which only new lands and new resources could ameliorate. The foreign policy sequence may also, in the short term, reflect the power struggle of Ribbentrop's personal foreign office organisation as it vied not only with other Nazi power groupings but with the established German Foreign Office and its career diplomats.

At first, Hitler's activities appeared to be concerned primarily with the reversal of the Versailles Treaty's provisions and with the incorporation in the Reich of lands inhabited by ethnic Germans. Thus was the Rhineland remilitarised, Austria seized, the Czech Sudetenland absorbed and Memel occupied (the Saarland became part of Germany by choice). But when Nazi policy became directed towards the subjugation of the entire Czechoslovak state, consisting of mainly non-German peoples, the picture also became one of militarist expansionism. The strike against Poland, which marked the beginning of the Second World War, confirmed the latter pattern.

The scale of Germany's territorial acquisitions in 1938 and early 1939 was vast. By the time of the incorporation of the Sudetenland, the Altreich had been augmented in area by roughly a quarter and its population by about one-sixth. The Saar, Austria and the Sudetenland contained in 1938 approximately 11.3 million inhabitants. But the real significance of the extended Reich lay in the industrial raw materials and manufacturing capacity that it brought. Austria had important resources of iron ore and lignite. In the Sudetenland, valuable coal and lignite deposits were acquired, while Bohemia and Moravia provided armaments works, iron and steel plants, chemical and engineering factories, as well as coal, lignite and wood. The first annexations also made the next conquests much easier, although their sequence was not planned for this reason.

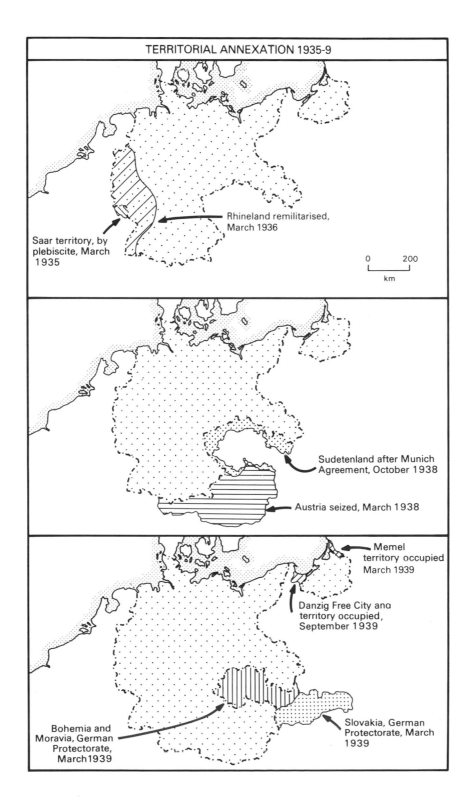

TERRITORIAL ANNEXATION 1935-9

Saar territory, by plebiscite, March 1935

Rhineland remilitarised, March 1936

0   200
km

Sudetenland after Munich Agreement, October 1938

Austria seized, March 1938

Memel territory occupied March 1939

Danzig Free City and territory occupied, September 1939

Bohemia and Moravia, German Protectorate, March 1939

Slovakia, German Protectorate, March 1939

Territorial Conquest

Although the Second World War is usually said to have begun on 3 September 1939, following upon Germany's invasion of Poland two days earlier, it fell short of being a 'world' war for some two years. Indeed, for almost a year it became for the English a 'phoney' war and for their German counterparts a 'sitzkrieg'. The first British bombs on Berlin fell on 25 August 1940, for instance. Initially it was not even a war in which a majority of European states were embroiled. Italian support for Germany was not immediately forthcoming. Literally days before the Polish invasion, Hitler had secured a non-aggression pact with Russia. Some countries, Sweden and Spain among them, never entered the war at all. It began as a world war only in so far as British colonies and dominions described a world-wide distribution and in so far as these interests became an immediate target for surface and submarine raiders.

The prosecution of the war was also distinctive. Gone was the dogged attrition of men which so characterised trench warfare. In its place the Germans introduced 'blitzkrieg': 'lightning war'. There were three central themes to blitzkrieg: surprise; rapid mobility of forces; and the crippling of the enemy by cutting supply and control lines. The Polish invasion saw blitzkrieg in operation for the first time and it proved a resounding success. The Polish Air Force was destroyed in two days, the Polish army as a viable fighting unit within a week, reeling under the isolating effects of two pincer movements by the German forces. Poland's fate was finally sealed by the entry of the Russian Army on to Polish soil in accordance with a secret plan agreed at the time of the German–Soviet non-aggression pact a few weeks previously. At the end of September Poland was partitioned, the western half going to Germany, the eastern to Russia.

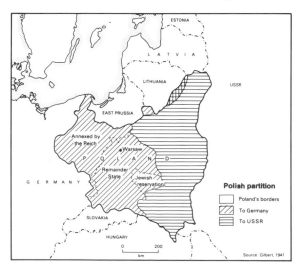

130

Germany's military success was in part explained by Poland's military weakness, the bulk of the latter's forces consisting of immobile, unmotorised infantry. But the tactical advantages of blitzkrieg, particularly in a relatively flat country like Poland, with vulnerable borders all round, were enormous. In the process, Poland became a formidable proving ground for modern tank warfare and for the German Panzers in particular.

Blitzkrieg also had a significance which extended far beyond the realm of the military tactician. It required only a limited economic commitment to war. The short, sharp shock of blitzkrieg needed armament in breadth, not in depth. This meant a wide, highly efficient range of air and ground forces, but with only limited capacity for replacement. Rapid conquest rendered armament in depth unnecessary. This pattern of war economy remained a crucial dimension of Nazi Germany for a little over two years, although as much the product of circumstance as conscious design. It was the first winter of the Russian campaign, in November

1941, that finally exposed its weaknesses.

With the liquidation of Poland, Hitler turned his attention to the west, although not until he had made an abortive effort to secure peace, notably with Britain. Plans for a lightning invasion of the Low Countries (Benelux) and France were slow to be formulated; execution in fact waited until the late spring of 1940, prior to which Hitler had moved to secure Germany's northern flank by occupying Denmark and Norway. The campaign in the west was just as successful as that in the east. The Netherlands capitulated within five days, Belgium in eight, and France in six weeks. The Germans succeeded in splitting the allied forces and Britain was pressed to engage in a risky though highly successful evacuation of Allied troops seaward from Dunkirk. Under the armistice signed with the French on 22 June 1940, Germany occupied a large part of France, including the entire northern and western coasts. In the remainder, a collaborationist French government was established at Vichy.

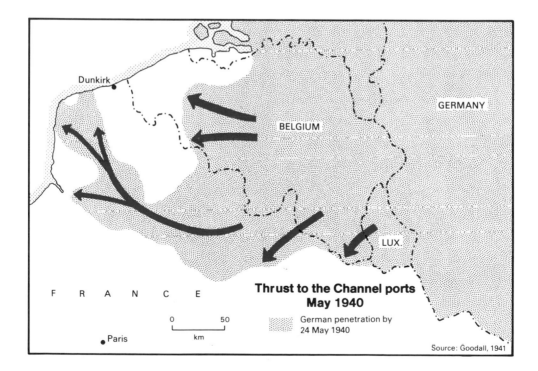

**Thrust to the Channel ports
May 1940**

0   50
km

German penetration by
24 May 1940

Source: Goodall, 1941

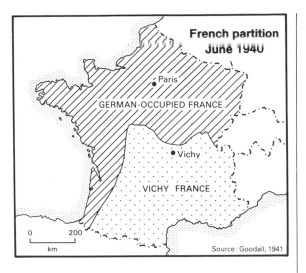

French partition June 1940

GERMAN-OCCUPIED FRANCE

Paris

Vichy

VICHY FRANCE

0 200 km

Source: Goodall, 1941

By mid-summer 1940, Hitler's Germany embraced a vast area of continental Europe and Scandinavia. Not only had a much extended German state been created (Grossdeutschland), but direct German influence stretched from France's Atlantic shores some 2,100 km eastward into the continent's interior and from the Pyrenees (dividing France from Spain) for some 3,200 km northward to beyond the Arctic Circle in occupied Norway. Here was a new German Empire won at breakneck speed. With so much of Europe under his control, Hitler and other leading Nazis saw it as only a matter of time before Britain, the one remaining belligerent, made overtures for peace. But German expectations proved fundamentally wrong. Under Winston Churchill's leadership from May 1940, the British remained intransigent against Nazi aggression. Thus Hitler moved towards a campaign to conquer Britain. By August 1940, in other words, the war was showing a logic of its own. An invasion of Britain represented a 'forward push' in pursuit of a resolution of hostilities. When it had to be abandoned for reasons of logistics, including bad weather, and the inability of the Luftwaffe

to wipe out the Royal Air Force, the focus became Russia, though not before Hitler had secured Germany's Balkan flank and made a successful thrust against British interests in North Africa.

German moves in the Balkans were precipitated in part by Russia's own territorial annexations on the eastern and southern flanks of the Reich. In June 1940 the Russians overran the three Baltic states of Estonia, Latvia and Lithuania and seized from Rumania the provinces of Northern Bukovina and Bessarabia, the latter having belonged to Russia prior to 1918. These moves reminded Hitler of the potential threat of war in the east and hence possible war on two fronts. More specifically, the Rumanian annexations threatened Germany's vital oil supplies from the Ploesti deposits. In a complicated piece of 'cloak-and-dagger' diplomacy, Hitler secured under German influence what remained of Rumanian territory, at the same time reinforcing Hungary's place in the Nazi orbit by the transfer of Transylvania from the Rumanians. This was achieved in August 1940 and by October German troops were occupying the Ploesti oilfields.

The second factor in Hitler's Balkan adventures was the role played by Italy. Mussolini's contribution to the Axis partnership was opportunist and often grossly miscalculated. Italy became formally active in the war after Hitler's successful invasion of France, capitalising on German success by securing minor territorial additions in the Alpes Maritimes. However, in October 1940 Mussolini engaged in an abortive invasion of Greece which eventually drew a British presence on Crete and on the Greek mainland. Faced with this threat, Hitler began planning for his own invasion of Greece. This was completed successfully in April 1941, having first crushed Yugoslavia when a *coup* there sabotaged plans for a peaceful accommodation with the Reich. Yugoslavia was divided up among Germany, Italy, Hungary and Bulgaria, only Croatia remaining as an autonomous (but puppet) state.

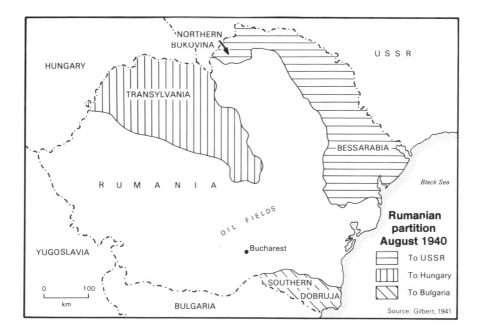

Rumanian partition August 1940

	To USSR
	To Hungary
	To Bulgaria

Source: Gilbert, 1941

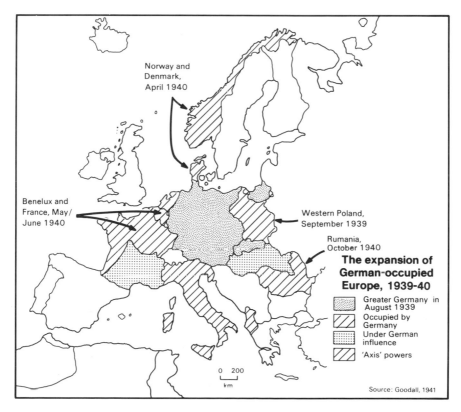

Norway and Denmark, April 1940

Benelux and France, May/ June 1940

Western Poland, September 1939

Rumania, October 1940

The expansion of German-occupied Europe, 1939-40

	Greater Germany in August 1939
	Occupied by Germany
	Under German influence
	'Axis' powers

Source: Goodall, 1941

The invasion of Russia, or 'Operation Barbarossa' to give it its German code-name, was launched on 22 June 1941. It had involved months of meticulous planning and aimed at the conquest of the entire area of European Russia, extending to the White Sea in the north and the Caucasus in the south. The sheer scale of these projected territorial acquisitions was monomaniacal. From the German border in the middle of what was originally Poland to the Volga River was roughly 1,600 km. It was not much further from the same border to France's Atlantic coast. From East Prussia, the Russian capital, Moscow, was some 950 km away. The length of Russia's entire European borders, from the Baltic to the Black Sea, was around 1,300 km, a formidable front for any attacking or even defending army. What is more, the front ultimately extended to almost 2,400 km as Russian territory was accumulated. The initial success of Barbarossa was startling. By mid-August, the German armies had almost reached the Dnieper River and the city of Kiev in the south, they had taken Smolensk in the centre, and they were within 160 km of Leningrad in the north. In places the front had advanced 700 km, and all in the space of around eight weeks. The Polish blitzkrieg was repeated over again, helped by largely uncoordinated Russian defence. By mid-October the Germans had taken the greater part of the resource-rich Ukraine, including Kiev, and were poised to enter the Caucasus, they were within 160 km of Moscow, and they were almost at the gates of Leningrad. But the approaching winter of 1941 was to be a watershed in Hitler's land war in Europe. Steadily crippled by the appalling weather conditions of a Russian winter, the Wehrmacht began to encounter strong Russian resistance. The Red Army's capacity for reinforcement far exceeded German assessments and expectations. Yet more significant was the evident failure of blitzkrieg. The entire German campaign had been developed on the assumption that Russia would be defeated by the autumn. It was manifestly not. Thus the strategy of lightning war had failed.

From the winter of 1941, Germany was forced into a war of attrition. It became a war which was to place severe strains on the German economy and ultimately to defeat it in the face of Allied resources. The Germans were to make further territorial gains in 1942, notably in the south beyond Rostov-on-Don and east to Stalingrad, but elsewhere they were pushed back from their autumn 1941 positions. The Russian recovery was slow and as late as July 1943 the battle fronts were not much different from their positions in the autumn of 1941. Phases of counter-attacks, from both sides, were interspersed with phases of uneasy equilibrium, while the weather continued to weave its own pattern into the sequences of military engagements. Not until mid-summer 1944 had the Red Army reinstated its prewar border with Poland. By this time, Hitler's western armies faced an Allied invasion in France and the feared land war on two fronts had become a reality. From mid-1943, Hitler's empire, which by then extended some 3,700 km east–west from the western coast of France to the Volga River at Stalingrad, was to suffer steady erosion from nearly all quarters of the compass. By April 1945 his German state had been wiped out altogether.

Allied Bombing

Bombing raids against Germany began in May 1940, following Hitler's invasion of the Low Countries and France. They continued largely uninterrupted for the ensuing five years, becoming much more intense after American entry into the war and after the successful D-Day landings in France in June 1944. In the single month of March 1945, British and American planes dropped on German cities twice the bomb tonnage that fell on Britain throughout the entire war.

Allied bombing took two basic forms: precision bombing of military, industrial and transportation targets; and general 'area' bombing of industrial and urban foci. The former required detailed and reliable information on target locations and generally had to be carried out in daylight, in other words requiring considerable fighter support. In many ways area bombing was a response to the difficulties of these contingencies. It was blanket in coverage, it was ideally suited for night attacks, and, in the British view, was a more potent destroyer of enemy morale. Area bombing, notably of urban–industrial concentrations, became the special preserve of Britain's RAF Bomber Command.

The efficacy of these two bombing strategies is not easily established. There is no consensus, for instance, on the degree to which the German war effort was retarded. The heavy British raids on German cities from the summer of 1943 onwards have been viewed by some commentators as having served to enhance Germany's war effort by allowing War Minister Speer and others to convince Hitler and leading Nazis that a much fuller mobilisation of the economy for war was urgently needed. However, Allied bombing can be held to account for

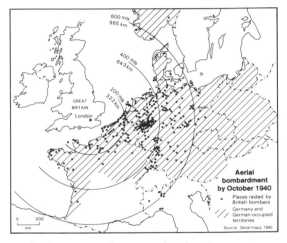

Aerial bombardment by October 1940
• Places raided by British bombers
Germany and German-occupied territories
Source: *Serial maps, 1940*

particular acute shortages in the German war economy. This was notably true of fuel oil. Attacks against synthetic oil plants at one stage brought production to a standstill (September 1944); and over the last six months of the war the German Army and the German Air Force often had more tanks and more aircraft than they had fuel to operate them. The urban–industrial concentrations of the Rhine–Ruhr area sustained some of the heaviest bombing. This reflected the great concentration of German industrial and raw material capacity in the area, but it had another, less immediately apparent significance. Much remaining German industrial capacity was in some way dependent on products from the Rhine–Ruhr. The dislocation of the area was thus an indirect path to retarding the broad mass of German industry, a feature which was enhanced as precision bombing of railway lines in and around the Rhine–Ruhr gathered force, so impeding the outward flow of goods, especially coal.

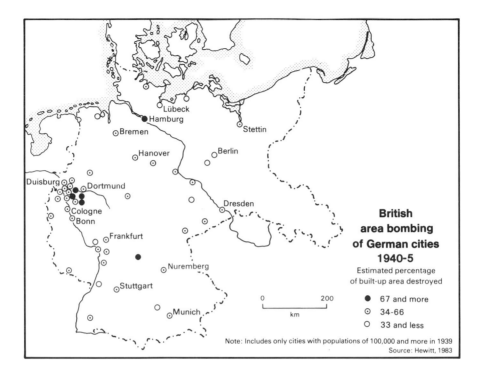

Total civilian deaths as a result of all bombing raids were approximately 600,000 with another 800,000 injured. Over 2 million homes were destroyed and some 7.5 million people rendered homeless. These figures were exceeded only in Japan.

The Allied Road to Berlin

If, in hindsight, the German failure to take Moscow in November 1941 appears as a turning point in Hitler's European war, this was hardly the perception of the Allies, the more so given Japan's surprise attack on the US fleet at Pearl Harbour in early December of that year and the consequent extension of war to a world theatre. Events in 1942 were even less encouraging. In the summer, Germany's North African armies under Rommel drove the British east to El Alamein, within 60 miles of the Egyptian port of Alexandria, and threatened British supply routes through Suez. In the Atlantic theatre, 6.25 million tons of Allied shipping were sunk by German U-boats in 1942. By late summer the monthly losses had reached 700,000 tons, a total that was beyond the capacity of Allied shipyards to replace. In the Far East, Japan was fast extending its empire with conquests in South-East Asia, including Burma, which posed a threat to British India. Finally, despite failure at Moscow, the German armies had penetrated the Caucasus almost to the Caspian by September.

To anyone unfamiliar with the subsequent history and outcome of the war, Hitler's empire by the late summer of 1942 would appear as the basis for a German-dominated Europe for years ahead. The resources of land and labour, the supplies of industrial raw materials and industrial plant, and the various other aggregates of economic power presented a formidable base from which to sustain it. Moreover, this was not an empire consisting of scattered territories, some of them separated by intervening seas. It was a contiguous land empire, protected by water on three of its four flanks. How, then, did this empire collapse? How was it that within three years of the German victories of mid-1942 the German state had ceased to exist?

The facts of defeat can be presented without difficulty. On the Russian front, Stalingrad became the pivot on which the two fighting forces advanced or retreated. Beginning in November 1942, the Russians seized the initiative and by the end of January 1943 the German forces at Stalingrad had been outmanoeuvred and had surrendered. The Caucasus were rapidly evacuated and almost the entire German front, from the Baltic to the Black Sea, began a steady retreat. In early spring and again in early July the Germans renewed their offensive, but with marginal success. This was followed by a Russian offensive which continued with only limited interruption into the depth of the next winter, bringing with it extensive territorial gains in the Ukraine, including Kiev. The German command made various attempts to stabilise the front here, but gains were won at tremendous loss of machines and men and rarely were they sustained. The winter of 1943/4 also saw Russian gains around Leningrad, but those in the Ukraine overshadowed all, and in February 1944 that area was again the focus of offensive. By April Odessa had been recaptured and the Crimea cleared of Germans. Then in June and July, in a series of ferocious advances, the Germans were driven to beyond Russia's old (1939) border with Poland. Henceforward the Russian campaign split into two basic parts: the drive across Northern Europe; and the operations in the Balkans. The latter made the more rapid progress. By August the Rumanian oilfields had been secured and Bucharest entered. Sofia fell in September and Bulgaria quickly joined in with the Red Army in the fight against

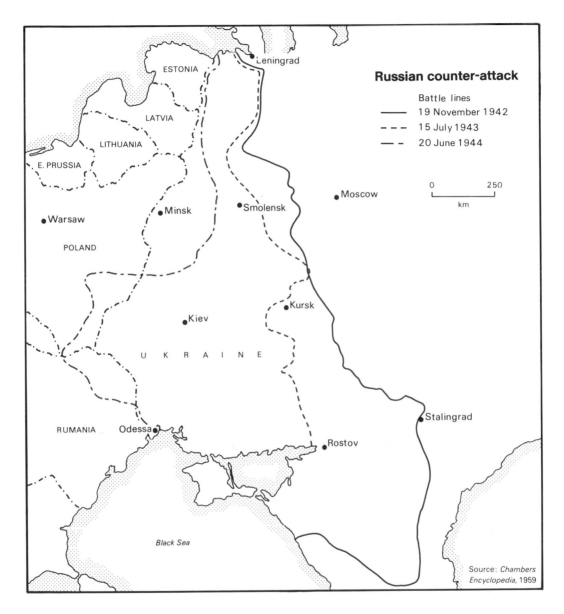

Russian counter-attack

Battle lines
— 19 November 1942
-- 15 July 1943
-·- 20 June 1944

0   250
└──────┘
km

Source: *Chambers Encyclopedia*, 1959

the German forces, as, by then, had Rumania. Progress subsequently slowed as the Germans took strong defensive action and Hungary was not finally won until February/March 1945. The Russians then advanced on Vienna and Prague, soon to converge with the armies of the Western Allies. Resistance on the northern front was stronger. A Russian attempt to seize Warsaw in late summer 1944 failed. But Russian fortunes here were assisted by Finland's desertion of the Axis cause which pushed the Germans back to Norway. The real assault on the Polish front came early in 1945. German defence proved locally strong but disorganised in aggregate. Berlin was soon surrounded, the city surrendering after fierce fighting early in May.

As the epic of Stalingrad unfolded in the late autumn and winter of 1942, the tide began rapidly to turn against the Germans in North Africa. In late August Rommel attempted to drive eastward to the Nile but the thrust proved unsuccessful. The Allies then counter-attacked in October and set in train a long rout of the German forces. Almost simultaneously, the Allies landed in Algeria and Morocco and threatened to strike a new blow to Axis positions from the west. Hitler responded by occupying Vichy France and flying in troops to seize French Tunisia. The North African campaign proved a relatively brief one, however. By the late spring of 1943 the Axis armies there had been defeated and North Africa became a springboard for attacks on the southern flanks of Hitler's Europe, its so-called 'soft under-belly'. The Italian and German forces were driven out of Sicily by mid-august 1943 and within weeks the Allies had landed in mainland Italy. The subsequent Italian campaign was protracted. The deposition of Mussolini and the surrender of the Italian government and its armies in September 1943 simply prompted a strong German military presence in Italy and Italian-held territory and the proclamation of a new Fascist state based in the north of the country, notionally led by Mussolini. Not until the beginning of May 1945 were the German troops in Italy forced into surrender. Italy thus became a war theatre in its own right.

The final element in the Allied campaign for the liberation of Nazi Europe came comparatively late. Ideas for an invasion of Europe from the west had been mooted early in the war, but it became a reality only in mid-summer 1944, despite persistent Russian pressure for a second European front. After months of meticulous planning and the accumulation of vast stocks of materials, a landing was successfully achieved on 6 June, D-Day. The Allied operation was greatly assisted by the superiority of its air and naval forces. Britain provided the base for the amphibious assault on the beaches of Normandy between the mouth of the River Orne

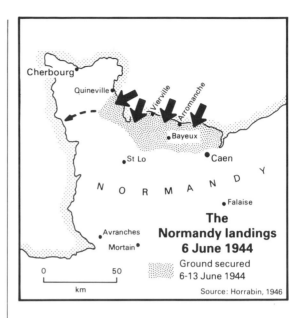

The Normandy landings 6 June 1944

Ground secured 6-13 June 1944

0   50
km

Source: Horrabin, 1946

near Caen and Quineville near the base of the Cotentin peninsula. The initial task became to secure an adequate bridgehead. This was achieved by late July. Thereupon the Allied armies broke out. The American forces thrust south towards Nantes and successfully isolated the Brittany peninsula, while British and Canadian forces engaged the Germans south of Caen. German opposition was strong and efforts were made to drive a wedge westward t the coast and so split the invading forces. However, American forces were quickly pulled round in a southerly arc to attack the German positions south of Caen and a lightning drive was also made upon the Seine and Paris. These moves were highly successful. The Seine was reached by mid-August and soon the German forces were in rapid retreat across it. As the campaign in Normandy began to meet its objectives, a second amphibious landing was being made near Cannes in south-eastern France by American troops. By early September this force had reached as far north as Lyons, French forces having landed in the interim and recovered Marseilles and Toulon.

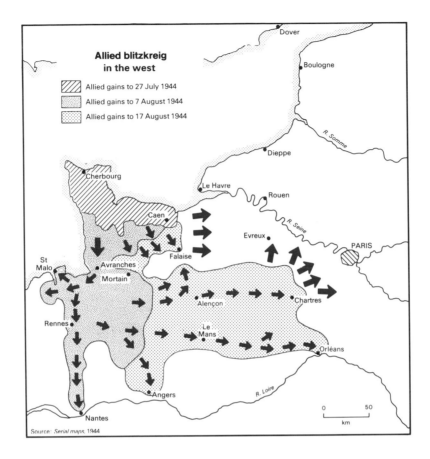

One of the Allies' most critical problems at this stage became the length of their supply lines and the need to secure ports of reinforcement further east in the Channel. The Germans frustrated the requirement by staging last-minute holds on vital ports and in the process destroying large parts of them. However, by late September 1944 German forces had been all but expelled from French soil and the Allies were pressing forward into the Low Countries and poised to enter Germany itself. There followed a period of consolidation in which preparations were made for the final thrust into the Nazi homeland and for the crossing of the natural defensive barrier of the Rhine. But in mid-December Hitler ordered a counter-attack. It was made through the Ardennes along a 65 km front from a base roughly parallel with the eastern border of Luxembourg. Within days the German forces had penetrated some 80 km. The victory was not sustained, though. Attacked by an Allied force from the south and subjected to intensive aerial bombardment, not to mention strong resistance along the front itself, the German thrust had been all but wiped out by late January 1945. Progress to the Rhine met with determined defence. The river was reached first in the south, second in the north and, finally, by early March, in its central course extending between the Ruhr and Frankfurt-am-Main. The task of literally crossing the Rhine slowed the Allied campaign once more, but by early April its armies were moving rapidly east to the Elbe and south-east towards the Austrian and Czech borders. Co-ordinated German defence had all but disappeared. By early May, the Western Allies were nose to nose with the Red Army.

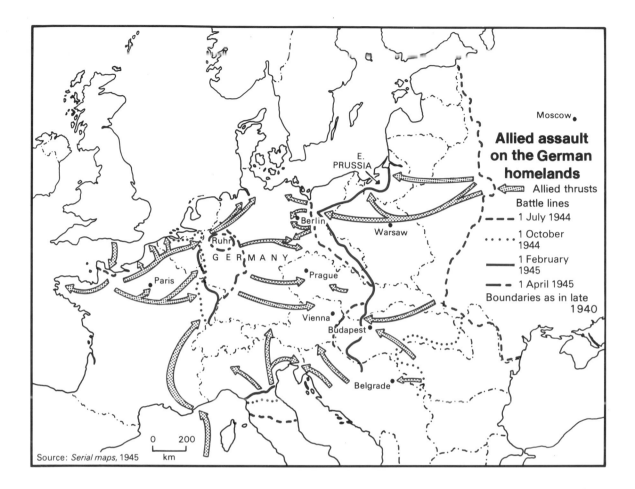

Source: *Serial maps*, 1945

The rapid contraction of Hitler's European empire and the occupation of the German state by the Allies stands as one of the most remarkable feats of modern warfare. Its explanation is far from simple. Numerical superiority in men and materials, together with technological advantages like radar, made a certain impact. By the late spring of 1943, for example, German U-boats were temporarily withdrawn from major Atlantic operations owing to disastrous losses in the face of superior Allied tracking methods. Another vital feature of German defeat was its management of the vast array of annexed and occupied territories. A more astute conqueror would have harnessed their resources of land, materials and labour to the full, and would have played up to the grievances of their indigenous populations. None of these conditions were met or even approached. The greater part of Germany's territorial acquisitions became locked into a system which progressively alienated — in some cases liquidated — local peoples, wrought havoc with much productive activity, and installed a chaos of conflicting authority from which little that was positive could emerge. The fruits of such policies were reflected in the strength of partisan activity in occupied Russia, for example, and in the fragility of the Axis alliance as soon as the spectre of defeat became apparent. A third dimension in Germany's rapid defeat was the extreme reluctance of Hitler and Nazi Party leaders to countenance a full-scale mobilisation of resources in favour of war. This is eloquently testified in the startling fact that the peak of German armaments production was not reached until the autumn of 1944, when Hitler's empire was in full retreat and much production capacity already lost to the Allies. The failure to mobilise female labour mirrored the pattern, as did the absence throughout the war of dual shift-working in much of industry.

Finally, no explanation of German defeat can neglect the personality and will of Hitler himself. This expressed itself in most of the facets already discussed above, but in others, for example the actual direction of the war, it had a most singular significance. Hitler's conception of war was a very restricted one. It centred around blitzkrieg: administering the lightning blow, the 'smash-and-grab' technique of aggression. When campaign conditions rendered such tactics irrelevant, the blitzkrieg mentality still remained the dominant force in the Hitler mind. To the utter dismay of many of his generals, the prevailing mould of the German war campaign after 1942 became the delivering of fatal blows to enemy forces. Counter-offensives like the one at Kursk on the Russian front in July 1943 were accorded totally unrealistic expectations. The Ardennes offensive of December 1944 fell into the same category. Defensive or holding strategies were pursued only when force of circumstances was undeniable, where, for example, events in the field were so rapid as to render Hitler temporarily out of direct control. Where events did not conspire to overtake his command, the approach became ideological rather than military. Von Paulus' Sixth Army at Stalingrad was to fight to the last man rather than surrender. To do otherwise was to undermine the Nazi view of the Germans as the *Herrenvolk*. The position of the army generals in all this was difficult and the problems intensified after Hitler assumed direct command of the army following its failure to take Moscow in the early winter of 1941. In the Normandy campaign, dissensions among the leading generals were exacerbated by Hitler's summary changes of confidence in them, dismissals being followed by reinstatements as each succeeding new command failed to stall the Allied assault.

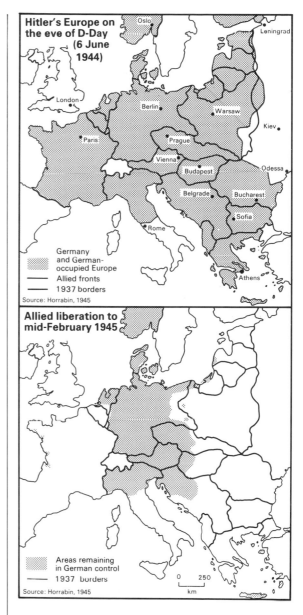

Hitler's Europe on the eve of D-Day (6 June 1944)

Germany and German-occupied Europe
Allied fronts
1937 borders

Source: Horrabin, 1945

Allied liberation to mid-February 1945

Areas remaining in German control
1937 borders

0   250
km

Source: Horrabin, 1945

German 15 cm Howitzer in action at Aisne, France, in 1940.

Part Six
The War Machine

Wartime Administration and Organisation

The outbreak of war brought no sudden fundamental changes to the Third Reich. Since 1933 Nazi Germany had existed in a state of emergency; the war merely intensified that state. For economy and society at large, the war brought home a situation which had long been prepared for: as seen, for example, in the militaristic training of the Hitler Youth, the drive for raw material self-sufficiency and, more widely, in rearmament. In the eyes of the Nazi leadership, moreover, the First World War had never been resolved to German satisfaction. But as the war progressed, as the tactics of blitzkrieg faltered, cracks appeared in the Third Reich's preparedness. In response, there was a steady extension in the power and jurisdiction of particular central authorities — in labour, in armaments, in raw material supply and in other sectors critical to the more rigorous conduct of the war. Yet, at the same time, often in contradiction, the authority of regional party leaders, Gauleiters especially, was reinforced. The pattern was most acutely expressed in the eastern occupied lands where party strongmen were quick to exploit the administrative vacuums which were presented following the turnover from military to civilian control. But the congruent state and party administrative structures (Reichsgaue) created for Austria, Western Poland and the Sudetenland in 1939/40 greatly augmented party authority within the Greater German Reich, as did the practice of allocating the administration of contiguous western occupied zones (such as Alsace-Lorraine) to the Gauleiters of adjacent Gaue.

At the outbreak of war the Ministerial Council for the Defence of the Reich appointed Reich Governors and Oberpräsidenten as Defence Commissioners in each of the 18 military regions (Wehrkreise). As most of these governors and presidents were Gauleiters, this had the appearance of enhancing party power at an early stage, but the difficulty was that the Wehrkreise bore little relation to either party regions or to the old Prussian provinces or Länder. The outcome was a maze of incongruent geographical jurisdictions which severely hindered the consistent exercise of authority. Only

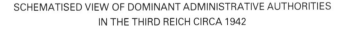

SCHEMATISED VIEW OF DOMINANT ADMINISTRATIVE AUTHORITIES
IN THE THIRD REICH CIRCA 1942

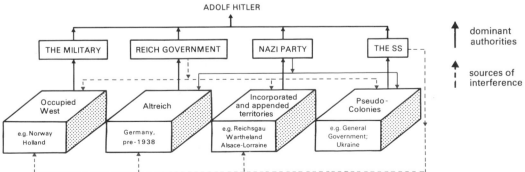

146

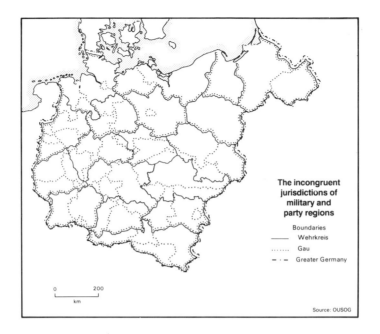

The incongruent
jurisdictions of
military and
party regions

Boundaries
——— Wehrkreis
······· Gau
— · — Greater Germany

0   200
km

Source: OUSOG

in late 1942 was this chaos resolved when the Gaue themselves became the Reich Defence Zones. Henceforward the power of the Gauleiters was manifest. Indeed, as the prospect of German defeat unfolded, some Gauleiters appeared to take on the role of absolute rulers, in the mould of 'Gau-Kings'. More and more they came to epitomise the operation of the Fuehrerprinzip as Hitler's delegate territorial leaders.

Even before the war, Hitler's participation in the day-to-day affairs of government had been steadily diminishing. With the outbreak of war, he effectively ceased to be Reich Chancellor, the task being delegated to the Cabinet Council for the Defence of the Reich, chaired by Goering. In practice, this body never operated as a council. As such it became quickly moribund. Decrees were issued under the Council's authority, but these primarily came from Goering or Frick and did not require agreement of the full council, merely counter-signatures of certain members. The outcome was inevitably to promote independence amongst Reich ministries and hence to encourage rivalries. These problems were compounded by the fact that

decrees did not extend automatically to cover the eastern zones of occupation or the various civilian and military administrations which obtained in the occupied west. This, in turn, was part of a wider problem of the increasing administrative disunity of the Third Reich: as between the Altreich of pre-1938, the incorporated territories like Danzig-West Prussia and Wartheland in which party and state administrations were fused (the so-called 'model Gaue'), appended territories such as Luxembourg or the Polish Government-General, and the pseudo-colonies of the east in what was formerly Russia. All displayed variant administrative forms which bred confusion and conflict; what is more, the situation became a self-polarising one. The supreme irrationality of Nazi administration, though, was perhaps to be found in the survival of the Gau units to the very end and in the enhanced functions ascribed to them from late 1942. Modelled largely on the Reichstag electoral districts, they were already anachronisms by the mid-1930s. They survived to the end because the essence of National Socialist power lay in personalities, not bureaucracies, in Gauleiters, not Gaue.

The Army

The army had long been a key power bloc in Germany. It remained so under the Nazi regime, but over time came more and more under Hitler's influence and direct control. The pattern showed first in 1938 with the formation of the OKW (Armed Forces High Command) of which Hitler made himself chief. It was dramatically extended when, with the first reverses of the Russian campaign in late 1941, Hitler also appointed himself Army Commander. Thereafter, the story became one of persistent interference and change in the army's command organisation and tactics. From the German side the land war was played out almost entirely according to the Fuehrer's will. The German Army's inability to stem the Allied invasion of France, the débâcle in the Ardennes in 1944/5 and the various battle failures in the east were all tied in some measure to Hitler's own prosecution of the war. And the diminishing authority of army leaders is no better demonstrated than in the Stauffenberg bomb plot of July 1944: the most determined assassination attempt on Hitler (and the nearest to being successful) emanated from within army ranks. The turnover of leading army personnel during the whole course of the war was formidable. Only one out of 18 field marshals survived to keep his position; no less than 10 were relieved of their commands and sent home. Likewise, out of 36 full generals, only 3 survived in post; the number relieved totalled 18.

THE HIGH COMMAND

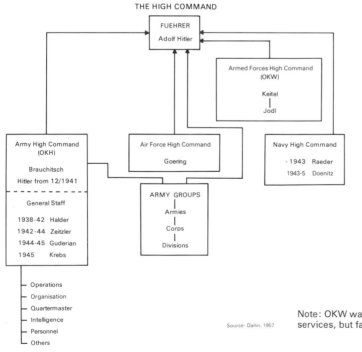

Source: Dallin, 1957

Note: OKW was supposed to co-ordinate the policy of all three services, but failed to do so in practice.

Neither the navy nor the air force enjoyed the position of importance occupied by the army, either before or during the course of the war. In terms of simple manpower, the army upon mobilisation in September 1939 had some 3.7 million troops; air force personnel numbered 400,000 and navy personnel just 50,000. This is not an entirely adequate perspective, though, because both the air force and the navy, by their nature, had far higher ratios of capital to men. Aircraft production as an individual armaments sector, for example, consistently absorbed the highest percentage of spending alongside other primary armaments sectors like tanks and munitions. Over 1942 to 1944, the figure averaged around 40 per cent. On the wider question of the prosecution of the war, however, it remains true that the army formed by far the dominant element. By 1942, for instance, the bulk of the German surface fleet had been effectively immobilised. The Atlantic U-boat packs, whilst enormously successful up to the summer of 1942, were soon blunted by Allied tracking, which resulted in their temporary withdrawal for several months in mid-1943. The air force fared somewhat better and, of course, fulfilled a significant adjunct role relative to army operations. But from midway through the war, its capacity was increasingly inadequate relative to the demands placed upon it; this was especially true in fighter defence against the Allied bombing campaign in the last years of the war. Thus it was the army which shouldered the burden of attack and defence, the latter especially. And it was relatively easier to reinforce, replace and re-equip the army than either of the other services.

The German Army also had an importance beyond its intrinsic utilitarian role. The power and traditions of the Prussian officer corps require little rehearsing here, save the necessity to underline Hitler's growing domination of the army leadership from 1938. But beyond this lay the relationship between Wehrmacht and the Nazi *Weltanschauung*. Until preparations for the invasion of Russia the military remained clearly separated from Nazi political ideology. But as the Russian war plans and the war itself unfolded in 1941, Hitler sought a fusion of ideological and military warfare. By and large he was successful. The majority of army leaders joined in the war of extermination against 'Jewish Bolshevism' and 'Asiatic barbarism', sometimes seeking their own specific justifications for doing so. This is not to say that the appalling conditions of the Russian front, the long-standing antagonism of German and Slav, and the intensity of Russian partisan activity were insignificant contributors to the inhuman sufferings of Russians, soldiers and civilian alike, at the hands of the German Army. Furthermore, the activities of the SS and its Einsatzgruppen, by comparison, were doubly savage. It is nevertheless true that the German Army in Russia fulfilled a task which its western counterpart hardly even addressed and that international codes of military conduct vanished on the Russian front as Hitler's infamous order to the army to liquidate all Russian political leaders and Commissars was carried out.

In the seven years of Nazi rule up to the end of 1939, the German Army had increased in size roughly 18 times over. Such a rapid rate of growth had produced inevitable problems in achieving a sufficient officer corps, not to mention the wider question of equipment. The age structure of the army upon mobilisation for war was also somewhat unsatisfactory. There were many veterans from the First World War, including officers. The reason was that the various industries associated with rearmament had absorbed men from the lower age cohorts who could not be removed without damaging effects; such skilled workers were not readily replaced. These different problems were far from resolved as the war unfolded. The concept of blitzkrieg and the remarkably short duration of the offensives against Poland, the Low Countries and France offered obvious mitigation. However, the manpower and the equipment needs for the attack on Russia were formidable, even allowing for a short war. The German Field Army in September 1939 numbered 2.76 million; by June 1941 it was 3.8 million and, of these, 3.3 million were deployed in Barbarossa. Henceforward, the needs of protracted land warfare on several fronts,

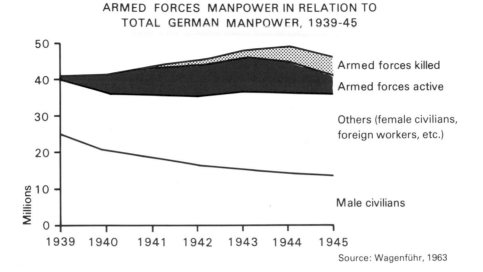

ARMED FORCES MANPOWER IN RELATION TO
TOTAL GERMAN MANPOWER, 1939-45

Source: Wagenführ, 1963

coupled with increasing levels of attrition, soon magnified the army's problems, often beyond anything previously encountered. The attrition is reflected in the relatively slower growth of the Field Army alongside the multiplying theatres of war. A year after the launch of Barbarossa, for instance, it was only 3.95 million. By the summer of 1943 it was only 4.48 million.

Hitler's relations with the army over this later period became increasingly strained and were in part responsible for the mushroom expansion of the Waffen-SS. At the opening of the Russian campaign it incorporated around 165,000 men. By April 1945 some 800,000 men had served in SS ranks and 40 SS divisions had been raised. Moreover, Hitler had also authorised the formation of an SS Army Corps. Previously, SS divisions had always been distributed singly throughout the army. SS divisions acquired reputations as formidable fighting forces, but this was not true generally, particularly of the much enlarged Waffen-SS after

1942 with its increasingly lower percentage of German nationals. For Himmler, the enlarged Waffen-SS offered an insurance towards SS domination in the Nazis' postwar European order. The 'watering down' of its elite quality was worrying but not without potential reward.

Perhaps one of the most striking features of the German Army during the Second World War was the infantry's reliance on horse transport. The pervasive image of the German military is one of superior mobility, of motorisation. This perception is encapsulated in the Polish blitzkrieg of 1939: the triumph of machine over muscle. And yet nearly twice as many horses were utilised by the German Army in 1939-45 as in 1914-18 (2.7 million against 1.4 million). By the winter of 1943/4, only 16 per cent of German divisions were fully motorised. The consequences were critical in the kind of mobile war which was fought with the Russians in the east.

The success of Albert Speer in achieving a quantum leap in armaments production after 1942 must naturally be set alongside the inadequacies of mobility. By 1944 the monthly tonnage of armoured vehicles (tanks, assault guns, etc.) was roughly fifteen times what it had been in 1940. However, against the forces assembled by Stalin, such an achievement does not look so impressive. In the great Russian frontal attack on Army Group Centre in mid-summer 1944, for example, the Soviets assembled nearly 200 divisions with 2.5 million men,

The vast scale of the armed forces commitment on the Russian front is reflected in the provisions of the German Labour Front through its Kraft durch Freude organisation. KdF homes acted as convalescent centres for injured soldiers.

6,000 tanks and assault guns, 45,000 guns and mortars and 7,000 aircraft. In 1944, German production of tanks, assault guns and similar armoured vehicles was but 1,500 a month. This had to service the demands of western and southern as well as eastern war theatres. The Germans also faced increasing quality hazards in their armament supplies, the consequence of the conscription of foreign labour in the armaments industries, including prisoners-of-war. Of equivalent note were the dramatic weapon failures, for instance the giant Ferdinand Tank first deployed in the Battle of Kursk in 1943. Even so, the technical superiority of some German weaponry was freely acknowledged by Allied forces right up to the closing months of the war.

The Kdf foreign organisation 1942

■ KdF homes
■ Ditto under construction

Berlin

Kiev

Kursk

0   500
km

Source: Dienst-gemeinschaft Kraft durch Freude im Kriegsjahr, 1942, DA Koblenz

The SS

The wartime years were ones of determined fulfilment for the SS. As the Reich's eastern borders were extended deeper into Europe towards Asia, there was opened up a massive trial ground in which the racial and ideological schemes of the SS could be tested and refined. The Third Reich's transition to war from 1938 was a watershed for the SS in that it changed from being primarily a support for the Nazi regime and a special Fuehrer executive to being also an organisation pursuing its own goals and particular conceptions of future German nationhood under Himmler's direction. There was, however, a dimension to the wartime SS which undermined the singularity of its purpose and the force of its authority. The SS grew enormously in size as the war progressed. In June 1944 it had reached around 800,000 men. By that time, some 100,000 had already perished in war action. By the close of the war up to 300,000 SS men were to have lost their lives. The bulk of wartime SS men were soldiers, in fact, serving in the Waffen-SS or the Wehrmacht. For the majority of them, the ideological and racist struggles in occupied lands were second-hand knowledge, activities in which they played little direct part. These tasks were performed by a tiny fraction of the SS, perhaps no more than 10,000 men, including officers. Even within this grouping there were SS men whose commitment fell some way short of the all-embracing views of Himmler and his closest SS officers. The war, in other words, saw a progressive watering down of the SS as the 'gene-pool' of a new Germany, as the vanguard of a superior Nordic/Aryan culture destined to dominate Europe and Eurasia. The vast eastern conquests may have afforded unprecedented proving grounds for the SS, but the hard core of true believers did not grow in tandem, indeed could not, given the manpower needs of war with Russia.

A vital facet of the SS from the late 1930s was the scale of its bureaucracy. The 'state within a state' syndrome is an understandable one, if not entirely appropriate. The central organ of this bureaucracy was the Reich Security Office (RSHA). Its title gave the impression of a formal state organisation. In fact it was an SS agency and represented the outcome of years of creeping infiltration by the SS apparatus into the various police organisations of the state. Himmler's installation in 1936 as Chief of German Police, alongside his position as SS Chief, had set the process firmly in train. By the beginning of the war, it was only the regional and local police administrations, involving the general Order Police, which remained outside direct SS control. Otherwise the RSHA incorporated the Gestapo, the Criminal Police (KRIPO) and the intelligence organisations, along with the SS Security Service (SD) built up by Heydrich. As war progressed, moreover, RSHA jurisdiction was extended to include departments such as that which oversaw occupation policies. But the significance of this giant central police apparatus went beyond the business of police activity *per se* and the safeguarding of the Nazi state. It was also aimed at moulding the new National Socialist order in a postwar Europe. In this sense the police organisation became a political agency in itself.

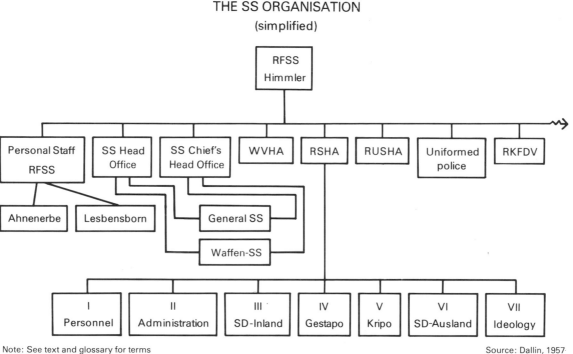

THE SS ORGANISATION
(simplified)

Note: See text and glossary for terms

Source: Dallin, 1957

Several of the remaining central offices of the SS bureaucracy reflected these longer-term goals. This was notably true of the Commissariat for the strengthening of German Nationhood (RKFDV), established in 1939, with the SS Chief as its first commissar. Himmler was charged with the task of resettling ethnic Germans within the Reich's borders and of weeding out ethnic groups which were considered undesirable. Beyond such SS main offices as that dealing with the recruiting and organisation of manpower, the other primary part of the SS bureaucracy was the Economic and Administrative Office. From 1942 this was the organisation (WVHA) which held the task of running the concentration and labour camps and of operating the growing range of SS economic enterprises. The concentration camp system underwent a phenomenal expansion over the course of the war. Whereas the camps had started life mainly as internment centres for political undesirables and opponents of the Nazi regime, from the late 1930s they became places for detaining *social* undesirables like vagrants, thieves, homosexuals, scaremongers, uncooperative nationals from seized or occupied territories, and, above all, *racial* undesirables ranging from gypsies to Jews. The camps grew because they became sumps for the 'cleansing' of European society according to Nazi racial dogma and because Hitler's successive conquests progressively enlarged the area in which this operation could take place. As the war unfolded, moreover, the camps increasingly became institutions for forced labour, servicing both the general demands of the war economy and the more specific requirements of the SS economic administration.

By 1943/4 there were 23 major concentration camps extending from the Low Countries and eastern France to the former Baltic states and eastern Poland. But added to these was a vast array of affiliated camps, perhaps numbering as many as 1,000 by 1943/4. Although the chronically inhuman conditions of detention were broadly similar across the

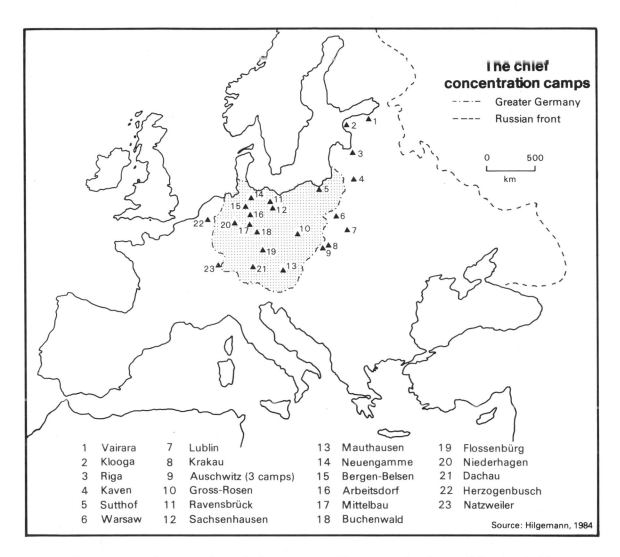

The chief concentration camps

-·-·- Greater Germany
---- Russian front

0 ————— 500 km

1	Vairara	7	Lublin	13	Mauthausen	19	Flossenbürg
2	Klooga	8	Krakau	14	Neuengamme	20	Niederhagen
3	Riga	9	Auschwitz (3 camps)	15	Bergen-Belsen	21	Dachau
4	Kaven	10	Gross-Rosen	16	Arbeitsdorf	22	Herzogenbusch
5	Sutthof	11	Ravensbrück	17	Mittelbau	23	Natzweiler
6	Warsaw	12	Sachsenhausen	18	Buchenwald		

Source: Hilgemann, 1984

range of camps — chances of survival were rarely much more than 30 per cent — some camps had special tasks. The most infamous of these was the extermination of the Jewish race, which fell to the camps in the east: namely Auschwitz, Chelmno, Treblinka, Sobibor, Majdanek and Belzec. Statistics about concentration camp detainees are few. Figures of the number of living inmates (in January 1945 there were some 714,000) are comparatively meaningless. To be alive in a concentration camp was exceptional. Millions perished or were murdered, unrecorded.

The extermination policies inevitably conflicted in some degree with the desire to use concentration camp labour in SS enterprises and with the more general demand for labour in the increasingly strained German war economy. As long as new detainees continued to arrive at roughly replacement rates or better, the dual purposes could be realised. When numbers declined, or when labour demands rose, conflicts with the Armaments Ministry and among the various arms of the SS bureaucracy became inevitable. The connection between the SS manufacturing enterprises and camp labour is reflected in their geographical coincidence. In 1943 the earth and stone-working division (DEST) of the SS Economic and Administrative Office had an annual turnover of 14.8 million RM. The armaments division (DAW) had a turnover of 23 million RM in the same year. Before the war, much SS economic activity was orientated towards craft enterprise or semi-luxury goods. The emphasis changed from 1939, with the armaments sector recording the most rapid expansion. In the last years of the war, the SS Economic and Administrative Office began hiring out concentration camp labour for use in state-run enterprises and in private industry. Such hirings brought significant profits to the SS, although these sometimes accrued not to the organisation itself but to leading SS officers. The average daily hire charge was 4 to 6 marks. In the last year of the war, up to 500,000 camp inmates toiled in this way, perhaps half of them for industrial giants like Krupps and IG-Farben.

General conclusions about the SS are not made with ease. It was an organisation which grew and changed incessantly, often inconsistently, and the exigencies of war wove their own complicating thread. In many ways the SS was a microcosm of the Third Reich itself. It became beset by the same kinds of overlapping and conflicting administrative jurisdictions. Its leading personnel were persistent opportunists, as were so many of Hitler's leaders, Himmler among them. The energy and dynamism generated within the Third Reich were replicated within the SS; the vast concentration camp system was alone testament enough to this. But

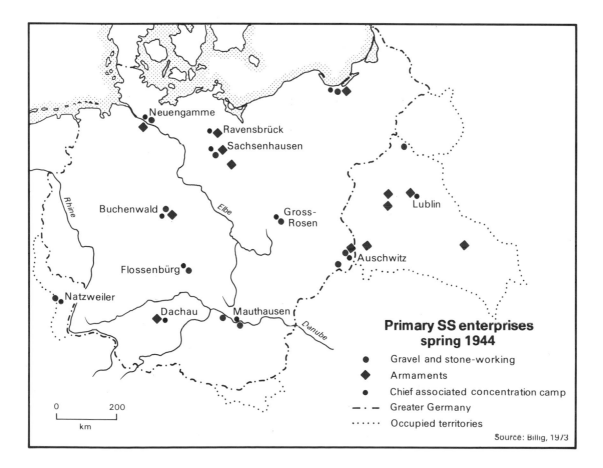

**Primary SS enterprises
spring 1944**

● Gravel and stone-working
◆ Armaments
● Chief associated concentration camp
—·— Greater Germany
········· Occupied territories

Source: Billig, 1973

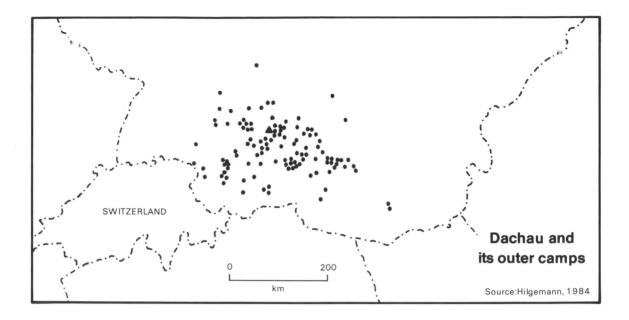

SWITZERLAND

0   200
km

**Dachau and
its outer camps**

Source: Hilgemann, 1984

PRINCIPAL NATIONALITIES AT DACHAU CONCENTRATION
CAMP AT THE TIME OF LIBERATION

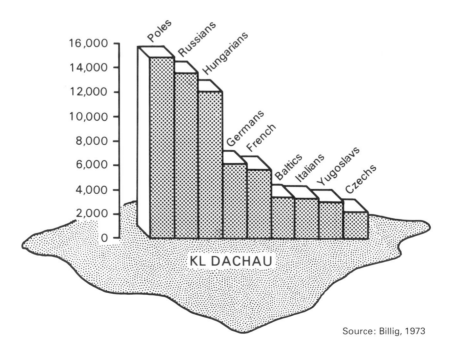

Source: Billig, 1973

the very elements which contributed to the momentum and force of the SS eventually proved its undoing. The system did not admit of consolidation. Power became too readily diffused and too idiosyncratic in exercise. The SS had no Speer to instil some semblance of central direction. Whereas the Reich was in some measure galvanised by the onset of total war, the SS was increasingly divided by it. The political and ideological goals became entangled with the opportunities for profits in servicing the war economy; with the increasing secularisation of the massive Waffen-SS as military reverse after military reverse made the war a patriotic rather than an ideological one; and with the complex manoeuvrings for retrenchment and survival as the domains of the SS in occupied Europe shrank and it was forced into open competition with the economic and military machines.

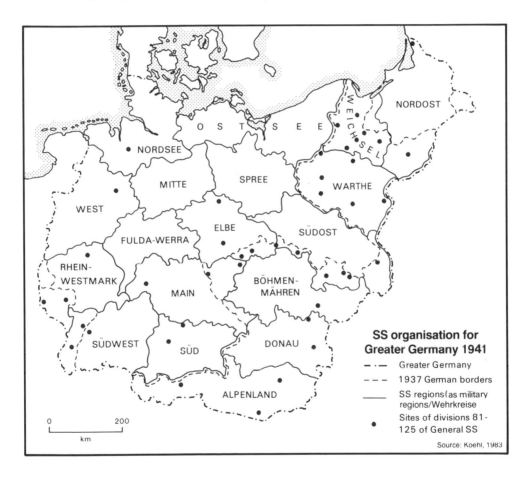

SS organisation for Greater Germany 1941

- — · — Greater Germany
- — — — 1937 German borders
- ———— SS regions (as military regions/Wehrkreise
- • Sites of divisions 81-125 of General SS

Source: Koehl, 1983

Policies of Occupation

The extension of Hitler's Germany deep into Eurasia, as well as the conquest of Western Europe and much of Scandinavia, posed immediate problems of administration. Once military victory had been secured and the military position stabilised in strategic terms, the question arose as to the nature of subsequent German control and organisation. The pattern that emerged was a complex one. It reflected needs of economic exploitation, the hunger for power among leading Nazi Party figures, the differing measures of civilian co-operation in occupied territories, and the ideological and racist ideals for a Nazi-dominated postwar Europe. As the war ran its course, moreover, policies of occupation evolved correspondingly. Increased civilian resistance and partisan activity, growing pressures for greater industrial production, Allied bombing raids and military reverses on land combined to intensify the force of occupation policies. Labour was conscripted on an increasing scale for work in Greater Germany, the whole of occupied Europe was combed for Jews and SS policies of extermination carried to their final conclusion, while police and SS terror broke new bounds of ferocity. In hindsight, the pattern of Nazi occupation organisation was haphazard and inefficient. But this was a predictable outcome given the conflicting power blocs which characterised the *Hitler state.* It also reflected the simple fact that trained administrative personnel were in short supply. Not only were Hitler's territorial plans for his new German Empire ill-formed and transitory, but so was the machinery for managing it.

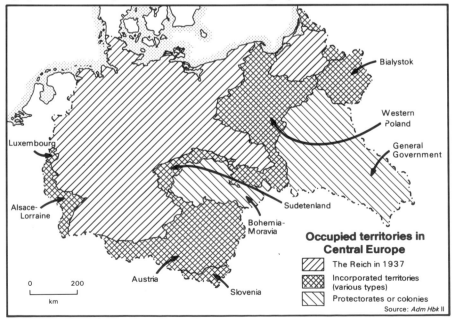

Occupied territories in Central Europe

Source: *Adm Hbk* II

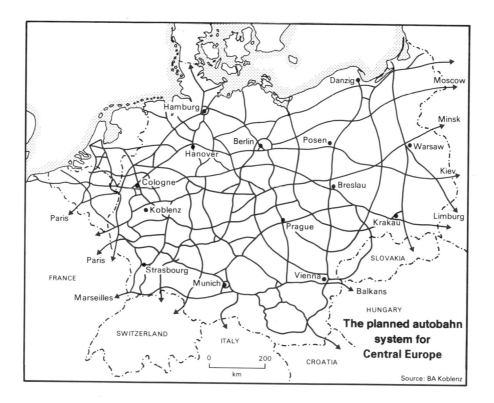

The planned autobahn system for Central Europe

Source: BA Koblenz

This map was published by the Reichsautobahnen Direktion as early as December 1941. For purposes of autobahn planning, the Polish General Government was included as part of Germany. The planned network also extended into Belgium and Holland. Much of the plan was a pipe-dream. The resources were never available to realise it.

In very broad terms, policies of occupation followed one of three models. In Norway, Denmark, Belgium, Holland and France, German control mainly consisted of installing a military or civilian commissioner to oversee what were otherwise relatively unchanged national administrations. Within this, there was considerable requisitioning of industrial and other economic capacity, but national and cultural identities did not become targets for Nazi Germanisation. A second category of Nazi occupation policy involved incorporation into the German state, to form Greater Germany. Austria was the first of these incorporated territories. Subsequently, they extended to include the Czech Sudetenland, Memel, Danzig, Eupen Malmedy, extensive parts of Western Poland, Luxembourg, Alsace-Lorraine, Slovenia and Bialystok. Some of these lands were formally incorporated under Reich law; others were incorporated on a *de facto* basis. Alsace and Lorraine, for instance, were administered by the Gauleiters of adjacent Gaue. Incorporation into Germany naturally carried with it certain penalties for the peoples and cultures involved. The consequences were greatest in the Polish areas, where native Poles were forcibly uprooted to make way for ethnic Germans from the Baltic states and south-east Europe. Wholesale Germanisation became the pattern, often with scant regard for humanitarian considerations. From the dismantled Polish state, Danzig-West Prussia and Wartheland became formally constituted Reichsgaue, administrative units in which state and party jurisdictions were coincident. Change was least in those territories which already had extensive German populations; here persecution and terror were little different from that already found within Germany itself.

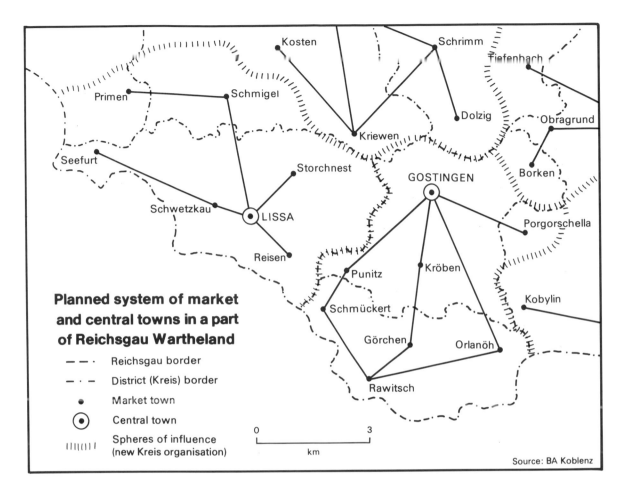

Planned system of market and central towns in a part of Reichsgau Wartheland

— — · Reichsgau border
— · — District (Kreis) border
· Market town
⊙ Central town
‖‖‖‖ Spheres of influence (new Kreis organisation)

0   3
km

Source: BA Koblenz

Although Wartheland enjoyed an existence of less than five years, and in all of that time Germany was at war, this did not prevent schemes for territorial reorganisation and changes in the urban system.

The third group of occupied territories formed what were ostensibly colonies. They consisted of the remnants of Poland and Czechoslovakia and, above all, vast tracts of conquered Russian territory. This was to be the great land empire in the east of which Hitler so often talked: the 'bread-basket' of the thousand-year Reich in which ethnic Germans and other pure-bred Nordic groups would be settled in fulfilment of Nazi ideals for a new-born peasantry. The ruthless corollary was enslavement and displacement of the indigenous peoples, the destruction of their society and the immediate liquidation of its political elites and Jewish populations. It was in Russia, in particular, that the full force of this Nazi ideology was felt. Special Gestapo and SS commandos (Einsatzgruppen) followed in the wake of victorious army units to purge the conquered areas of Bolsheviks and other enemies of the Nazi state. On Hitler's express orders, all political leaders and commissars in Russia were to be summarily executed. The Jews in these Russian territories suffered a similar fate. Some 2.25 million perished, either massacred by the Einsatzgruppen or deported to concentration and extermination camps.

To a growing degree, the Einsatzgruppen emerged as upholders of political security in the eastern territories and as an authority which overrode that of the military. Thus was formed the basis for SS domination in the east. The military was not fully acquiescent in this role. In Poland as well as in Russia, it relinquished the 'normal' administrative role of a victorious army and thereby paved the way for SS rule. But in Russia in particular, all kinds of conflicts arose over who had authority in the rear of the battle areas, a position which became compounded as the front line was forced into retreat. The military's somewhat tangential role in eastern occupation policy contrasted with its largely undisputed dominance in the western occupied areas.

The administration of occupied Russia

— — Front line, autumn 1942
- - - Administrative areas
- · - International borders

• Moscow

REICHSKOMMISSARIAT OSTLAND

GREATER GERMANY

BIALYSTOK

MILITARY AREA

GENERAL GOVERNMENT

REICHSKOMMISSARIAT UKRAINE

HUNGARY

RUMANIA

0   200
km

Source: Hilberg, 1961

The structure of administration for Hitler's eastern conquests never proceeded far beyond temporary expedient. In Russia there were created the Reichskommissariats Ostland and Ukraine, headed by prominent Gauleiter. Erich Koch (East Prussia) took control of the Ukraine, while the Ostland went to Lohse, Gauleiter of Schleswig-Holstein. Nazi 'philosopher' Alfred Rosenberg became Reich Minister for the Occupied Territories in the east, thereby laying the claim for state as compared to party control. Hitler's initial scheme for Russia envisaged a total of four Reichskommissariats, taking in Muscovy and the Caucasus, but these last two never materialised. In the Reichskommissariat Ostland, there was some use of native personnel in the civil administration formed by the Germans. But in the Ukraine German personnel carried out the task alone.

Even Goebbels was led to describe Rosenberg's charge as the 'Ministry of Chaos'.

THE CHAOTIC NAZI BUREAUCRACY IN OCCUPIED RUSSIA

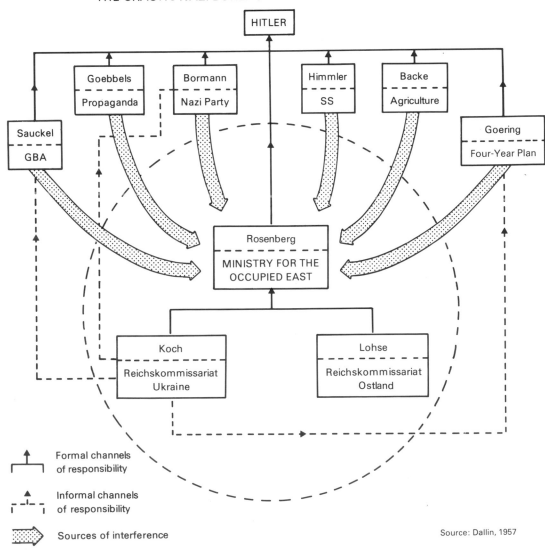

Source: Dallin, 1957

162

SIBERIA

M O S C O W

O S T L A N D

U K R A I N E

TURKESTAN

**The planned
German empire
in Russia**

———— Borders of
Reichskommissariat

- - - - Borders of
Generalkommissariat

C A U C A S U S

0   400
km

TURKEY

Source: Dallin, 1957

In the rump Czechoslovak state, labelled by the Germans the Protectorate of Bohemia-Moravia, a rather greater degree of native autonomy was allowed. The Germans installed a Reich Protector, but permitted a series of Czech departments of government. Even so, German control of political power and security limited the extent to which Czech wishes were carried out. What remained of the Polish state was translated by the Germans into the 'General Government'. This territory enjoyed a much lesser degree of autonomy than Bohemia-Moravia. Some Poles were employed in the lower ranks of administration, but the entire machinery of government was otherwise German, as were its principal personnel. Far more than the Czechs, the Poles were viewed as an inferior, subject race. And the General Government, although initially the focus of economic exploitation, soon followed the fate of the rest of Poland under a campaign of racial and cultural repression, spearheaded by the SS. The highly improvised nature of Hitler's plans for the government and administration of the east played readily into the hands of the party Gauleiters and Himmler's SS. Ultimately, though, it was the various offices of the SS machine which more often than not exercised the primary authority, notwithstanding the deep internal rivalries.

Armaments

The realities of German armaments production over the five and a half years of war were not fully appreciated until several decades after the war's end. And even today grey areas remain as a result of deficiencies in the historical record. The almost universal perception of the Western powers was that Germany was rearming 'in depth' from the very early years of the National Socialist regime. This view persisted through the first years of the war and was not properly confounded even when the scale of armaments production advanced rapidly from 1942 onwards, reaching its peak only in July 1944, by which time many of Hitler's European con-

quests (and hence additional resource bases) had been lost to the Allied advance. The mistake reflected a basic inability to comprehend the 'blitzkrieg' style of warfare which Hitler employed with such success between September 1939 and late 1941. The public rhetoric of Nazi leaders and the warlike activities of organisations like the Hitler Youth may have sounded otherwise, but the accompanying diagrams reveal very clearly that in armaments Germany was far removed from total war when seen alongside the other combatant powers and against the performance it registered between 1942 and 1944.

RATES OF ARMAMENTS PRODUCTION
OF COMBATANT POWERS (1944 = 100)

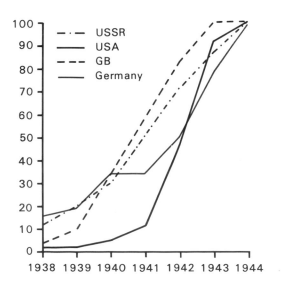

Source: Noakes and Pridham, 1974

PROPORTION OF GERMAN INDUSTRIAL PRODUCTION
DEVOTED TO WAR MATERIALS (at 1943 prices)

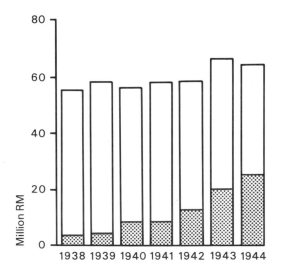

Source: Wagenführ, 1963

164

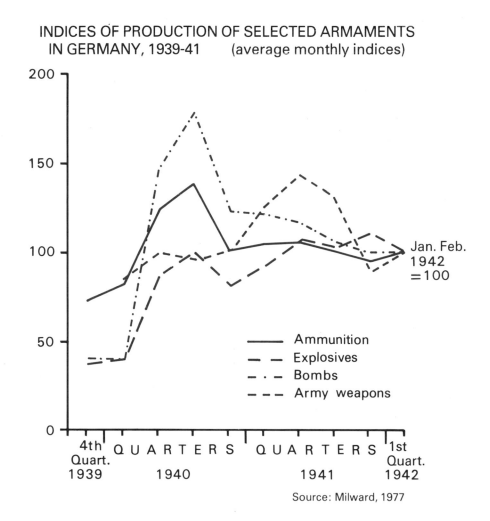

INDICES OF PRODUCTION OF SELECTED ARMAMENTS IN GERMANY, 1939-41 (average monthly indices)

Jan. Feb.
1942
=100

Ammunition
Explosives
Bombs
Army weapons

4th Quart. 1939   Q U A R T E R S   Q U A R T E R S   1st Quart. 1942
1940   1941

Source: Milward, 1977

The remarkable success and speed of Hitler's early campaigns and the fact that Germany alone set the nature and pace of events in the first years of war combined to enhance the strategy of blitzkrieg, whatever its underlying tactical and economic advantages. The attempts to shift armament priorities between army, navy and air force in accordance with Hitler's planned offensives were viable so long as the initiative remained in German hands. The weakness of blitzkrieg, especially as it operated in the Third Reich, was that it contained little margin for expansion. Counter-initiatives which accorded ill with Hitler's campaign plans or German offensives which lost their momentum

proved its undoing. A few of the danger signs were apparent in the Battle of Britain and in the subsequent preparations for a seaborne invasion of Britain. But they assumed real significance in the early autumn of 1941 as the Russian campaign faltered and, later, as the Soviet armies began their own attacks. Blitzkrieg might have been less readily confounded if there had been a more rigorous and efficient system for managing it. But in true National Socialist mould, it was prey to the competitive struggles of the different service chiefs and to *ad hoc* methods of arms procurement both within and between the service sectors.

The transfer from blitzkrieg to armament in depth was not a rapid one, for it required a far greater measure of central direction and control than existed up to the autumn of 1941. It also needed the understanding and co-operation of the population and the party. Moves in the former direction had begun in early 1940 when Fritz Todt was appointed to resolve a crisis over copper supplies. Success in this task led to his appointment as Minister for Armaments and Munitions in March 1940 and to the progressive rationalisation of armaments production, planning and research which was to bear such fruit under the later direction of Albert Speer, the man who took over the ministry following Todt's untimely death in a plane crash in early 1942.

The central feature of German armaments administration in the second half of the war was the system of committee organisation. This acted to co-ordinate the armaments demands of the three services, to rationalise those demands in relation to the factors of supply and to achieve a more efficient functional and geographical organisation of arms production and development. Albert Speer thus came to preside over an administrative regime which, with the progressive addition of wider controls like those over general raw material allocation and planning, became the central force in the German war economy, eclipsing Goering's Four-Year-Plan Organisation in much the way that that same office had earlier superseded various functions of the Economics Ministry. The OKW's War Economy and Armaments Office met a rather similar fate with the rise of Speer's Ministry.

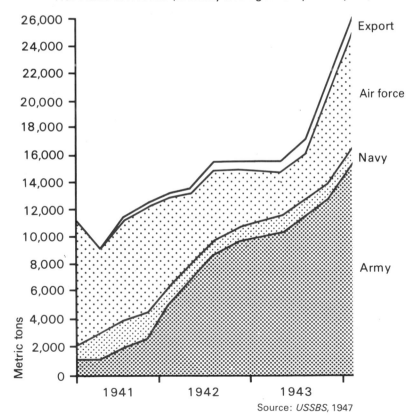

TNT ALLOCATIONS (monthly averages for quarter year)

Source: *USSBS*, 1947

INDICES OF ARMAMENTS PRODUCTION IN GERMANY
(January-February 1942 = 100)

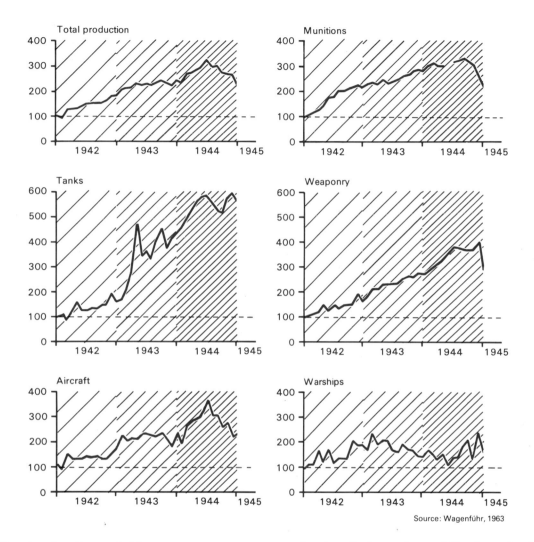

Source: Wagenführ, 1963

The singular facet of this great armaments expansion was its reliance on private industry. Speer's ministerial empire operated primarily as a guiding force in a production project which handed the basic tasks of armament manufacture, research and development to factory managers and industrialists. The spectacular feats of armaments production from 1942 onwards would have been impossible without the agency of private enterprise. Speer's scheme can be described as the mobilisation of self-interest and the armaments indices tell their own story. Over 1943 to 1944, German armaments production increased roughly threefold at a time when Allied bombing was gathering steadily in momentum. Tank production registered the most remarkable advances, notably after winter 1942, as the war against Russia became one of attrition.

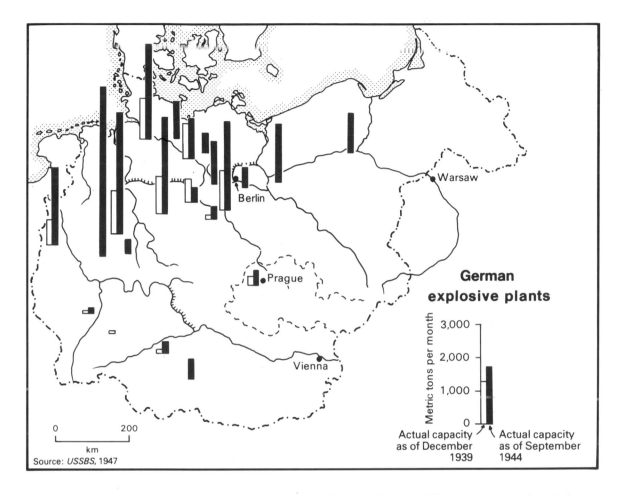

German explosive plants

Metric tons per month
3,000
2,000
1,000
0

Actual capacity as of December 1939

Actual capacity as of September 1944

0   200
km
Source: *USSBS*, 1947

Unlike so much basic industry, the German explosive industry was a relatively well-dispersed one and new plants established during the course of the war reinforced this. The aggregate growth in capacity between December 1939 and September 1944 was approximately fourfold.

In some ways, the Speer ministry represents an aberrant organisational form in Hitler's Germany in that its executive structure was relatively unambiguous. The conflicting and overlapping competencies that characterised so many other institutions of the *Hitler state* were much less evident, a reflection of Speer's political skills, his confident relations with Hitler, and the harsh requirements of defensive war on two fronts. But the passage was not uniformly easy. In the management of labour for the armaments sector, Speer had to bow to the will of the General Plenipotentiary for Labour appointed by Hitler in spring 1942. Similarly, Speer and his committee system regularly met opposition from party officials, the Gauleiters especially, over requirements to cut raw material allocations for consumer goods production and over the need for transfers of industrial plant in order to achieve a more rational spatial organisation of arms production. There were also persistent battles with the SS, as in the case of control of the great Skoda armaments works in Czechoslovakia. Hence political limitations remained to deflect the goals of the centre-piece of the German war machine. And parallel limitations sprang from the priority Hitler demanded for his secret weapons programme.

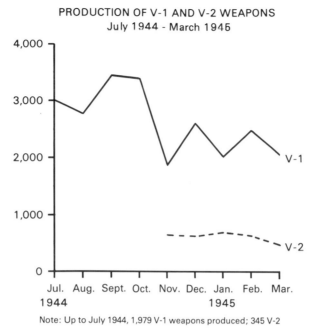

PRODUCTION OF V-1 AND V-2 WEAPONS
July 1944 - March 1945

Note: Up to July 1944, 1,979 V-1 weapons produced; 345 V-2

Source: Wagenführ, 1963

The V-bombs

The course of wars has in varying measure been affected by the development of novel forms of weaponry. The successful development and use of the atomic bomb by the Americans were decisive in forcing the Japanese surrender in August 1945. In Germany, the last years of the war saw much expenditure and research effort on the development and production of the V-1 and V-2 bombs, weapons intended for long-range bombardment. The V-1 was a pilotless jet-propelled aircraft which was launched from specially constructed ramps. It had a maximum flying time of about one hour, whereupon it literally fell to the ground with its warhead. The V-2 was a rocket which used liquid oxygen and alcohol as its fuel. This gave rise to a gas velocity nearly twice that obtained from the combustion of gunpowder and meant that after 60 seconds' flight the rocket had reached a height of 22 to 23 miles. By this time the fuel had been expended and the rocket fell in a relatively uncontrolled fashion, though approximating a parabolic path. It could carry a warhead of up to a ton in weight.

The first of the V-1 weapons was launched shortly after the Normandy landings in June 1944 and was directed at London. Subsequently, both weapons were used against London and also against the port of Antwerp. Their impact on the final course of the war and on Germany's fortunes was negligible, though. Despite sustained production to the very last months, the weapons lacked accuracy and reliability. An even more critical handicap was the location of many launching sites on the Channel coast beyond Germany's borders; later in 1944 these steadily fell into Allied hands. The Nazi propaganda machine, however, cast the weapons as likely to change the course of the war. Taking its cue from Hitler, who had referred to a battery of secret weapons late in 1942 and who was to maintain a blind faith in their strategic power to the end, Goebbels' Propaganda Ministry made them a continuous focus of faith against defeat, not only to the mass of the people, but to soldiers and military leaders.

The Supply of Materials

Long before the war the National Socialist leadership had been conscious of the uncertain supply and/or shortage of a variety of materials, agricultural as well as industrial. In both sectors, policies had been enacted to ameliorate these and also to replace imports with increased domestic output, particularly those imports originating from countries thought likely to be unreliable with the prospect of war. The success of these measures was highly variable between sectors. Moreover, the territorial annexations and conquests from 1938 onwards to some extent undercut their purpose. The industrial and raw material capacities of a long line of European states soon became at Nazi Germany's disposal. And states which threw in their lot with Germany added to the total. Rumania dominated the latter group with its large mineral oil output, most of which became available to the German cause. With so large an area of Europe under German control or influence, one might have supposed that problems of material supply would have become a feature of the past, especially given the Nazis' callous attitudes to indigenous populations and economies in some of the occupied lands. This was not true, however. The reasons were basically two-fold. The transition from 1942 towards an economy much more fully geared to war and to armament 'in depth' placed greatly enhanced demands on material supply and began to expose critical weak links. But it was not simply a problem of resource bottlenecks. Equally difficult was the full mobilisation of available resources. This required co-ordinated control and planning which looked to maximum efficiency in the recovery, allocation and use of resources. However, the nature of the Nazi state made this an idle dream. It was approached in the mid- to late years of the war as a result of Speer's success in establishing some central direction of the war economy, particularly in the quarterly allocation of primary materials like coal, iron and steel. Even then, however, deficiencies in the quantity and quality of labour remained to frustrate the position. There were also persistent weaknesses in transportation, not to mention the increasing effects of Allied bombing after 1942 which would have strained even the best co-ordinated of war economies. By 1942 Germany was in fact working a railway network in continental Europe which was almost two-thirds the size of that operated by the USA. This stretched the manpower resources of the Reichsbahn almost to breaking point; and there were parallel shortages of motive power and rolling stock. Russian broad-gauge tracks might be converted to narrow gauge relatively easily, but stock could not be so readily altered and resulted in limited resources being stretched over an even greater network. It is difficult to overestimate the functions of the railway system in wartime. It was the lifeline for the supply of armaments and stores to combat areas. It conveyed vital raw materials to Germany from occupied countries. Servicemen, labour conscripts, prisoners-of-war and concentration camp victims were all among the railways' clientele. Within Germany, the railways performed the vital task of servicing the complex industrial machine, particularly the high geographical concentration of activity in the Rhine–Ruhr, which, by definition, multiplied and elongated trade linkages and in so doing was to prove so devastating a handicap in the face of Allied bombing and, later, Allied invasion.

INDEX OF TOTAL INDUSTRIAL PRODUCTION (1943 =100)

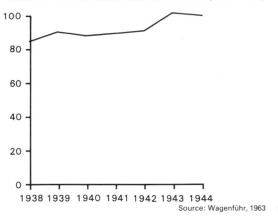

Source: Wagenführ, 1963

INDICES OF MAJOR PRODUCTION GROUPS (1943 = 100)

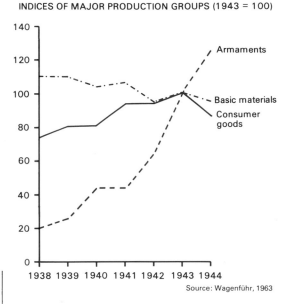

Source: Wagenführ, 1963

The requirements of war naturally made heavy additional demands upon basic industries like coal-mining, iron-working and steel manufacture. Armaments production, meanwhile, brought with it a whole range of demands for non-ferrous metals; chromium, for example, was vital to the manufacture of armour plate, indeed of most alloy steels altogether. Also needed were oil supplies in growing quantities — for aviation spirit, carburettor and diesel fuel especially. Coal and lignite (brown coal) were materials in which Germany was fairly well endowed and the Nazis' territorial acquisitions added to this stock considerably. The lignite beds of Bohemia and Moravia, for instance, alone had an annual output of some 11 million tons. Within the Altreich, though, coal production barely increased at all over the course of the war. Production in 1938 was some 186 million tons; by 1943 it was only 190.4 million tons. Surprisingly little attention was given to coal planning, despite the build-up of coal-devouring branches of the chemical industry. In 1943 the annexed territories yielded an additional 88 million tons and the occupied areas a

further 77 million. But the latter figure would have been yet higher had it proved possible to exploit the coal deposits of the Russian Donetz basin more rigorously. In total, it seems that they extracted less than a tenth of prewar production levels in the Donetz. The real Achilles' heel of coal supply, however, was its dependence on railway transportation for distribution, and when the railway system became exposed to heavy air raids, that distribution broke down. This was notably true by the late autumn of 1944 and particularly affected the Ruhr, which provided some two-thirds of German output. In contrast to coal, there was a radical increase in lignite production within the Altreich — from 195 million tons in 1938 to 253.4 million by 1943. Most of this increase came from central Germany. The primary uses of lignite were for electricity generation and domestic heating.

Iron and steel

The raw material with which Germany was not well endowed, particularly for war production purposes, was iron ore. The German ores were mostly low grade and low in phosphoric value, phosphorus content being important for armaments manufacture. Germany was traditionally a strong importer of quality ore, notably from Sweden. And since the Swedish ores were rich in phosphorus they assumed vital significance in the German war economy, in some measure accounting for Hitler's 1940 campaign to secure the Norwegian flank. Nazi territorial annexation and conquest also brought significant spoils of iron ore. The Austrian reserves yielded an output of some 2 million tons at the time of annexation. But far greater were the reserves in the Lorraine region of France, with a prewar yield of about 18 million tons.

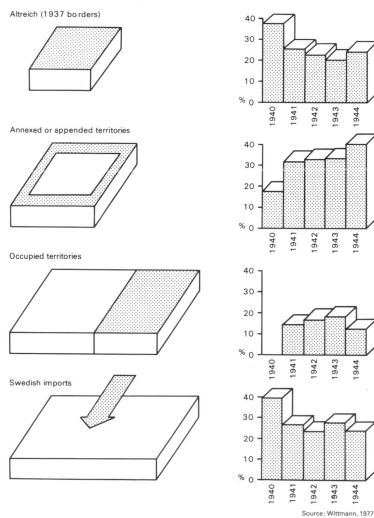

SOURCES OF IRON ORE, 1940-4

Source: Wittmann, 1977

The extent to which Nazi Germany came to depend on ore supplies from outside its 1937 borders is apparent in the accompanying diagrams. Discounting imports from neutral states, the figure was around 51 per cent in both 1943 and 1944. In 1943, in fact, only one-fifth of the Nazi empire's ore supply was accounted for by Germany proper. Over the course of the war there was almost a 50 per cent drop in ore tonnage produced in the Altreich. The consequences of this external dependence in the face of Allied advances from east and west in 1944 were understandably acute. And with German prospects of winning the war receding rapidly, neutrals became less and less willing to maintain previous levels of ore supply.

Iron ore was translated into a variety of ferrous products, but the most significant in terms of war economy was steel, notably high-grade steels and steel plate. In 1937, raw steel output was just short of 20 million tons. By 1943 the Nazis had some 35 million at their disposal, roughly two-thirds of which came from the Altreich, the remainder from the annexed and conquered territories. In the event, though, the demand for high-grade steels and steel plate was never satisfied. There was a persistent shortfall which stemmed fundamentally from deficient production capacity, not deficient material availability. This reflected a basic lack of plant investment in the interwar period and the general reluctance of the Nazi economic leadership to maintain much manufacturing capacity beyond the borders of Greater Germany where it was not only less secure but more open to SS domination and manipulation.

Other metals

Steel production problems were reinforced by increasing difficulties over the supply of chromium. For these, Nazi Germany relied heavily on neutral Turkey and Albania. Turkey in 1943 supplied almost 5,000 tons, roughly double the production of Greater Germany and the occupied territories put together. The figure rose to nearly 12,000 tons in 1944. The enforced German withdrawal from south-east Europe interfered with chrome supplies, both in their acquisition and in their carriage to Germany itself.

Aluminium was another material vital to the German war effort, notably for aircraft production. Soon after the occupation of Norway in 1940, plans were laid to create a massively enlarged aluminium industry there, making use of the large and cheap supplies of hydro-electricity. Norway had no bauxite reserves, though. These had to be imported from France and Hungary; and herein lay the weak link of production plans, that is aside from the costs and manpower requirements of constructing eight new hydro-electric power stations and ten new smelting plants.

173

Oil supplies

Of all Nazi Germany's material demands, however, the greatest challenges and the greatest difficulties were presented in oil supply. In perspective the response was an impressive one. With limited supplies of mineral oil within its borders, synthetic oil production had been a feature of the industry since the mid-1920s, and by the middle years of the war output was roughly five times that of mineral oil. Even before the outbreak of war, Germany had achieved the largest synthetic oil industry in the world, despite failures to meet planned targets. Austria yielded mineral oil to Nazi Germany, as did various other annexed or occupied territories. But the bulk of the remaining deficit was met by Rumanian mineral oil production. By 1941 nearly 3 million tons were being imported for Reich use and for the active armed forces. This compared with 2.5 million tons of synthetic production.

Throughout the early years of the war, there were minor difficulties over oil supplies — related, for example, to transportation problems, irregularities of demand and diverse jurisdictional conflicts within the Nazi organisation. But these were nothing compared to the havoc wrought by Allied bombing from the spring of 1944. In the view of some commentators, this became the most serious single threat to the German war economy. Synthetic oil capacity, concentrated as it was in the Ruhr and in the central industrial belt, proved a relatively easy target. Some two-thirds of the hydrogenation capacity was actually contained within only seven plants. The impact of bombing on fuel production is demonstrated in the accompanying graph. Aviation fuel output, the bulk of which derived from synthetic production, dropped catastrophically. As the need for fighter protection against bombing raids on the plants grew, so the raids were progressively destroying the fighters' own fuel. Reconstruction work was pressed with all speed but barely kept ahead of renewed attacks. From the summer of 1944 onwards, therefore, Hitler's Reich and the armed forces in particular faced critical fuel shortages. This could not fail to hasten the pace of defeat.

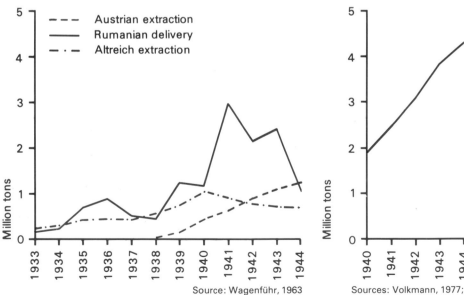

MINERAL OIL SUPPLY

- – – – Austrian extraction
- —— Rumanian delivery
- – · – Altreich extraction

Million tons

Source: Wagenführ, 1963

SYNTHETIC OIL PRODUCTION
(Greater Germany)

Million tons

Sources: Volkmann, 1977;
Statistisches Handbuch, 1928-44

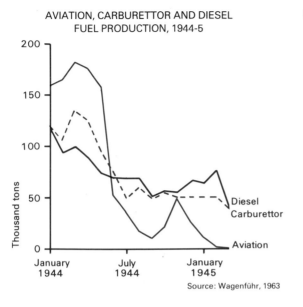

AVIATION, CARBURETTOR AND DIESEL FUEL PRODUCTION, 1944-5

Source: Wagenführ, 1963

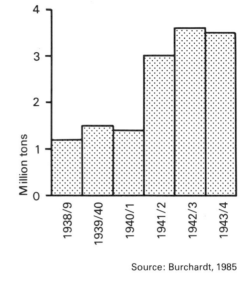

BREAD GRAINS FROM OCCUPIED TERRITORIES

Source: Burchardt, 1985

The supply of food

By the last winter of the war, food supplies had also been reduced to a critical level; the average daily calorie intake for civilians was below the minimum considered necessary for long-term survival (1,800 per day). Until that time, however, Nazi Germany had been relatively well provided with food, especially when set against the chronic food shortages suffered in the later years of the First World War. Rationing was instituted immediately the war broke out in 1939 and remained effective up to 1943/4, when black marketing began to assume growing significance in the face of contracting official allocations. The most serious setback to food supply was probably that occasioned by the severe winter weather of 1941-2 which killed much winter grain and damaged potato crops and stores. Occupied territories yielded grain and other food commodities. Indeed, the decision to drive the German attack on Russia south-east to the Ukraine in summer 1941 was ostensibly to secure the rich food resources of that region. In fact, however, the greater part of the Russian grain harvest collected by the Germans went to supply the army. And in spite of instituting one of the most vicious occupational regimes, German rule in Russia actually yielded a limited reward. It is estimated, for example, that net German imports in agriculture totalled only RM 3,500 million, a fraction of what the Nazi state obtained from France alone. The scale of bread grain imports to the Reich from occupied territories is illustrated in the accompanying diagram. By 1942/3 they met just short of a third of demand. The pattern for meat and fat was not dissimilar. The steady attrition of Hitler's land conquests from 1943 inevitably spelt a progressive diminution in these food supplies. And the position was made doubly difficult by the need to supply the armed forces at the front from German sources, where previously they had subsisted directly from the territories under occupation.

175

The Supply of Men

The civilian labour force in Germany fell from 39.1 million to 28.4 million between May 1939 and September 1944. In a country which was already experiencing a labour crisis in 1938/9, the consequences for the operation of the war economy were severe. Nor was it simply a question of deficient numbers. The quality of the labour force became equally problematic. The pace at which workers could be trained in vital industrial skills became steadily inadequate as armament production accelerated. Wehrmacht conscription added to the difficulties. Even early on in the war, newly trained young men were liable to call-up; and emergency drafting in later years probed yet more widely into the profile of skilled labour. By the autumn of 1944, in fact, some 13 million had been called up, while the number of those lost in combat totalled 3.9 million.

For reasons examined earlier, there was little mobilisation of women to make up for the losses to the civilian labour force. Indeed, in the first two years of war, there was a fall in female labour strength. However, the regime was very effective in adding to its labour force by drafting in foreign workers from occupied or allied countries and by utilising prisoners-of-war. The latter soon became part of a massive, inhumane slave labour programme. By spring 1941 there were some 1.5 million foreign workers engaged in Germany, and in some Labour Ministry regions they represented over 10 per cent of the workforce. At the same time there were just over 1 million employed POWs. By early 1943 the figures had risen to 4.8 million foreign workers and 1.75 million POWs. But even though the total foreign and POW labour force may have reached nearly 8 million, this was still short of replacement level. Moreover, POW labour was no substitute, man for man, for ordinary labour, a feature compounded by appalling living conditions in the POW camps. There were also serious inadequacies in the way the regime used its foreign labour. Skilled men, for instance, were often employed in non-skilled positions, many in agriculture. Muscle power typically took precedence over trade skill, with inevitable longer-term detriment.

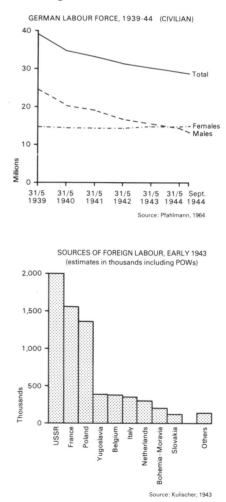

GERMAN LABOUR FORCE, 1939-44 (CIVILIAN)

Source: Pfahlmann, 1964

SOURCES OF FOREIGN LABOUR, EARLY 1943
(estimates in thousands including POWs)

Source: Kulischer, 1943

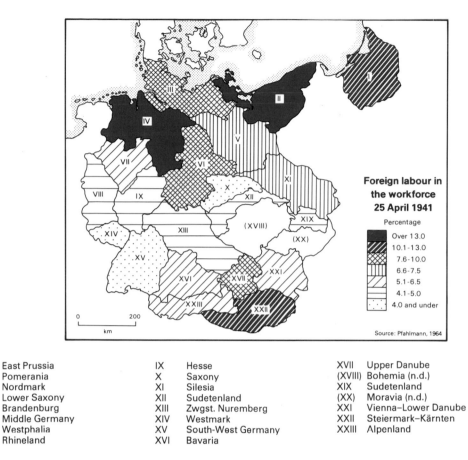

Foreign labour in the workforce 25 April 1941

Percentage

Over 13.0
10.1-13.0
7.6-10.0
6.6-7.5
5.1-6.5
4.1-5.0
4.0 and under

Source: Pfahlmann, 1964

I	East Prussia	IX	Hesse	XVII	Upper Danube
II	Pomerania	X	Saxony	(XVIII)	Bohemia (n.d.)
III	Nordmark	XI	Silesia	XIX	Sudetenland
IV	Lower Saxony	XII	Sudetenland	(XX)	Moravia (n.d.)
V	Brandenburg	XIII	Zwgst. Nuremberg	XXI	Vienna–Lower Danube
VI	Middle Germany	XIV	Westmark	XXII	Steiermark–Kärnten
VII	Westphalia	XV	South-West Germany	XXIII	Alpenland
VIII	Rhineland	XVI	Bavaria		

Note: Regions are those of Reich Labour Ministry. POWs included.

The efficiency of wartime labour utilisation became a particular worry for Albert Speer and his Armaments Ministry. The central powers that Speer managed to assemble over raw material allocation, weapon supply to the different services and the organisation of production never extended to labour. In 1942 this became the province of a General Plenipotentiary for Labour, Fritz Sauckel, former Gauleiter of Thuringia. Sauckel enjoyed rather similar central power and was able to streamline and speed up the movement and allocation of labour, particularly that from occupied territories. In four recruiting campaigns from spring 1942 to December 1944, he procured over 5 million foreigners and POWs. But Sauckel's relationship with the Speer ministry was an uneasy one; and it deteriorated steadily as prospects of defeat loomed. Speer argued for the retention of industrial workers in occupied areas as the most effective means of maximising armaments output. Sauckel differed, and in January 1944, for example, won Hitler's sanction for the deporting of roughly a million French workmen to the Reich over the course of that year. The haphazard use of foreign worker skills was also a product of Sauckel's intervention. As a long-standing party figure, he belonged to a group who were suspicious of the role occupied by the business interests with which Speer's ministry was inextricably bound. And the antipathy developed a mutual character as industrialists increasingly perceived financial ruin as the only outcome of total German defeat.

Civilian Conditions

Two factors were critical to the determination of civilian conditions in wartime Germany. The first was the uncompromising desire to avoid the experience that Germany had in the First World War, when food supplies declined drastically, the cost of living rose much more quickly than incomes, and soldiers' families, in particular, were reduced to the barest of subsistence levels. The second was the National Socialists' need to maintain the support of the population at large. As a novel and radical regime, it relied on the general acquiescence of the people to maintain some degree of stability; there was not the innate stability that existed in Britain. The outcome was that, until the later years of the war, Nazi Germany did not experi-

ence the full rigours of war economy. The prewar level of consumer goods production, for example, was maintained to a considerably greater degree than in Britain. Assigning the value of 100 to the base year of 1938, British production had fallen to 81 by 1941, German to only 97. Even as late as the fifth year of the war, some 43 per cent of those employed in Nazi Germany were engaged on tasks for civilian consumption. Speer's ministry fought hard to reduce the level in favour of war production. It was really successful only in the textile sector, where production of men's clothing, for instance, fell some 80 per cent from 1943 to 1944.

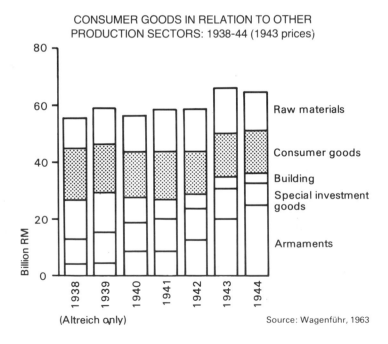

CONSUMER GOODS IN RELATION TO OTHER
PRODUCTION SECTORS: 1938-44 (1943 prices)

Raw materials

Consumer goods

Building

Special investment goods

Armaments

Billion RM

(Altreich only)

Source: Wagenführ, 1963

178

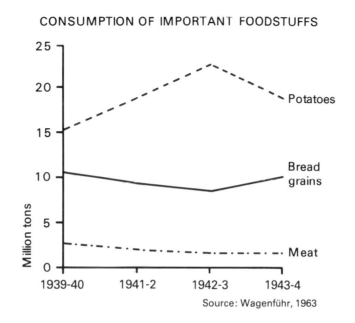

CONSUMPTION OF IMPORTANT FOODSTUFFS

Source: Wagenführ, 1963

Food rationing was adopted in Germany immediately on the outbreak of war, with differentiations made for regional food preferences. This, coupled with fair grain stocks, sufficient labour and fertiliser allocations, and imports, contributed to a reasonably stable food situation until all but the last months of the war. Predictably, given Germany's prewar agricultural pattern, there were cutbacks in meat and fat supplies, but consumption of bread grains and potatoes was more than maintained up to 1944.

The cost of living index increased by only 12 per cent during the course of the war and was nearly matched by the increase in wages. This was achieved by state control of prices and wages, and assisted by the relatively favourable supply positions in food and other goods. Given that rationing prevailed, however, many Germans found themselves with more money than they could spend. The institution of a wide-ranging and relatively generous set of payments to families of serving men tended to reinforce the pattern.

Another significant contrast between the German and British war economies was in the use of women for war work. This was instituted in Britain at an early stage and proved a vital supplement to the labour force. In Nazi Germany the employment of women was objected to on a variety of grounds including concern for soldiers' morale. What is more, the favourable financial supports given by National Socialism to 'the family' resulted in an outflow of women from employment. Speer's ministry reckoned that between July 1939 and February 1942 some 80,000 left *industrial* employment to stay at home. Over the entire course of the war the total number of women in the labour force remained static at about 14.5 million. This has to be set alongside the increasing demands of the armed forces draft, which, after two and a half years of war, had absorbed some 7.5 million men.

Civilian existence in wartime Germany, then, was not a harsh one, except for political dissidents. However, this became less and less true from 1943 as Allied bombers started to raze the face of many German cities and the death toll of the Wehrmacht climbed. In the last years of the Russian campaign, whole army divisions were almost wiped out, leaving few German families unaffected. Ultimately there were 3.5 million dead servicemen.

179

German Resistance to National Socialism

Assessments of resistance within the Third Reich face formidable problems of interpretation. Major incidents such as the von Stauffenberg bomb plot of 20 July 1944 and earlier army attempts either to assassinate or to arrest Hitler are clear enough testament, but resistance at grass-roots level is not nearly so easily apprehended or appraised. It is represented in the detainees in concentration camps from the regime's earliest days, in arrests for political crimes, in seizures of 'illegal' literature and in various forms of uncooperative action within such institutions as the Church and the civil service. But it is difficult to evaluate these. And one should beware of forgetting the resistance that for one reason or other went largely unrecorded; concentration camp detainees and political arrests represent only the detected resistance.

The most significant German resistance can be conveniently separated into two camps: that of the conservatives or right wing, largely repre-

sented by leading members of the army and of the German elite; and that of the left wing in which the outlawed German Community Party (KPD) dominated. The strength of communist opposition within the broader frame of left-wing resistance is demonstrated in the available statistics. In 1936, for example, some 11,700 were arrested as against only 1,400 for the Social Democratic Party (SPD) and associate groups. The adjacent graph for 1938-9 replicates the pattern. The conclusion of a Nazi–Soviet pact in August 1939 naturally stemmed the force of communist opposition. But after the invasion of Russia in June 1941, it again gathered momentum, especially as reflected in the communist press. Communist arrests in 1941 totalled over 11,000, almost a return to the level of 1936.

For reasons given above, a map of 'set-piece' incidents of this kind can be misleading. But it does show that resistance was relatively widespread rather than geographically confined.

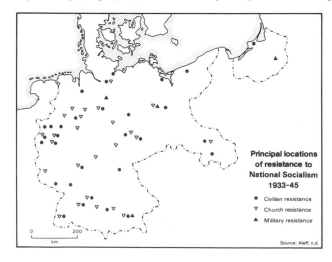

Principal locations of resistance to National Socialism 1933-45

- Civilian resistance
- Church resistance
- Military resistance

0   200
km

Source: Aleff, n.d.

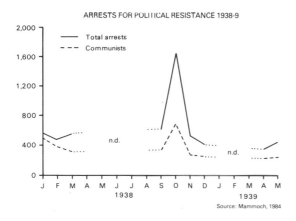

ARRESTS FOR POLITICAL RESISTANCE 1938-9

Total arrests
Communists

n.d.

n.d.

J F M A M J J A S O N D J F M A M
1938 1939

Source: Mammoch, 1984

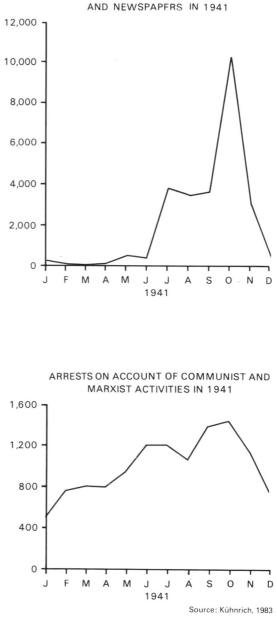

GESTAPO SEIZURES OF COMMUNIST FLY-SHEETS
AND NEWSPAPERS IN 1941

J F M A M J J A S O N D
1941

ARRESTS ON ACCOUNT OF COMMUNIST AND
MARXIST ACTIVITIES IN 1941

J F M A M J J A S O N D
1941

Source: Kühnrich, 1983

The conservative opposition, in which members of the army figured strongly, was best placed of all Nazi political opponents to achieve positive results, but it laboured under one very important shadow, the cause of patriotism. In France, resistance could hardly be construed as anything but patriotic. In Germany the synonymity was non-existent. When Hitler's policies were winning, resistance looked like treason. For this reason a number of serious army plots to arrest Hitler ultimately evaporated due to lack of support. This was notably true in the crisis over the Sudetenland and in the subsequent capitulation of the Western powers to Hitler's demands. The startling successes of the German armies, first in Poland, then in Scandinavia and later in Western Europe, dampened the force and conviction of military opposition yet further. Not until 1942, when the tide of the war was beginning to move in favour of the Allies, was activity renewed. It culminated in the abortive July 1944 *coup* when Hitler survived a bomb placed in his East Prussian headquarters. This plot had been preceded by several others which had sought (unsuccessfully) to eliminate Hitler. Its failure was followed by a ruthless Nazi vendetta, which was soon to liquidate a major part of the conservative opposition, including most of the members of the Kreisau Circle, a remarkable resistance group which subscribed to liberal principles and had been secretly deliberating on the nature of a post-Hitler Germany.

The Holocaust

If there is any one single act for which the Nazis will be remembered, it is the systematic extermination of the Jews of Europe. Even today, over forty years later, the 'Holocaust' remains a subject of intense debate and dispute in the Western world at large. And the pattern is likely to continue for several more decades given the serious problems of political and emotional engagement which persist as long as interpreters remained connected with the reality of the event.

There is no reliable figure for the number of Jews who perished in Nazi hands, nor for the other racial and social 'undesirables' who fell to the same lot. Estimates of total Jewish deaths range between 4 million and 6 million. Perhaps a quarter of these lost their lives at the hands of the Einsatzgruppen, particularly in Poland and in Russia. The rest were shot or gassed in notor-

ious death camps like Auschwitz, or else worked to death in servitude to the SS.

The war saw a progressive brutalisation in Nazi policies towards the Jews — not as a result of a clearly laid out plan, but as a function of conflicting objectives among the various Nazi power blocs which found resolution only in more and more radical measures. Emigration ceased and large numbers of the Jewish populations of Germany, Austria and the newly conquered parts of Poland were rounded up and shipped to the areas of Poland not incorporated in the Greater German Reich, the so-called 'remainder state'. Here they were 'concentrated' in ghettos, the largest being Lodz (established February 1940) and Warsaw (established November 1940). The area south of Lublin also became a major reception zone for Jewish deportees, and for some months in 1940 the intention was that this would become a reservation for Europe's entire Jewish population. Once in the Polish ghettos, the Jews became slave labourers, working in poor conditions and with inadequate food.

This map should be viewed as a characteristic piece of Nazi propaganda. It is misleading rather than inaccurate, as the map in section 1 of Part Three has already shown. Jewish populations were heavily concentrated in towns and cities.

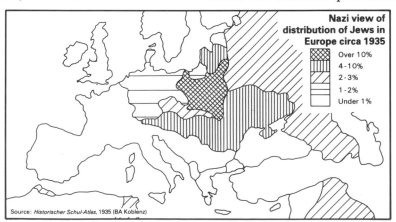

Nazi view of distribution of Jews in Europe circa 1935

- Over 10%
- 4-10%
- 2-3%
- 1-2%
- Under 1%

Source: *Historischer Schul-Atlas*, 1935 (BA Koblenz)

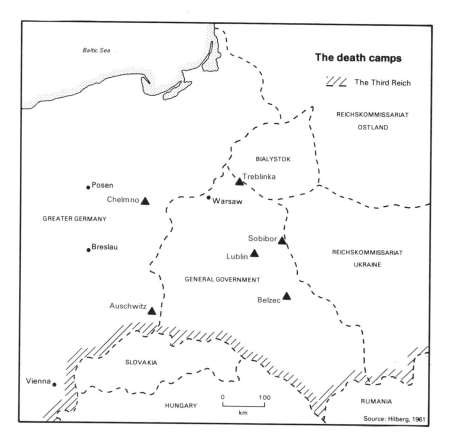

The death camps

/// The Third Reich

REICHSKOMMISSARIAT
OSTLAND

BIALYSTOK

Treblinka ▲

• Posen

Chelmno ▲

• Warsaw

GREATER GERMANY

Sobibor ▲

• Breslau

Lublin ▲

REICHSKOMMISSARIAT
UKRAINE

GENERAL GOVERNMENT

Auschwitz ▲

Belzec ▲

SLOVAKIA

Vienna •

0   100
km

HUNGARY

RUMANIA

Source: Hilberg, 1961

The genesis of the 'final solution' to the Jewish question and the seat of its responsibility are themes which remain indistinct, in spite of a plethora of investigation. At all events, Himmler and Heydrich had assembled four Einsatzgruppen by May 1941 for use in different sectors of Russia after the invasion. These groups began operating very soon after the Barbarossa campaign opened on 22 June 1941. Within months they had killed some 600,000 Jews. A second major phase of killing opened in the spring of 1942.

The Einsatzgruppen dealt only with Jews in the area of occupied Russia. For those in Poland and the remainder of occupied Europe, including those still in Germany performing vital munitions work, a more thorough method of liquidation had to be found. Gas had been used by the Nazis between 1938 and 1941 in connection with the euthanasia experiments for the mentally handicapped and chronically sick. Some of the staff involved in that programme were transferred to assist in dealing with the Jews and to help set up gas chambers for mass killing. Hitler probably decided upon a policy of systematic genocide in the summer of 1941. The first extermination camp was opened at Chelmno within the borders of Greater Germany in December 1941. Further camps followed at Belzec in the Polish General Government (opened March 1942), at Sobibor on the border between the General Government and the Reichskommissariat Ukraine (opened May 1942), and at Treblinka, north-east of Warsaw (opened July 1942). To these four camps must be added two existing SS concentration and labour camps which were subsequently equipped with extermination facilities: Lublin and Auschwitz.

Over the course of 1942 and 1943, the Nazi campaign against the Jews was accelerated. Satellite states in south-east Europe were increasingly drawn into it, while in western occupied zones Jews were steadily rounded up preparatory to railway transportation east. Jews still performing vital munitions work in Berlin and in areas like the Polish General Government were similarly evacuated. The fact that neither their labour nor their skills could be adequately replaced was immaterial in the eyes of Himmler and other Nazi fanatics like Goebbels. Thus developed some of the bitterest internal rivalries of the Nazi regime. At a time when Speer and all the various representatives of his Armaments Ministry were seeking to maximise war production, Himmler and the SS were depleting the labour force, absorbing vital railway capacity and consuming precious building materials in the making of their camp installations. Given the primacy of the SS in occupied Europe, especially in the east, it was the crusade to wipe out the Jewish race rather than victory in war which generally held sway.

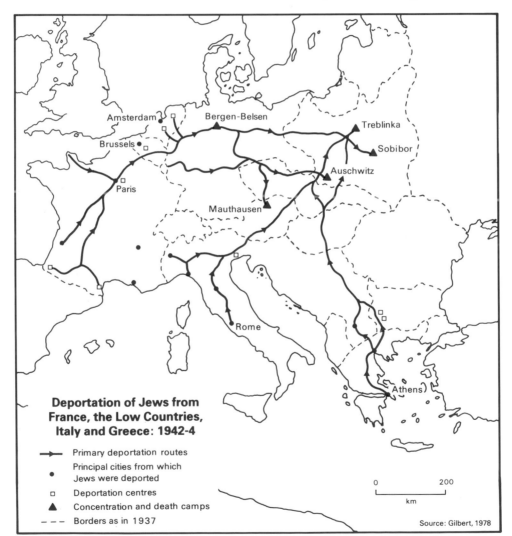

Deportation of Jews from France, the Low Countries, Italy and Greece: 1942-4

→ Primary deportation routes

• Principal cities from which Jews were deported

□ Deportation centres

▲ Concentration and death camps

– – – Borders as in 1937

0   200
km

Source: Gilbert, 1978

One of the crematoria at Auschwitz-Birkenau

Auschwitz became the biggest of the extermination camps, as well as providing workforces for numerous SS enterprises. Mass transports of Jews began arriving there in March 1942. By late autumn of 1944, as many as two million Jews may have perished there — either worked to death, shot, gassed, or killed in grotesque medical experiments by SS doctors invariably undertaken without any form of anaesthetic.

Auschwitz's one-time camp commandant, Rudolf Hoess, became the Nazis' ultimate technocrat of death. His advocacy of Zyklon-B crystals [hydrogen cyanide] as the most efficient method of gassing is by now infamous. In the earlier euthanasia experiments and in the lesser extermination camps, carbon monoxide was used. Hoess maintained that Zyklon-B was quicker and more efficient. And as it was already used in the camps as a fumigant, there were few problems in obtaining additional supplies. One Hamburg chemical firm was eventually to supply Auschwitz with two tons of the crystals a month. Auschwitz also had a physical capacity for extermination which outstripped its sister camps. At Treblinka, the ten gas chambers accommodated only 200 apiece. Hoess built four chambers each capable of accommodating 2000 and in his testimony at Nuremberg reckoned that up to 16,000 camp inmates were processed daily. Auschwitz was also distinguished from several of the other extermination centres in the way it sought to disguise the gas chambers and the associated crematoria — with the aid of gardens, for example. However, even Hoess' zealous pursuit of the speediest and most efficient machinery of death failed in the handling of the dead bodies. The crematoria proved incapable of disposing of corpses fast enough.

Throughout their deliberations over the Jewish race, Nazi leaders sought to maintain a cloak of secrecy, particularly as the policy of large-scale physical extermination became a reality. The language of euphemism as seen in terms like 'final solution' and 'special treatment' was one symptom of the trend. But Heydrich, Himmler's deputy in the overseeing of the Jewish question, soon realised that more concrete disguise would be necessary given the sheer scale of the extermination and the many Reich and SS agencies which would inevitably become involved. One of his principal solutions was the setting up of a special Jewish ghetto at Theresienstadt in northern Bohemia. It was intended for Jews over sixty-five years of age, the inmates having first been persuaded to make over their assets to the Reich Association of Jews in return for housing, food and welfare.

Theresienstadt subsequently became a propaganda stage for the Nazis' treatment of Jews. The camp was emphasised as humane. Photographic records were released which showed senior Jews engaging in self-government. Even a Red Cross inspection was arranged in an attempt to convince ordinary Germans as well as the wider world of the sincerity of the enterprise. In reality, of course, Theresienstadt proved very close to being a concentration camp. And above all it operated as a transit centre for the death camps further east.

Jews being marched through Warsaw by German soldiers, winter 1940

186

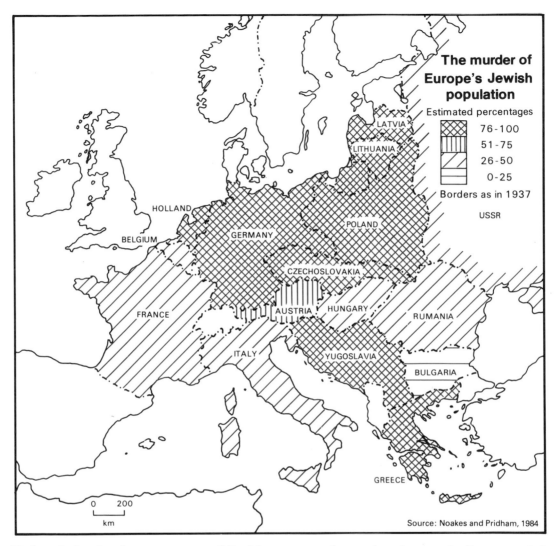

The murder of Europe's Jewish population

Estimated percentages

	76 - 100
	51 - 75
	26 - 50
	0 - 25

Borders as in 1937

Source: Noakes and Pridham, 1984

If the whole ghastly programme of Jewish extermination was instituted by Hitler and his closest Nazi leaders and the genocide act itself carried out by the regime's elite guard, it remains true that thousands of ordinary Germans knew what was happening and many thousands more had a good general idea of the Nazis' treatment of the Jews. The Wehrmacht had extensive, often first-hand, knowledge, particularly in the case of the Einsatzgruppen operating in Russia in the rear of the advancing army groups. Railway employees involved in the mass transit of Jews to the extermination camps knew that human bodies were being incinerated there. Auschwitz, moreover, was on the borders of the heavily populated industrial area of Upper Silesia. There were ordinary Germans working in the factories associated with the concentration camps there, notably those of the IG-Farben organisation; and the smoke and stench from the crematoria were evident for miles around. Some were revolted by what they witnessed themselves or learned about second hand; some closed their eyes and sought refuge in Nazi propaganda; many knew but simply did not believe.

Epilogue

The *Hitler state* ceased to exist when the Fuehrer committed suicide in his Berlin bunker on 30 April 1945, although Admiral Doenitz, Hitler's chosen successor, tried in vain to prolong the Third Reich's existence from his headquarters at Flensburg on the Danish border. The policy of the Allies towards a defeated Germany had been set out as early as January 1943 at the Casablanca conference. It called for Germany's unconditional surrender and the occupation of all German territory for an undefined period. The territorial losses sustained by Germany's neighbours from 1937 were to be rectified and the entire German war machine dismantled.

The actual occupation of Germany from April 1945 involved a four-power division among the USSR, the USA, Britain and France; Greater Berlin, located deep inside the Soviet zone, became a four-power city, with access for the Western powers along specially defined routes. From the start, native Germans were permitted a considerable measure of administrative autonomy, although this did not prevent the four powers from pursuing distinctive general occupation policies, especially in the Soviet area where Stalinist ideology invariably prevailed. Subsequently this divergence sharpened and, coupled with a steady deterioration in relations between the Soviets and the Western Allies, became the stage-set for the emergence of two separate German states by 1949: the Federal Republic in the British, French and American zones; the Democratic Republic in the Soviet zone.

German suffering in the immediate postwar years was great. In 1945, national income per capita was down to less than a quarter of the prewar level; even by 1948 it had risen to only two-thirds. There was chronic economic dislocation and there were desperate housing shortages in the many bombed cities. Problems also arose from the quadripartite occupation system. The malfunctioning of the German state was great enough from physical destruction of its fabric, without introducing arbitrary geographical divides. This applied particularly in the movement of food. However, the most potent indicator of German plight was the problem of expellees. The annexation by Poland and the USSR of parts of the prewar German Reich, together with the untenable position of ethnic Germans beyond the Reich's prewar borders, precipitated a massive westward flight of refugees. By 1960 as many as 12 million people may have figured in this largely forced migration, while several million more perished in the process of expulsion. In many parts of north Germany, eastern refugees came to form major components of the total population. In Mecklenburg, 42.5 per cent of the population were expellees in 1946.

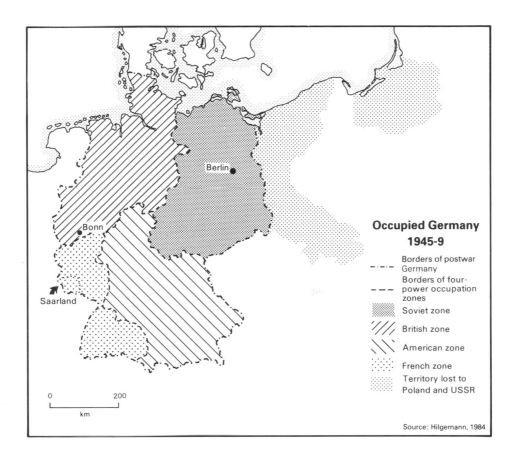

Occupied Germany 1945-9

- –·–·– Borders of postwar Germany
- – – – Borders of four-power occupation zones
- Soviet zone
- British zone
- American zone
- French zone
- Territory lost to Poland and USSR

Source: Hilgemann, 1984

Economic hardships and the severance of so many Germans from their homelands were obvious enough foci for renewed political extremism. And in spite of extensive denazification and re-education by the Western Allied powers, right-wing nationalism remained alive in western Germany, in later years making only the barest of attempts to disguise its Nazi inspiration and connections. Indeed, the NPD (National Democratic Party) was to become labelled by liberal opponents the NSDAP without the SA. But there was one vital facet of the first postwar decades which distinguished them from Weimar: the so-called West German economic miracle. From 1949 the Federal Republic sustained an extraordinarily rapid economic recovery — such that the gibe of the man in the street became: 'We may have lost the war but we won the peace.' It consistently out-performed its European partners and became a linchpin of the postwar Western European economic system. Recovery in the Democratic Republic was more strained and produced a steady migration of people to the Federal Republic through the 'safety valve' of Berlin. This was halted, however, with the erection of the Berlin Wall in August 1961, which sealed the old Soviet sector from the rest, creating a divided city. Since then, the Democratic Republic has enjoyed a greater measure of stability and prosperity. There have also been attempts to reconcile the otherwise growing tensions between the two German states, although hopes that there will ever again be a single Germany are now exceedingly remote. The legacy of National Socialism has, in these terms, been formidable.

References

Unpublished sources

BA Koblenz: Bundesarchiv Koblenz
Bodleian: Bodleian Library, University of Oxford
OUSOG: Oxford University School of Geography Library

Official published sources: German

Die Kunst im Dritten Reich: monthly Nazi periodical devoted to all forms of art and to architecture
Der nationalsozialistische Schulungsbrief: monthly Nazi periodical devoted to education and schools
Statistisches Jahrbuch: annual statistical yearbook
Wirtschaft und Statistik: monthly digest of economic commentary, including statistics

Official published sources: British, American and Allied

Adm Hbk: British Admiralty Handbooks for Germany (4 vols., HMSO, London, 1944-5) (produced by Naval Intelligence Division based at the University of Cambridge)
Germany Basic Handbook: Economic surveys for the British Foreign Office and Ministry of Economic Warfare (21 vols., HMSO, London, 1944-5)
Serial Maps: *Serial Map Service*: monthly digest of commentary and maps relating to the Second World War, beginning September 1939 (Phoenix Book Company)
Statistisches Handbuch: Statistical summary covering Germany from 1928 to 1944, produced for the American occupying forces (Munich, 1949)
Trial of German Major War Criminals: a verbatim record of the Nuremberg proceedings (22 vols., HMSO, London, 1946–50
USSBS: *United States Strategic Bombing Survey* (208 vols., Washington, DC, 1945-7). For a valuable guide to these reports, see G. Daniels (ed.), *A guide to the reports of the United States strategic bombing survey* (Royal Historical Society, London, 1981)

Other published sources

Aleff, E. (n.d.) *Terror und Widerstand, 1933-1945*, Berlin
Bessel, R. (1984) *Political violence and the rise of Nazism: the storm troopers in eastern Germany, 1925–34*, New Haven, Conn.
Billig, J. (1973) *Les camps concentrationaires dans l'économie du Reich Hitlérrien*, Paris
Broszat, M. (1968) 'The concentration camps, 1933–45' in H. Buchheim, M. Broszat, H. Krausnick and H.A. Jacobson, *Anatomy of the SS state*, London
—— (1981) *The Hitler state: the foundation and development of the internal structure of the Third Reich*, London
Burchardt, L. (1985) 'The impact of the war economy on the civilian population of Germany during the First and Second World Wars' in W. Deist (ed.), *The German military in the age of total war*, Leamington
Coon, C.S. (1939) *The races of Europe*, New York
Dallin, A. (1957) *German rule in Russia, 1941–5 — a study of occupation policies*, London
de Martonne, E. (1930) *L'Europe central*, vol. IV, Paris
Dickinson, R.E. (1938) 'The economic regions of Germany', *Geographical Review*, 28, 609–26
Farquharson, J. (1976) *The plough and the swastika: the NSDAP and agriculture in Germany, 1928-1945*, London
Forstmeier, F. and Volkmann, H.E. (eds.) (1977) *Kriegswirtschaft und Rüstung, 1939–45*, Düsseldorf
Gilbert, E.W. (1941) *How the map has changed, 1938–1940*, Oxford
Gilbert, M. (1978) *The Holocaust*, London
Goodall, M.A. (ed.) (1941) *The war in Maps*, London
Grünberger, R. (1970) *Hitler's SS*, London
Grunfeld, F.V. (1974) *The Hitler file: a social history of Germany and the Nazis, 1918–45*, London
Hewitt, K. (1983) 'Place annihilation: area bombing and the fate of urban places', *Annals of the Association of American Geographers*, 73, 257–84
Hilberg, R. (1961) *The destruction of the European Jews*, Chicago
Hilgemann, W. (1984) *Atlas zur deutschen Zeitgeschichte, 1918–1968*, Munich
Hinz, B. (1979) *Art in the Third Reich*, Oxford
Horrabin, J. (1940–6) *An Atlas History of the Second Great War*, 10 vols., London
Kater, M. (1983) *The Nazi Party: a social profile of members and leaders, 1919-1945*, Oxford
Klein, B.H. (1959) *Germany's economic preparations for war*, Cambridge, Mass.
Koehl, R.L. (1983) *The Black Corps: the structure and power struggles of the Nazi SS*, Madison, Wis.
Kühnrich, H. (1983) *Die KPD im Kampf gegen die faschistische Diktatur, 1933–45*, Berlin

Kulischer, E.M. (1943) *The displacement of population in Europe,* Montreal

Kwiet, R. and Eschwege, H. (1984) *Selbstbehauptung und Widerstand: Deutsche Juden im Kampf um Existenz und Menschenwürde, 1933–45,* Hamburg

Mammoch, K. (1984) *Widerstand, 1933–39,* Berlin

Milatz, A. (1965) *Wähler und Wählen in der Weimarer Republik,* Bonn

Milward, A.S. (1977) *War, economy and society, 1939–45,* London

Noakes, J. and Pridham, G. (eds.) (1974) *Documents on Nazism,* London

——, —— (eds.) (1984) *Nazism, 1919–1945 — a documentary reader, volume 2: State, economy and society, 1933–39,* Exeter

Orlow, D. (1971, 1973) *The history of the Nazi Party, 1919–1945,* 2 vols., Newton Abbot

Petzina, D. (1968) *Autarkiepolitik im Dritten Reich: der nationalsozialistische Vierjahresplan,* Stuttgart

Pfahlmann, H. (1964) *Fremdarbeiter und Kriegsgefangene in der deutschen Kriegswirtschaft, 1939–1945,* Würzburg

Stolper, G. (1940) *German economy, 1870–1940: issues and trends,* New York

Volkmann, H.E. (1977) 'NS-Aussenhandel im "geschlossen" Kriegswirtschaftraum 1939–41' in Forstmeier and Volkmann, 1977

Wagenführ, R. (1963) *Die deutsche Industrie im Kriege 1939–45,* Berlin

Wittmann, K. (1977) 'Deutsch-schwedische Wirtschaftsbeziehungen im Zweiten Weltkrieg' in Forstmeier and Volkmann, 1977

Glossary

Altreich — Old Reich — term used by Nazis to refer to the land area of Germany before 1938

Einsatzgruppen — Commando groups — special Gestapo and SS 'killing' squads

Freikorps — Free Corps — volunteer defence units organised by former army officers from 1918

Gaue — Regions — the name given to the regional/territorial divisions of the Nazi Party

Gauleiter — Region leader — the Nazi Party's regional/territorial leader

Gleichschaltung — Political co-ordination — the process whereby all institutions and organisations were harnessed in the service of Nazism

Herrenvolk — Master race or master people — part of Nazi racial terminology

Kampfbund — Combat league — association of militant right-wing groups

Kreise — Districts — term used to denote area subdivisions of the party Gaue; used also in local government administration

Kreisleiter — District leader — Nazi Party leader in a Kreis

Länder — States of the federation — the name given to the former sovereign states of Germany under the Weimar Republic

Reichsbahn — German State Railways

Reichsrat — State Council — the council or assembly of the Länder under the Weimar Republic

Reichstag — Imperial Diet — the German National Assembly or Parliament

Reichswehr — Imperial forces — the term used for the German Army until the mid-1930s

Stahlhelm — Steel helmet — Nationalist, ex-soldiers' organisation, founded 1918

Waffen-SS — Army formations of SS

Wehrkreise — Military districts — the army's regional administrative divisions

Wehrmacht — the German armed forces

Weltanschauung — World outlook — term much used in Nazi ideology

Zentrum — Catholic Centre Party

193

Select Bibliographical Guide

The following list provides suggestions for further reading for those unfamiliar with the history of the Third Reich. It is confined to books; for guidance on the voluminous periodical literature, readers should consult the recent historiographic surveys.

The Weimar Republic

Eyck, E. *A history of the Weimar Republic* (2 vols., Oxford, 1962, 1964)
Hiden, J. *The Weimar Republic* (London, 1974)
Nicholls, A.J. *Weimar and the rise of Hitler*, 2nd edn (London, 1979)

General and introductory accounts on Hitler and the Third Reich
Bullock, A. *Hitler: a study in tyranny* (Harmondsworth, 1962)
Shirer, W.L. *The rise and fall of the Third Reich* (London, 1960)
Trevor-Roper, H.R. *The last days of Hitler*, 2nd edn (London, 1950)
Williamson, D.G. *The Third Reich* (London, 1982)

Recent surveys and reviews of the historical literature

Hiden, J. and Farquharson, J. *Explaining Hitler's Germany* (London, 1983)
Hildebrand, K. *The Third Reich* (London, 1984)
Kershaw, I. *The Nazi dictatorship: problems and perspectives of interpretation* (London, 1985)
Laqueur, W. (ed.) *Fascism: a reader's guide* (Harmondsworth, 1979)

Some major perspectives on the Third Reich

Bracher, K.D. *The German dictatorship: the origins, structure and consequences of National Socialism* (London, 1971)
Broszat, M. *The Hitler state: the foundation and development of the internal structure of the Third Reich* (London, 1981)
Hirschfeld, G. and Kettenacker, I.. (eds.) *Der 'Führerstaat': Mythos und Realität* (Stuttgart, 1981)

Neumann, F. *Behemoth: the structure and practice of National Socialism* (London, 1942)
Rich, N. *Hitler's war aims* (2 vols., London, 1973, 1974)

The Nazi Party

Hamilton, R.F. *Who voted for Hitler* (Princeton, 1982)
Kater, M. *The Nazi Party: a social profile of members and leaders, 1919–1945* (Oxford, 1983)
Orlow, D. *The history of the Nazi Party, 1919–1945* (2 vols., Newton Abbot, 1971, 1973)

Society under Nazism

Grünberger, R. *A social history of the Third Reich* (London, 1971)
Hinz, B. *Art in the Third Reich* (Oxford, 1979)
Mosse, G.L. *Nazi culture* (London, 1966)
Schoenbaum, D. *Hitler's social revolution: class and status in Nazi Germany, 1933–9* (London, 1967)
Stachura, P.D. (ed.) *The shaping of the Nazi state* (London, 1978)

Economy under Nazism (including the war)

Forstmeier, F. and Volkmann, H.E. (eds.) *Kriegswirtschaft und Rüstung, 1939–45* (Düsseldorf, 1977)
Gillingham, J.R. *Industry and politics in the Third Reich: Ruhr coal, Hitler and Europe* (London, 1985)
Milward, A.S. *The German economy at war* (London, 1965)
—— *War, economy and society, 1939–45* (London, 1977)
Nathan, O. *The Nazi economic system: Germany's mobilization for war* (Durham, NC, 1944)
Overy, R.J. *The Nazi economic recovery, 1932–8* (London, 1982)
Petzina, D. *Autarkiepolitik im Dritten Reich: der national-sozialistische Vierjahresplan* (Stuttgart, 1968)
Wagenführ, R. *Die deutsche Industrie im Kriege 1939–45* (Berlin, 1963)

The army

Cooper, M. *The German Army, 1933–45: its political and military failure* (London, 1978)

195

Deist, W. (ed.) *The German military in the age of total war* (Leamington, 1985)

O'Neill, R.J. *The German Army and the Nazi Party, 1933–39* (London, 1966)

The SS and the war machine

Buchheim, H., Broszat, M., Krausnick, H. and Jacobsen, H.A. *Anatomy of the SS state* (London, 1968)

Dallin, A. *German rule in Russia, 1941–5 — a study of occupation policies* (London, 1957)

Georg, E. *Die wirtschaftlichen Unternehmungen der SS* (Stuttgart, 1962)

Gilbert, M. *The Holocaust* (London, 1978)

Hilberg, R. *The destruction of the European Jews* (Chicago, 1961)

Homze, E.L. *Foreign labour in Nazi Germany* (Princeton, 1967)

Koehl, R.L. *The Black Corps: the structure and power struggles of the Nazi SS* (Madison, Wis. 1983)

Kogon, E. *The theory and practice of Hell* (London, 1950)

Laqueur, W. *The terrible secret* (London, 1980)

Reitlinger, G. *The SS: alibi of a nation, 1922–45* (London, 1956)

Speer, A. *The slave state: Heinrich Himmler's masterplan for SS supremacy* (London, 1981)

Geographical accounts of Germany in the Nazi era

The British *Admiralty Handbooks* (see under references) summarise a vast body of English and German contemporary material. Other useful works are:

Dickinson, R.E. *Germany* (London, 1953)

Mellor, R.E.H. *The two Germanies* (London, 1978), part I

An atlas of modern German history (in German) which includes much material on the Nazi period is:

Hilgemann, W. *Atlas zur deutschen Zeitgeschichte, 1918–1968* (Munich, 1984)

Index

WE SHALL OVERCOME

VOICES OF THE CIVIL RIGHTS MOVEMENT

A PRIMARY SOURCE EXPLORATION OF THE STRUGGLE FOR RACIAL EQUALITY

by Lori Mortensen

Consultant:
Lyde Cullen Sizer, PhD
Professor of U.S. Cultural and Intellectual History
Sarah Lawrence College
Bronxville, New York

CAPSTONE PRESS
a capstone imprint

Fact Finders Books are published by Capstone Press,
1710 Roe Crest Drive, North Mankato, Minnesota 56003
www.capstonepub.com

Library of Congress Cataloging-in-Publication Data
Mortensen, Lori, 1955–
  Voices of the civil rights movement / Lori Mortensen.
      pages cm.—(Fact finders. We shall overcome)
  Summary: "The civil rights movement brought about major changes in the United States, including the legal end of segregation between African-Americans and white Americans. Explore the points of view of the activists who fought for change and the people who opposed them through powerful primary sources and historical photos"— Provided by publisher.
  Includes bibliographical references and index.
  ISBN 978-1-4914-2044-7 (library binding)
  ISBN 978-1-4914-2219-9 (paperback)
  ISBN 978-1-4914-2234-2 (ebook PDF)
1. African Americans—Civil rights—History—20th century—Juvenile literature. 2. Civil rights movements—Southern States--History—20th century—Juvenile literature. 3. Southern States—Race relations—Juvenile literature. I. Title.
  E185.61.M87 2015
  323.1196'073075—dc23   2014019814

Editorial Credits
Adrian Vigliano, editor; Cynthia Akiyoshi, designer; Wanda Winch, media researcher; Gene Bentdahl, production specialist

Photo Credits
AP Images, 14, Bill Hudson, 20, Horace Cort, 21; Arkansas Democrat-Gazette: cover (newspaper background); Corbis: Bettmann, 9, 24, Hulton-Deutsch Collection, 13, Jack Moebes, 7, Steve Shapiro, 27; Getty Images: The LIFE Images Collection/Don Cravens, cover (left), 8, 10, 11, The LIFE Picture Collection/Grey Villet, 23; LBJ Library: Yoichi Okamoto, 28; Library of Congress: Prints and Photographs Division, cover (bottom, right), 4, 5, 6, 15, 16, 17, 18, 22, 25; Newscom: KRT, 26, Zuma Press/The Commercial Appeal, 19; U.S. Air Force photo: MSgt. Cecilio Ricardo, 29

Printed in Canada.
092014   008478FRS15

A NOTE ABOUT PRIMARY SOURCES

Primary sources are newspaper articles, photographs, speeches, or other documents that were created during an event. They are great ways to see how people spoke and felt during that time. You'll find primary sources from the time of the civil rights movement throughout this book. Within the text, these primary sources are colored blue and set in italic type.

TABLE OF CONTENTS

Chapter One
SEPARATE AND NOT EQUAL

In 1865, toward the end of the Civil War (1861–1865), the 13th Amendment to the U.S. Constitution **abolished** slavery. In 1868 the 14th Amendment promised equal rights to all citizens. But these new laws did not erase more than 200 years of racial hatred and **prejudice** toward black people.

After the war southern states made "Jim Crow" laws. These laws separated black people from white people. Blacks had to sit in the backs of buses and trains. Blacks had to use separate facilities that were usually old and run-down. Many businesses refused to serve nonwhite citizens.

▶ Under Jim Crow laws, black or "colored" people were not treated like equal citizens.

Mobs and hate groups used the threat of lynching to enforce Jim Crow laws.

A National Crime

Black people who broke **segregation** rules could be fined and arrested. Sometimes black people were attacked or even killed by mobs. Guilt or innocence did not matter. Instead of going to trial, white mobs killed blacks at public **lynchings**.

During the 1890s Ida B. Wells, a black journalist, spoke out against these brutal killings. She even met with President William McKinley. *"Our country's national crime is lynching,"* she said. More people began speaking up and taking action to challenge segregation. People who supported segregation spoke up too. The fight over civil rights seemed to grow louder every day.

abolish—to put an end to something officially

segregate—to keep people of different races apart in schools and other public places

prejudice—an opinion about others that is unfair or not based on facts

lynch—to be killed by a mob without a trial, usually by hanging

5

Chapter Two

TIRED OF GIVING IN

On December 1, 1955, in Montgomery, Alabama, Rosa Parks got on a bus. Jim Crow laws said black passengers had to sit in the back. If the bus filled up, they had to give up their seats to white passengers.

That day, a white passenger needed a seat. The driver told Parks to get up. Parks recalled her confrontation with the bus driver, **"*When he saw me still sitting, he asked if I was going to stand up and I said, 'No, I'm not.' And he said, 'Well, if you don't stand up, I'm going to have to call the police and have you arrested.' I said, 'You may do that.'*"**

▶ Rosa Parks' arrest was the event that started the Montgomery Bus Boycott.

Bus companies posted signs with instructions separating black people from white people.

Parks was arrested for *"refusing to obey orders of bus driver."* Local black leaders learned of Parks' actions. They asked all black people to **boycott** the buses in Montgomery. Thousands of people stopped riding the buses. Some of the leaders formed a group called the Montgomery Improvement Association (MIA) to coordinate the boycott.

Some people claimed Parks didn't get up because she was tired. *"No, the only tired I was,"* Parks explained, *"was tired of giving in."*

boycott—to refuse to take part in something as a way of making a protest

FACT

Many call Rosa Parks the mother of the civil rights movement.

Chapter Three
THEY CAN WALK

Clyde Sellers was the Police Commissioner of Montgomery in 1955. When black people boycotted city buses, he vowed to arrest anyone who broke segregation rules.

"You know," said Sellers during an interview, *"the Nigras in Montgomery were treated better than any place else. They got everything from the whites—they went to the whites for everything they wanted and they got it ... [the whites] don't want to do it anymore."*

▶ During the boycott protesters found other ways to travel. Many people rode bicylces, found carpools, or simply walked.

Sellers saw only one solution. *"We have laws requiring segregation on the buses, and if they want to ride the buses they will have to obey the laws. They can walk until they are ready to obey the law."*

The bus boycott went on for 12 months. One night in early 1956 boycott leader Martin Luther King Jr.'s home was bombed. After the bombing Sellers met with King and said, *"I will certainly do everything in my power to bring the guilty parties to court and put them in prison ... I do not agree with you in your beliefs, but I will do everything within my power to defend you against such acts as this."*

Chapter Four

FATHER OF THE CIVIL RIGHTS MOVEMENT

Following Rosa Parks' arrest, local black leaders gathered to plan a boycott. During this meeting the MIA was formed, and a young minister named Martin Luther King Jr. was appointed president of the organization.

King agreed to lead a bus boycott to protest inequality. On December 5, 1955, King spoke to a crowd of thousands of boycotters. He urged people to use carpools and other options to stay off the buses until they reached their goal.

▶ Boycott leaders organized a carpool system for people to use instead of buses.

King told the crowd, "*Automobiles will be at your service ... Now my automobile is gonna be in it ... and I'm not concerned about how much gas I'm gonna use. I want to see this thing work. And we will not be content until oppression is wiped out of Montgomery, and really out of America.*"

▶ Police arrested 26-year-old King for leading the boycott. It was the first time King received national attention for his work in the civil rights movement.

King's voice became a powerful force in Montgomery. Under his leadership, the boycott gained national attention. Soon lawyers were arguing for and against bus segregation in front of the Supreme Court.

In November 1956 the Supreme Court struck down laws requiring segregated seating on public buses. The boycotters had won.

"I Have a Dream"

After leading the bus boycott in Montgomery, King became a major leader in the civil rights movement. He worked with other leaders to organize nonviolent protests to fight against segregation.

On August 28, 1963, more than 250,000 people marched in Washington, D.C.

"I have a dream," King said in his speech to the crowd, *"that my four little children will one day live in a nation where they will not be judged by the color of their skin, but by the content of their character."*

King shared his vision of the future. He imagined the day, *"when all of God's children, black men and white men, Jews and Gentiles, Protestants and Catholics, will be able to join hands and sing in the words of the old Negro spiritual: Free at last, Free at last, Great God a-mighty, We are free at last!"*

King's powerful words rang in the nation's ears. His speech inspired people to keep fighting for civil rights.

Suffering for the Cause

King suffered many assaults and arrests during his fight for civil rights. On April 4, 1968, King was shot and killed while standing on a motel balcony in Memphis, Tennessee. His friend and fellow civil rights leader, Ralph Abernathy, was by his side. *"I have suffered as much as Martin Luther King,"* said Abernathy. *"Only I didn't get the bullet. And I would have taken the bullet if I could have."*

Chapter Five

BY ANY MEANS NECESSARY

After a lifetime of **discrimination**, Malcolm X grew impatient with injustice. He rallied blacks to fight racism, *"by any means necessary"* and called Martin Luther King Jr. a *"fool."*

King believed peaceful protest was an effective tool. Malcolm X believed nonviolent protests taught blacks to be defenseless. While King fought for integration, Malcolm X fought for blacks to live separately and govern themselves.

"I am a Muslim," said Malcolm X, *"because it's a religion that teaches you an eye for an eye and a tooth for a tooth. It teaches you to respect everybody, and treat everybody right. But it also teaches you if someone steps on your toe, chop off their foot. And I carry my religious axe with me all the time."*

▶ Malcolm X held up a newspaper while addressing a crowd in New York City in 1963. He encouraged blacks not to wait to get involved in the fight for equal rights.

▶ Malcolm X and King met only once, as King was leaving a press conference in March of 1964. Malcolm X died less than one year later—he was assassinated on February 21, 1965.

Malcolm X's revolutionary stand against injustice united blacks all over the world—and created enemies. His message frightened white society. Some people in the black community thought violence would damage the progress made through peaceful protests.

Some of Malcolm X's views changed over time. In 1964 Malcolm X said he wanted to find ways to work with other civil rights leaders. He said, *"Dr. King wants the same thing I want—freedom!"*

discriminate—to treat people unfairly because of their skin color or class

Chapter Six

ARGUING FOR FREEDOM

Thurgood Marshall's words hushed the courtroom. He said that the real reason for continuing to have segregated schools was to keep people who had been slaves *"as near that stage as is possible."* He concluded by saying, *"this Court should make it clear that that is not what our Constitution stands for."*

In 1952 Marshall began arguing a case before the Supreme Court for a group of black families. These families did not want their children forced to attend a black school far from their homes. This case, *Brown v. Board of Education*, challenged a ruling from 1896 that said "separate but equal" was constitutional.

▶ The Supreme Court's *Brown* decision provided a legal basis for the civil rights movement over the next 10 years.

FACT

In 1967 Marshall became the first black person to serve on the Supreme Court.

On May 14, 1954, the Supreme Court agreed with Marshall. *"... in the field of public education,"* wrote Chief Justice Earl Warren, *"... separate educational facilities are inherently unequal."* The ruling cleared the way for school **integration**. This was a huge victory for the civil rights movement.

Historian Roger Wilkins remembered Marshall by saying, *"Segregation was crushing; It crushed black people's belief that what they said and did and thought counted for something. Thurgood Marshall led a team of lawyers before an all-white court and gave us one of the three or four most important constitutional decisions this country has ever seen."*

integrate—to bring people of different races together in schools and other public places

17

Chapter Seven

NOT AS LONG AS I AM GOVERNOR

The Supreme Court's 1955 ruling to integrate public schools outraged many people in the South. While some states began taking steps to integrate, many refused and made laws against integration. In 1957 a federal court ordered Little Rock, Arkansas to comply with the 1955 decision. The school board began by enrolling nine black students at Central High School. The students were called the Little Rock Nine.

Governor Orval Faubus decided to fight school integration. He knew a big fight would help him win an upcoming election. Faubus said, *"No school district will be forced to mix the races as long as I am governor of Arkansas."*

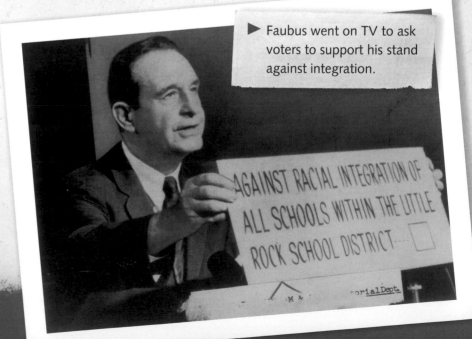

► Faubus went on TV to ask voters to support his stand against integration.

▶ One of the Little Rock Nine, Elizabeth Eckford, walked to school as angry white protestors followed her.

The day before school started, Faubus ordered the Arkansas National Guard to surround the school. *"It will not be possible,"* he explained during a televised speech, *"to ... maintain order and protect the lives and property of the citizens if forcible integration is carried out."* Faubus later won the election and served six terms in a row. *"It's true in politics as it is in life,"* he said, *"that survival is the first law."*

Chapter Eight
SEGREGATION AT ALL COSTS

Martin Luther King Jr. called Birmingham, Alabama, *"the most segregated city in the United States."* That was exactly how the city's commissioner of public safety, Eugene "Bull" Connor, wanted to keep it. *"Negroes and whites will not segregate together as long as I am commissioner,"* he declared.

Civil rights leaders knew Birmingham was an important battleground. On May 2, 1963, more than 1,000 children marched through the streets singing freedom songs. To turn them back, Connor brought out fire hoses and police dogs. The hose blasts knocked marchers to the ground. The dogs lunged and bit.

▶ Images from Birmingham shocked people around the country. It was a major turning point for civil rights.

► Connor (center) directed the arrest of a group of black demonstrators on April 10, 1963.

Photos from Birmingham outraged many Americans and exposed the battle for civil rights like never before. *"… the water ripped clothing and sent children rolling down the street,"* said a reporter.

Connor's violent methods made some Americans sympathetic to the goals of the civil rights movement. President Kennedy proposed legislation that would lead to the Civil Rights Act of 1964 that banned discrimination. *"The civil rights movement should thank God for Bull Connor,"* said Kennedy. *"He's helped it as much as Abraham Lincoln."*

Chapter Nine

HATE CAN DESTROY YOU

After three white men murdered her mother, Daisy Bates hated white people. Her father said, *"Hate can destroy you. Don't hate white people just because they're white ... Hate the humiliations ... discrimination ... the insults hurled at us—and then try to do something about it."*

Bates did do something.

In 1957 she was a leader in the local chapter of the National Association for the Advancement of Colored People (NAACP). She fought for school integration. She became an adviser to the nine black students who would enroll at Central High School in Little Rock, Arkansas.

▶ Daisy Bates (back row, second from right) posed for a picture with the Little Rock Nine.

▶ Hate groups broke Bates' front window. She fixed the glass with tape and kept fighting for equality.

Hate groups burned crosses on Bates' lawn as an act of intimidation. A rock with the note, *"Stone this time. Dynamite next"* shattered her window. But she was determined to keep fighting for civil rights.

"I never know when they're going to pass here and blow this house to bits," she said, *" ... nevertheless, I feel if I'm going to live in this town and with myself, I must oppose hatred and prejudice in any way that I can."*

Chapter Ten
IF NOT US, THEN WHO?

On May 20, 1961, a group of Freedom Riders sat together on a bus as it rolled toward Montgomery, Alabama. The group was heading to a segregated bus terminal. Freedom Riders were civil rights activists who rode buses into the South. They rode in mixed racial groups to challenge segregation on interstate buses.

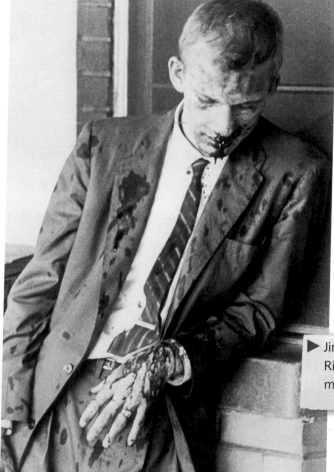

One Freedom Rider, Genevieve Houghton, said, *"We were to go through various parts of the South, gradually going deeper and deeper ... and see whether places were segregated, whether people were being served when they went to get something to eat, or buy a ticket, or use the restrooms."*

▶ Jim Zwerg was one Freedom Rider who was attacked by a mob in Montgomery.

► A journalist snapped photos of John Lewis and Zwerg beaten by the mob. Their bloodied faces were shown around the world.

When a bus of Freedom Riders arrived in Montgomery, an enraged mob attacked with bats and pipes. Police arrived about 10 minutes later. They did almost nothing to stop the mob's attack.

But the movement grew and hundreds of people became Freedom Riders. *"If not us, then who?"* said Freedom Rider John Lewis. *"If not now, then when?"*

On September 22, 1961, the Interstate Commerce Commission outlawed discrimination on interstate buses and at bus stations. The Freedom Riders had achieved their goal.

Chapter Eleven
SEGREGATION FOREVER

In 1962 George Wallace ran for governor of Alabama. Many voters in Alabama liked Wallace and they showed it with their votes. He spoke against black voting rights and school integration. He won the election.

After his election Wallace gave his inaugural address. He said, *"I draw the line in the dust ... I say segregation now, segregation tomorrow, segregation forever."*

In March 1965, about 600 peaceful civil rights demonstrators began marching from Selma to Montgomery, Alabama. Wallace ordered state troopers to stop them.

▶ State troopers sent by Wallace attacked John Lewis and the other marchers. Lewis said, *"I don't see how President Johnson can send troops to Vietnam ... and can't send troops to Selma."*

▶ In 1963 Wallace stood in the doorway of a University of Alabama building. He was trying to stop two black students from enrolling.

Alabama state troopers met the demonstrators at the Edmund Pettus Bridge. When the marchers refused to leave, troopers attacked with clubs, whips, and tear gas.

"All I remember is screaming," recalled marcher Joanne Bland. *"They ran those horses up into the crowd and were knocking people down ... Blood was everywhere."*

But Wallace did not apologize. He continued to speak out for segregation. He said, *"The president wants us to surrender this state to Martin Luther King and his group of pro-Communists who have instituted these demonstrations."*

Chapter Twelve
A CHANGING NATION

On July 2 President Johnson signed the Civil Rights Act of 1964. This outlawed discrimination in certain areas of public life, such as public education and accommodations. Congress ratified the 24th Amendment, eliminating poll taxes in federal elections that prevented many blacks from voting. The next year Johnson signed the Voting Rights Act of 1965, protecting blacks' right to vote.

Martin Luther King Jr. talked about the United States' beginning in his "I Have a Dream" speech. King said, *"When the architects of our republic wrote the magnificent words of the Constitution and the Declaration of Independence, they were signing a ... promise that all men—yes, black men as well as white men— would be guaranteed the 'unalienable rights' of 'life, liberty, and the pursuit of happiness.'"*

▶ President Johnson signed the Civil Rights Act of 1964 in a televised ceremony at the White House.

▶ On November 4, 2008, Barack Obama became the first African-American president of the United States. This would not have been possible without the courageous voices of the civil rights movement.

The people of the civil rights movement raised their voices to demand their rights. Slowly the nation began to change. Changes did not come easily, but they did come. People began thinking differently about discrimination. Opportunities for African-Americans increased. The changes of the civil rights movement affect people today and will affect generations to come.

Selected Bibliography

Bausum, Ann. *Freedom Riders: John Lewis and Jim Zwerg on the Front Lines of the Civil Rights Movement.* Washington, D.C.: National Geographic, 2006.

"City Threatens Arrests Here to Enforce Bus Segregation." *The Associated Press.* April 24, 1956. http://www.montgomeryboycott.com/city-threatens-arrests-here-to-enforce-bus-segregation/

Fine, Benjamin. "Arkansas Troops Bar Negro Pupils; Governor Defiant." *The New York Times.* September 5, 1957. http://www.nytimes.com/learning/general/onthisday/big/0904.html#article

Freedman, Russell. *Freedom Walkers: The Story of the Montgomery Bus Boycott.* New York: Holiday House, 2006.

Kasher, Steven. *The Civil Rights Movement Photographic History 1954-68.* New York: Abbeville Press, 1996.

"The Montgomery Bus Boycott: December 1955–December 1956." PBS/WGBH, August 23, 2006. http://www.pbs.org/wgbh/amex/eyesontheprize/story/02_bus.html

Partridge, Elizabeth. *Marching for Freedom: Walk Together, Children, and Don't You Grow Weary.* New York: Viking, 2009.

Van Delinder, Jean. "Brown v. Board of Education of Topeka: A Landmark Case Unresolved Fifty Years Later." *Prologue Magazine,* 2004. http://www.archives.gov/publications/prologue/2004/spring/brown-v-board-1.html

Walker, Paul Robert. *Remember Little Rock: The Time, the People, the Stories.* Washington, D.C.: National Geographic, 2009.

Williams, Juan. "Daisy Bates and the Little Rock Nine." NPR, September 21, 2007. http://www.npr.org/templates/story/story.php?storyId=14563865

Glossary

abolish (uh-BOL-ish)—to put an end to something officially

assassinate (us-SASS-uh-nate)—to murder a person who is well known or important

boycott (BOY-kot)—to refuse to take part in something as a way of making a protest

discriminate (dis-KRI-muh-nayt)—to treat people unfairly because of their skin color or class

integrate (IN-tuh-grate)—to bring people of different races together in schools and other public places

lynch (LINCH)—to put someone to death, often by hanging, by mob action without legal authority

prejudice (PREJ-uh-diss)—an opinion about others that is unfair or not based on facts

segregate (SEG-ruh-gate)—to keep people of different races apart in schools and other public places

Critical Thinking
Using the Common Core

1. Many activists were arrested or violently attacked during the civil rights movement. Discuss some of the reasons why people might accept great risks to take a stand for civil rights. (Key Ideas and Details)

2. Why do you think some people were so opposed to integration? Discuss the different reactions these people had. Were their reactions justified? Support your answer with examples from the text and other sources. (Integration of Knowledge and Ideas)

Internet Sites

FactHound offers a safe, fun way to find Internet sites related to this book. All of the sites on FactHound have been researched by our staff.

Here's all you do:
Visit *www.facthound.com*
Type in this code: 9781491420447

Check out projects, games and lots more at
www.capstonekids.com

Index